MEDITERRANEAN
THE BEAUTIFUL COOKBOOK

AUTHENTIC RECIPES FROM THE MEDITERRANEAN LANDS

Winter Squash with Sharp Ricotta (recipe page 205)

AUTHENTIC RECIPES FROM THE MEDITERRANEAN LANDS

MEDITERRANEAN
THE BEAUTIFUL COOKBOOK

RECIPES AND FOOD TEXT BY
JOYCE GOLDSTEIN

REGIONAL TEXT BY
AYLA ALGAR

FOOD PHOTOGRAPHY BY
PETER JOHNSON

STYLED BY
JANICE BAKER

HarperCollins*Publishers*

First published in USA 1994
by Collins Publishers San Francisco.
Reprinted 1994.
Produced by Weldon Owen Inc.
814 Montgomery Street
San Francisco, CA 94133 USA
Phone (415) 291-0100 Fax (415) 291-8841

Weldon Owen Inc.:
Chairman: Kevin Weldon
President: John Owen
General Manager: Stuart Laurence
Co-Editions Director: Derek Barton
Publisher: Jane Fraser
Managing Editor: Anne Dickerson
Editorial Assistant: Jan Hughes
Copy Editor: Sharon Silva
Proofreader: Sharilyn Hovind
Production: Stephanie Sherman, Mick Bagnato,
James Obata
Design: Tom Morgan, Blue Design
Design Assistant: Jennifer Petersen
Design Concept: John Bull, The Book Design Company
Map: Kenn Backhaus
Illustrations: Diana Reiss-Koncar
Index: Ken Dellapenta
Assistant Food Stylists: Liz Nolan, Marianne Rudd
Assistant to Photographer: Simon Edie

For information address HarperCollins Publishers, Inc.,
10 East 53rd Street, New York, NY 10022.

Library of Congress Cataloging-in-Publication Data:

Goldstein, Joyce, Esersky.
Mediterranean, the beautiful cookbook :
authentic recipes from the Mediterranean
regions / recipes by Joyce Goldstein ; text by
Ayla Algar ; food photography by Peter Johnson ;
styled by Janice Baker.
p. cm.
ISBN 0-00-255370-8
1. Cookery, Mediterranean.
2. Mediterranean Region—Description and
travel. I. Algar, Ayla Esen. II. Title.
TX725.M35G65 1994
641.59182'2—dc20 93-42641
CIP

ISBN 0-06-757590-0 (pbk.)

Printed by Toppan in China

A Weldon Owen  Production

Endpapers: Mosaic detail from the ancient city of Ephesus, Turkey.

Pages 2–3: The Mediterranean Sea, bound by three continents, was thought to be the center of the world by many ancient civilizations.

Right: The ancient Egyptian temple of Queen Nefertari, in Nubia, had to be moved to higher ground in the 1970s to escape the rising waters of the Nile after it was dammed.

Pages 8–9, left to right: Pita Bread (recipe page 82), Spinach Pies (recipe page 74), Meat Pies (recipe page 87).

Pages 12–13: The glistening village of Cesares, nestled in the gentle slopes of the Andalusian countryside in Spain, has a view to the south of Gibraltar and North Africa.

Top to bottom: Tomato Soup (recipe page 107), Vegetable Soup with Basil and Garlic (recipe page 107)

CONTENTS

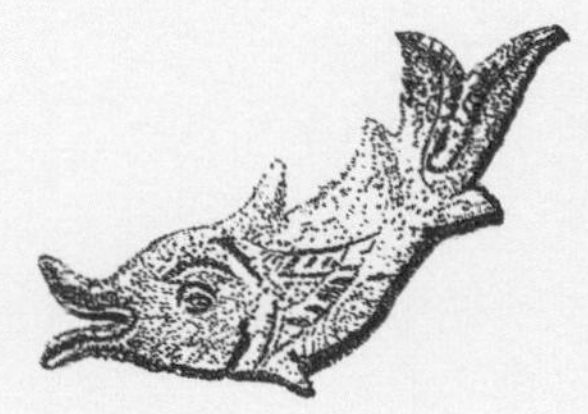

Through the ages, volcanic activity has continually altered the rugged island of Santorini, Greece.

INTRODUCTION

Assertions that a given place is the center of the world have more to do with theological self-perception than with geographical or historical reality. The spread of the globe is too vast and the history of humankind too complex for anywhere to have been the nub for all things. Within the Old World, however, a certain centrality may be claimed for the Mediterranean. Its waters wash the shores of three continents, Europe, Asia and Africa, and since antiquity most of the principal currents of world history have flowed across its surface. Little in either European or Middle Eastern history and culture can be comprehended without reference to the civilizations that arose or grew to maturity in the Mediterranean basin.

Despite these manifold connections, the Mediterranean constitutes a coherent, almost self-contained world of its own, being in essence an inland sea. Were it not for the separation of Africa from Europe at the Strait of Gibraltar, opening a chink onto the oceanic vastness of the Atlantic, the Mediterranean would be entirely landlocked. One of its two other outlets, the Suez Canal, is recent and human-made; and the other, the Dardanelles, with its continuation, the Bosporus, is little more than a channel leading to the Black Sea, which can legitimately be regarded as an annex of the Mediterranean. Other seas lying within the Mediterranean realm—the Tyrrhenian, the Adriatic, the Aegean—are mere inlets or subdivisions of the mother sea; they are cartographical conventions rather than independent geographical realities. This coherence of the Mediterranean world has meant that the peoples inhabiting its shores have often had more in common with one another, despite differences of language and religion, than with their conationals living in their respective hinterlands. Exposure to comparable climatic and geographic environments preconditioned them for the culinary interchanges that came about as the result of migration, conquest and trade. It is here that the ultimate origin of the ensemble of traditions we call Mediterranean cuisine is to be sought.

The Mediterranean world is defined, self-evidently, by the sea that lies at its heart, with the predictable consequence for cuisine that full use has always been made of its abundant fish and shellfish. This prominence of the fruits of the sea has been reinforced by another factor of geography, the relative paucity of pastureland, which tends to make beef a rarity on Mediterranean menus. Sheep farming, by contrast, is not so dependent on lush pastures, and lamb and mutton therefore enjoy some prominence in the diet. This is often limited by economic circumstance; it is not for nothing that the slaughter of a lamb has always counted as a lavish gesture of hospitality. For all the sun-drenched ease we associate with the Mediterranean—in reality little more than a vacationer's fantasy—there is an undertone of harshness to the region's beauty. The lands that ring the sea—both the mountainous peninsulas that line its northern shores and the relatively narrow coastal plains that run along its eastern and southern shores—are for the most part arid, lacking all but a fraction of the rainfall that is lavished on northern Europe; they do not yield a livelihood readily and unsparingly to their inhabitants. It is indeed remarkable that agriculture has flourished in

Ghardaia is the Algerian center for carpets; markets like these abound in North African cities.

FRANCE
PYRENEES
ANDORRA
NICE
MONACO
MARSEILLE
Ligurian Sea
Corsica
ROME
ITALY
Adriat
BARCELONA
MADRID
SPAIN
VALENCIA
Balearic Islands
Menorca
Mallorca
Ibiza
Sardinia
NAPLES
Tyrrhenian Sea
MÁLAGA
Straight of Gibraltar
TANGER
Mediterr
PALERMO
Sicily
SKIKDA
ALGIERS
TUNIS
RABAT
FÈS
CONSTANTINE
MALTA
MOROCCO
ATLAS MOUNTAINS
TUNISIA
SFAX
ALGERIA
GRAND ERG OCCIDENTAL
GRAND ERG ORIENTAL
TRIPOLI
LI
BACKHAUS

Black Sea
BELGRADE
TERRITORIES OF THE FORMER
YUGOSLAVIA
SPLIT
DUBROVNIK
ALBANIA
Sea
TIRANË
ISTANBUL
ANKARA
TURKEY
Aegean
Sea
GREECE
IZMIR
ATHENS
Ionian Islands
Ionian
Sea
TAURUS MOUNTAINS
ANTALYA
Rhodes
NICOSIA
CYPRUS
SYRIA
LEBANON
BEIRUT
DAMASCUS
Crete
JERUSALEM
ISRAEL
anean Sea
ALEXANDRIA
BANGHAZI
CAIRO
Suez Canal
EGYPT
Gulf of Suez
BYA
LIBYAN
DESERT
Nile
Red
Sea

Situated on the inlet of a wooded promontory, the picturesque fishing village of Portofino typifies the ports of northern Italy.

the Mediterranean, the result not only of skillful cultivation but also of the peasant tenacity and hardiness of its peoples. Discernible beneath the surface of virtually all Mediterranean cuisines is this same peasant character, which has bestowed on the cooking of the area some of its best qualities: boldness of taste, purity of ingredients and simplicity of conception.

As Fernand Braudel, magisterial authority on all things Mediterranean, has remarked, "In the Mediterranean, to live is to exchange"; ports and peoples, contemplating each other across its waters, could live in no other way. The process of exchange has generally followed two principal axes, running between east and west and north and south. Moving along the first of these axes, Phoenicians, Greeks and Arabs—in order both of chronology and of significance—thus disseminated both crops and culinary techniques in the western reaches of the Mediterranean. As for the ports of the northern Mediterranean—Montpellier, Marseilles, Venice, Genoa—they all built their prosperity on trading in foodstuffs with the eastern and southern shores.

Trade is, of course, the primary form of interchange, and for many centuries the principal commodity in the trade of the Mediterranean consisted of spices. Spices in the ancient, classical and medieval worlds were not thought of simply as seasonings, but as a much broader category embracing all "particularly luxurious and fine substances used in food," especially imported ones. Few Mediterranean cuisines could be described today as pungent, but the historical importance of spices, in the capacious sense of the word, was great throughout the Mediterranean world. They impinged even on its political and military destiny. One of the several worldly motives that underlay the Crusades was gaining control of the eastern Mediterranean ports that served as termini for caravans laden with Asian spices, and it was the hope of gaining direct access to those same spices that helped impel a badly disoriented Columbus across the Atlantic.

It is not our intention to sing the praises of empires, ancient or modern, but there can be no denying their role in promoting the interchange of people and materials that is crucial in the emergence of any worthwhile cuisine, a role second only to that of trade. Bringing diverse territories under unified political control, empires have brought the products of each to the attention of the other, and the well-stocked markets that grew up in the great imperial cities—Rome, Baghdad, Constantinople—constituted a standing invitation to culinary experimentation and indulgence. Courts and palaces not only bestowed the imprint of imperial prestige on culinary styles; they sometimes participated actively in their elaboration. Nero, for example, is said to have invented aioli, certainly a greater achievement than fiddling while Rome burned, and it is to the initiative of another highly arbitrary ruler, the Ottoman Sultan Murad IV, that the invention of *hünkâr beğendi* ("the sovereign approved")—lamb on a bed of smoked eggplant cream—is attributed. Both anecdotes may be apocryphal, but they serve to exemplify the general principle of personal contributions to gastronomy by emperors. (We must of course exclude coprophagous monsters like the Roman emperor Commodus.)

For all their extensive voyaging around the Mediterranean, with culinary consequences on which we occasionally remark, the Phoenicians and Greeks were primarily traders and colonists, not empire builders. It was instead the Romans who first built an empire that knit together all the shores of the Mediterranean. They certainly developed the wheat fields of Spain, Sicily and North Africa; appreciated fine olive oil; used spices with what seems to have been a reckless, self-defeating abandon; and were, in general, adventurous eaters, ready to try almost anything. It is difficult, however, to be enthusiastic about a cuisine that regarded dormice cooked in honey as a delicacy; that thought of "hares and sow's udders, boars and antelopes, fowls and flamingoes and gazelles" as fit material for "a magnificent feast" (Juvenal); and that showed a general dislike for natural and unadulterated flavors. The use of complex sauces to disguise such flavors, considered the height of skill in certain cuisines, is relatively rare on the Mediterranean table; where it is to be found, it can be considered an echo of Roman taste. Somewhat more common, at least on the northern shores of the Mediterranean, is the mixing of different meats in the same dish, which may also point to the existence of a Roman substratum.

The Byzantines—lords of Constantinople, the "Second Rome"—sought in many ways to perpetuate or revive Roman tradition; to the kitchen, however, they brought their own skills and tastes, discussed later in our section on Greece.

The imperial concept of rule was, strictly speaking, unknown to the Arabs, and the political fragmentation of the Islamic world began quite early. The lands conquered by the Arabs were, however, truly imperial in their extent and diversity, rivaling Rome in this respect, and the Arab contribution to the cuisine of the Mediterranean world was certainly greater than that of the Roman Empire. The first emergence in the West of "sophisticated cuisine, typical of all advanced civilizations," came, according to Braudel, in the fifteenth century, the result, in large part, of several hundred years of gradual impregnation by Arab influences. There is a general reluctance to go beyond Judeo-Christian tradition and Greco-Roman civilization as sources for the intellectual and material culture of the West, and it is in keeping with this reluctance that food historian Reay Tannahill describes the fifth to the tenth centuries as "the silent centuries" of European cuisine. But silence prevailed only in northern Europe; in Arab-ruled Spain and Sicily veritable symphonies of gastronomy were being composed. The Arabs are often thought of as essentially nomadic, and the general poverty of nomad cuisine is well-known. But the fact is that the early Arabs, energized by Islam, excelled as traders, agriculturists and city builders, three essential attributes for any people wishing to excel in cuisine. The nature of their contribution is detailed in several sections that follow; here, let us evoke only rice, described by historian, Lucien Lefebvre as "the blessing brought by the Arabs."

Lying just over the horizon of the Mediterranean world, Persia (or Iran, as we are now accustomed to calling it) deserves a special mention. In its days of imperial glory, it often encroached directly on the Mediterranean world: Persian armies advanced all the way to the Asiatic shores of the Bosporus, and Egypt came intermittently under Persian rule. Integration into the Islamic world, from the seventh century onward, deprived Persia of an independent military or political role, but the dissemination of its culture actually increased and its culinary impact on the Mediterranean was manifold. Persia was the homeland of many of the fruits and vegetables the Arabs introduced to Syria, North Africa, Spain and Sicily. It had itself acquired many of these from

Because much of Algeria contains vast uninhabitable stretches of desert, most of the population lives near the life-giving Mediterranean Sea.

India or China, so that it functioned as a kind of waystation for the produce of Asia on its journey to the Mediterranean. Many of the irrigation techniques used to such good effect by the Arabs, notably the digging of subterranean channels, had been learned from the Persians. The classical cuisine of the Arabs, in both its eastern (Syro-Iraqi) and western (North African) styles, was of largely Persian inspiration, something that could still be verified today by placing a Moroccan *tagine* next to a traditional Persian *khoresh.* Nor is there any reason to suppose that the Persian influence was always indirect, mediated by the Arabs. Persian scholars and musicians are known to have made it all the way to Spain, so why not a few Persian cooks as well?

The tricontinental Ottoman Empire was the last and in many ways the greatest of the Mediterranean empires. Heir not only to the entire civilization of classical Islam but also to many Byzantine traditions (excluding, of course, the specifically religious), the Ottomans produced a powerful and rich synthesis of culinary styles that penetrated deep into Europe and triumphed throughout much of the Arab world.

In the Mediterranean world of exchanges, Jews often played a special role as traders, migrants and refugees. They lived on the sea's eastern, southern and northern shores, and were present in both the Muslim and Christian worlds, often acting as intermediaries between the two, although they were infinitely better integrated in the former than the latter. After the fall of Rome, Jews ensured the continued cultivation of the citron throughout the Mediterranean basin, needing it as they did for the ritual purposes spelled out in the Talmud, thus preparing the way for the large-scale cultivation of citrus fruits by the Arabs. Much of the trans-Pyrenean trade that conveyed to Europe the agricultural wealth of Arab Spain was conducted by Jews, and down to the early eleventh century it was also Jews who predominated in the spice trade with the eastern Mediterranean. When the Jews were expelled from Spain, they are said to have avenged themselves on their tormentors by introducing chocolate to France and thus breaking the Spanish monopoly on this commodity (although the same achievement has been attributed to a Hapsburg princess, Anne of Austria).

The Erechtheum, built in Athens in the 5th century B.C., *marks the height of the Golden Age of Greece.*

A more palpable legacy of the Jewish departure from Spain is the cuisine of those Jews who took refuge in Ottoman Turkey; its constituent dishes, designated even today in Istanbul by their ancient Ladino names, echo the culinary traditions of Arab Spain while bearing a distinctively Jewish imprint. It has been hypothesized that the Jews of Sicily, permitted to remain on the island for almost two centuries after the end of Arab rule, played a similar role in the preservation of Sicilian Arab cuisine, and even transmitted it to northern Italy by means of the merchants with whom they traded. If this hypothesis is true, the Jews would have served as the penultimate link in a chain of transmission that began in Baghdad and ended in Venice. In general terms, Jews enriched the repertoire of Mediterranean cuisine by creating variations on many regional dishes in accordance with the requirements of dietary law.

Together with empires and trade—from neither of which can it be fully dissociated—religion has played a cardinal role in the shaping of Mediterranean cuisine. A similar statement might be made about virtually any part of the globe. There is a certain mystery about the sustenance of life just as there is about its origin, and it would be possible to write a sacred ethnology of food. But the interconnections of food and religion in the Mediterranean world are particularly dense and numerous. They begin, perhaps, with the legends of the Egyptian and Greek gods, but are equally prominent in the three Abrahamic religions. The sacred connotations of bread provide a connecting thread among most Mediterranean traditions (with the possibly significant exception of Roman religion). Egypt and Greece made ritual offerings of bread to their gods, and Judaism bakes special breads for Passover and other high days. Bread is of course central to the Christian Eucharist (together with wine, the second element in the Greek trinity of bread, wine and olive oil), and Christmas, Easter and the saints' days are still celebrated around the Mediterranean with the consumption of special breads and pastries. Islam inculcates respect for bread, to the degree that it is a religious duty to pick up a crust that has fallen by the wayside, but special types of bread for religiously significant days are baked only in Turkey, perhaps in unconscious imitation of Greek Orthodox practice. Particular breads and pastries often migrate across religious borders. Many of the rich, flaky pastries bequeathed by the Arabs to the cuisines of Spain and Sicily became, after their expulsion from those lands, the special preserve of Christian monastic communities. A common item in Turkish bakeries is the sweet braided bread known as

Mediterranean ports such as Mallorca's Porto Colom have served to export the region's products throughout the world for a millennium.

paskalya çöreği, or "Easter bread," which happens to be almost identical to the Jewish challah.

Judaism brought to cuisine its own set of dietary rules, which not only banished the pig from the menu but also forbade certain combinations of foodstuffs. The prohibition of cooking on the Sabbath gave rise to what might be called the Jewish hotpot, buried in warm ashes before the onset of the Sabbath to cook overnight and known accordingly to the Sephardic Jews of the Mediterranean by the Hispano-Arabic term *adafina,* "the buried." Christendom, heir to the omnivorous traditions of the Greeks and Romans, made little distinction between permitted and forbidden foods, but the regular abstention from meat it demanded of the faithful favored the consumption of fish. Islam contents itself with prohibiting the pig, among animals conventionally consumed in the West, although it has reservations concerning the rabbit and shellfish. The fast of Ramadan is the most rigorous exercise in abstention prescribed by any of the Abrahamic religions, but the deprivation of the day is frequently offset by feasting at night, even in the least affluent Muslim communities.

The practice of serving tea and coffee has developed into a fine art in many Mediterranean countries; here, Moroccans partake at a festival in Fès.

In a very fundamental sense, the Atlantic has for long been vivifying the Mediterranean. Every second, about one million cubic meters of Atlantic water flow into the Mediterranean past Gibraltar, while beneath the surface a slightly inferior quantity of Mediterranean water flows out into the Atlantic; it is this interchange that permits the Mediterranean to remain more or less stable. There has also been a culinary interchange between the Mediterranean and the Atlantic, or rather with the New World lying beyond the Atlantic, and it is this process that has enabled the Mediterranean world to complete its complement of necessary ingredients. Which Mediterranean cuisine could, for example, dispense with the tomato? Despite the ubiquity of the tomato, the process of its acceptance was by no means swift, nor was the route of transmission direct. Seville witnessed the European landfall of the tomato, but it was in northern Italy that it first entered the cooking pot. It was also by way of Italy that haricot beans traveled to Provence, and the bell pepper is said to have made a lengthy detour via the Persian Gulf and Ottoman Turkey before being welcomed in Europe.

Europe in return made its own donations to the diet of the Americas, in addition to which the voyages of discovery profoundly affected the cuisines of both Africa and Asia. It can be said, indeed, that the "discovery" of the New World resulted in a new world order of food, which permits us to insert the Mediterranean in a truly global pattern of change.

The tracing of cultural influences is a delicate and imprecise task. National pride is often at stake, and definitive, explicit documentation is rarely available. This is true even of literature and the arts, where a concrete body of data may be analyzed. The case of cuisine is still more difficult, for cooks do not leave permanent monuments of their art. The etymology of the names of foodstuffs and dishes is perhaps our best and most reliable guide. If an item in a given national cuisine is identified by a name borrowed or derived from a foreign language, it is reasonable to suppose that the item itself is also a borrowing, particularly if the donor language is that of a triumphant empire or civilization. Examples of this are the Arabic loanwords found in Spanish, Italian and to a lesser degree French (not to mention English), and the Turkish names embedded in the menus of Greece and the Balkans. But the etymological evidence is not infallible. The precise sense of food names may change even within the same language, a possibility that is heightened by the process of being absorbed into another language. Some names are, moreover, etymological mysteries, present in many languages and cuisines, but not indisputably indigenous to any of them. No one can pretend to be sure whence came *moussaka,* the name or the dish, and no satisfactory conclusion can be seen for the wranglings of philhellenes and Turcophiles over the genesis of *baklava*.

The task of the culinary historian is, in any event, not in the last resort to demonstrate in mechanical fashion who took what from whom. Cuisines, like other cultural enterprises, are the result of cumulative and collaborative efforts, expended by varying peoples in varying ways and to varying degrees at varying times. Preeminence indeed goes to certain societies and cultures, but there is no cuisine that has been exclusively a donor or exclusively a recipient. To doubt this would be to misread the whole history of Mediterranean cuisine.

Beyond differences of language and religion, and beneath the whole pattern of interchange, there are certain perennial features of life in the Mediterranean that have helped to maintain its cuisine as a living tradition. First comes an unconscious aesthetic of everyday life and the enjoyment of simple, accessible pleasures, foremost among them being the taking of food, especially in outdoor settings of natural beauty. Then comes the importance of family and religion—twin foci of loyalty—one narrow, the other broad. Loyalty to the nation-state, even in countries such as France and Spain where it took root relatively early, has never ranked very high in the value system of the Mediterranean peoples; the attachment has been rather to something more immediate and familiar, and to something more elevated and universal. Especially in the Mediterranean world, the family is above all the unit that prepares and eats food together (preferably in the company of guests); it is the cornerstone of all culinary tradition. Fast food, by contrast, is the culinary accompaniment to the breakup of families. The Mediterranean emphasis on religion, while not without its drawbacks, complements the succession of seasons with its own measurement of time, feasts and fasts that both support and give meaning to the sustenance of life.

There are numerous developments that threaten this pan-Mediterranean ethos. The frenetic pace of modern life and economic need draw women increasingly outside the home, and it is only through great feats of self-sacrifice that they can perpetuate the culinary traditions of their mothers and grandmothers. Tradition is also threatened by the tourist-fueled onslaught of international fast food; the Golden Arches of McDonald's are rearing up around the Mediterranean like the triumphal arches of a globally uniform consumerism. The ingredients of Mediterranean cuisine are no longer, in many places, what they used to be: battery poultry yields the same unsatisfactory results as elsewhere; the use of chemical fertilizers is introducing the Mediterranean to the joys of the anaemic and tasteless tomato; and the precious stock of its fish and seafood is being depleted by pollution so severe that its glistening and historic waters are now being compared to an open sewer.

There is a sense in which the future of Mediterranean cuisine does not depend entirely upon the region itself. Much talk is heard today in the United States of the healthful properties of the Mediterranean diet. It is lauded for spurning the use of red meat in large quantities; showing great favor to fish and seafood; using olive oil instead of animal fat; and emphasizing the importance of legumes and fresh vegetables. (This hygienic listing excludes, of course, another common feature of Mediterranean cuisines—indulgence in rich and sugary pastries!) Concern for the consequences of diet on health is itself an originally Mediterranean phenomenon. It was the Greeks who first sought to discover the essentials of a healthful regimen; their findings were confirmed, extended or modified by the Arab physicians who, either in person or through their writings, were responsible for the foundation of European dietetics in Cordoba, Salerno, Montpellier and elsewhere. If the diet of late twentieth-century *Homo americanus* is indeed to be modified by drawing on Mediterranean models, it will not only be because of the intrinsic appeal of those models, but also because of the lasting cultural influence of the Mediterranean world, long after the centers of world power have drawn far distant from its shores.

The introductory lecture is now over. Let us now embark on our voyage through the culinary history of the Mediterranean, with its seven ports of call.

The vibrant open markets of Old Nice are perfectly suited to the sun-drenched climate of the Mediterranean.

SPAIN

SPAIN

Andalusia and Catalonia

Spain, it is said, owes the origin of its name to an animal, the rabbit. According to Pliny, it made its initial appearance in Spain and then hopped across the Pyrenees into France, from where it proliferated throughout Europe. The rabbit was but the earliest culinary gift of Spain, and arguably the least significant. The greater contributions came first during the brilliant centuries of Arab rule, and then during the colonization of Hispanic America. It can even be said that the entire geopolitical history of Spain, and especially its Mediterranean shores, could be written in terms of the movement of foodstuffs and dishes.

A few basic elements of Spanish cuisine were already in place before the beginning of Roman rule in the early second century B.C. The olive had been brought from the eastern Mediterranean one or two centuries earlier; grafted onto the primitive oleaster, it was quick to flourish. The Phoenicians similarly brought the chick-pea (garbanzo) from the east. The fish off the Andalusian coast were already being harvested, and some of the techniques still used today for salting fish may go back to pre-Roman times.

The Romans, as true imperialists, developed Spanish agriculture primarily to serve the needs of the metropolis.

Previous pages: Cape Formentor, the northernmost tip of Mallorca, boasts rugged countryside and breath-taking views of the sea. Left: Labyrinthine archways and columns in Córdoba's Mezquite are the legacy of early Moorish occupation; the Mosque was begun in 785 and completed two centuries later.

APPETIZERS

Garlic is among the most ancient cultivated plants in the Mediterranean.

Appetizers

Whether they are called *mezes,* antipasti, tapas or hors d'oeuvres, these appetizers are some of the most interesting and delicious dishes of Mediterranean cuisine—an enticing beginning for any repast. In the Mediterranean, meals are to be shared and enjoyed and hosts pride themselves on how many delectable little dishes they can offer to their guests. A table laden with an array of appetizers is symbolic of abundance and hospitality.

Commonly, these dishes are brought to the table a few at a time, or they are set out as part of a large assortment to which guests help themselves. Some of them can be expanded into main courses and, in fact, a selection of these plates can be a satisfying meal on their own.

The first category of appetizer is the purée, or what some might call a spread or dip. The Near East and Greece are home to some of the best: *hummus* made with chickpeas (garbanzos), tahini and garlic; Syrian *muhammarah,* a mixture of pomegranate and walnuts; smoky *baba ghannouj* made with roasted eggplant; Greek fava (broad) bean purée with olive oil and slivers of red onion; *skordalia* of potato or bread crumbs and a generous measure of garlic; creamy *taramasalata* made from prized fish roe. All are meant for serving with pita bread. The French *tapénade,* a spunky olive spread, is ideal on grilled country bread or it can be used as a sauce for grilled fish or vegetables.

North African vegetable salads make a particularly tasty and colorful appetizer assortment: spicy slivers of carrot; olive-strewn cauliflower; a plate of glistening grilled peppers, eggplant and tomatoes; bowls of olives; lemon wedges with an aromatic dressing. Served with Tunisian semolina bread (recipe on page 84), and followed by *b'stilla* (recipe on page 87), a North African feast is at hand.

An Italian antipasto table might include the Sicilian sweet-and-sour eggplant dish known as *caponata* or an Apulian grilled eggplant salad, sautéed slices of golden pumpkin squash with mint and garlic, marinated sardines or anchovies, crispy rice croquettes, slices of fresh mozzarella or pecorino cheese drizzled with olive oil, paper-thin sheets of house-cured prosciutto, and a slice of *scacciata* (recipe on page 74), the double-crusted pizza of Calabria and Sicily.

It is in Spain, with its tapas bars outfitted with long counters on which are laid seemingly countless platters brimming with foods, that the appetizer assortment has been elevated to an institution. Each bar is known for a specialty. People go from place to place, sipping glasses of well-chilled *fino* sherry and tasting and sampling tapas. These might include *pa amb tomaquet,* grilled bread rubbed with garlic, olive oil and tomato; wedges of *tortilla,* an omelet ribboned with golden brown potato and onion slices, marinated sardines or cooked vegetables dressed *"à la grecque"* with a Greek-style marinade that has been adopted by the French and the Spaniards as well. Salt-cod *buñuelos* and shrimp fritters, pine nut–dotted meatballs, a rice salad, some *manchego* cheese, a few slices of sausage, a mound of fried almonds, and a bowl of olives might complete the tableau.

Previous pages: Marinated Octopus Salad (recipe page 52)

Olive trees have thrived in the Peloponnese since the Greeks began exporting olive oil in the 11th century B.C.

The *meze* table, depending upon the country, would have an assortment of purées—*hummus, fava,* a rich *baba ghannouj*—crunchy *falafel* with a lemony tahini dressing, cheese-filled fried eggplant sandwiches, deep-fried mussels with walnut *tarator* sauce or rice-stuffed mussels in the shell, stuffed grapeleaves, marinated octopus, shrimp and beets with garlicky almond *skordalia,* just to mention a few. Maybe even hard-cooked eggs dipped in toasted coriander and cumin seeds.

The combinations and variations are countless. You can pair room-temperature salads—the traditional Greek mix of ripe tomatoes, cucumbers, romaine, Kalamata olives and tart feta cheese or the equally venerable Provençal *salade niçoise* of beans, potatoes, tomatoes, tuna and olives—with such hot dishes as fried mussels; croquettes of salt cod, rice, or potato; little meatballs or fried cheese. Or, at the height of tomato season, make *tabbouleh* or *fattoush,* similar in that they both bring together tomatoes, cucumbers, onions, mint, parsley and lemon, but different in that one uses bulgur (cracked wheat) and the other toasted pita bread. And don't overlook the savory pastries in the next chapter for a wealth of delicious small foods enclosed in dough.

At one time Europe depended so heavily on spices, they became common currency; here, an Egyptian merchant offers a variety of the once-traded seasonings.

For a more substantial plate, prepare Circassian chicken, the Turkish classic that combines chicken in a fragrant nut sauce, or add shellfish or tuna to an Andalusian rice salad. For rice in yet another form, set out a plate of rice-filled *dolmas* and bowls of yogurt and lemon wedges or meat-and-rice *dolmas* served warm with *avgolemono* sauce and pita bread.

In the Mediterranean eggs are not for breakfast. They appear on the menu as an appetizer or main dish, customarily served at room temperature. Street vendors sell them hard-cooked for dipping into spice mixtures. *Tortillas* in Spain, *frittate* in Italy and all manner of savory *omelettes* in France and North Africa can be substantial enough for dinner or lunch, or they can appear cut into appetizer portions on the buffet table.

This chapter is about temptation, about stimulating the palate and the appetite. Start here and move on to other courses, or stay here and eat from a bountiful table.

TUNISIA

CHALDA BROUKLOU SFAXINYA

Cauliflower Salad from Sfax

Sfax, the second largest city in Tunisia, is an agricultural center noted especially for the cultivation of olives. This salad plays the mildness of potatoes and cauliflower off against the heat of harissa.

1 cauliflower, broken into florets
8 small red potatoes or new potatoes, unpeeled
salt to taste, plus 1 teaspoon salt
1 teaspoon *harissa* mixed with 3 tablespoons water (see glossary)
1 teaspoon ground caraway
1 teaspoon ground coriander
¼ cup (2 fl oz/60 ml) olive oil
2–3 tablespoons fresh lemon juice
grated zest of 1 lemon
sharply flavored black olives for garnish (optional)

Bring 2 saucepans three-fourths full of water to a boil. Add the cauliflower to one pan and the potatoes to the other, and salt to taste to each. Bring to a boil and cook until they are just tender; the cauliflower will take 10–15 minutes and the potatoes about 30 minutes. Do not overcook; drain well.

Cut the potatoes into bite-sized chunks about the same size as the florets. Place the vegetables in a serving bowl. In a small bowl stir together the diluted *harissa,* caraway, coriander, the 1 teaspoon salt, oil, and lemon juice and zest. Pour the mixture over the vegetables and toss well to combine. Let stand for 1 hour, then readjust the seasoning as the potatoes will absorb most of the salt.

Just before serving, garnish with olives, if desired. Serve at room temperature.

SERVES 6–8

Clockwise from left: Cauliflower Salad from Sfax, Olive Salad, Lemon Salad, Tomato and Sweet Pepper Salad

MOROCCO

SALATIT MISCHWIA

Tomato and Sweet Pepper Salad

This North African salad can be served as a starter or as an accompaniment to meat and fish dishes.

6 ripe tomatoes, peeled, seeded and diced
3 sweet green peppers (capsicums), roasted, peeled, seeded and diced (see glossary)
2 tablespoons fresh lemon juice
1 teaspoon salt
½ teaspoon freshly ground pepper
3 tablespoons olive oil
2 tablespoons chopped fresh flat-leaf (Italian) parsley
1 small hot chili pepper, seeded and finely minced (optional)
peel from ¼ preserved lemon, rinsed and finely diced (optional; see glossary)
½ teaspoon ground cumin (optional)
1 clove garlic, very finely minced (optional)

Place the tomatoes, green peppers, lemon juice, salt, ground pepper, oil and parsley in a salad bowl. Toss to mix.

If you like, add the chili pepper, preserved lemon, cumin and/or garlic to the mixture. Toss once again and serve at room temperature.

SERVES 6

MOROCCO

SALATIT LIMOUN

Lemon Salad

A specialty of the colorful city of Fès, this salad is quite tart. It can also act as a sauce for simple baked or broiled fish.

4 lemons
1 onion, finely chopped
4 tablespoons chopped fresh flat-leaf (Italian) parsley
1 teaspoon paprika
¼ teaspoon cayenne pepper
2 teaspoons ground cumin
12 black olives, pitted and chopped
salt
olive oil

Peel the lemons and remove all of the white pith. Separate into segments by cutting through and removing the membrane. Dice the segments and place in a salad bowl.

Add the onion, parsley, paprika, cayenne, cumin and olives to the lemons and toss to mix. If you think the salad needs salt, add a little. Then drizzle on just a bit of olive oil, toss lightly to coat and serve slightly chilled or at room temperature.

SERVES 4

MOROCCO

MESLALLA

Olive Salad

Although considered a salad in Morocco, this lively mixture may seem more like a condiment. Think of it as a North African tapénade *and serve it as you like. In a similar Cypriot dish that is served as a spread with bread, the olives are chopped and mixed with ¼ cup (2 fl oz/60 ml) each olive oil and vinegar; 2 cloves garlic, finely minced; and 2 teaspoons ground coriander. Be sure to use an assortment of olives—black, green, purple—for a colorful salad.*

2 cups (10 oz/315 g) mixed olives
juice of 2 large lemons (about ½ cup/4 fl oz/125 ml)
1 teaspoon paprika
½ teaspoon cayenne pepper
1 clove garlic, finely minced
1 teaspoon salt
3 tablespoons olive oil
3 tablespoons chopped fresh flat-leaf (Italian) parsley

Rinse the olives briefly under running water, then pit and place in a salad bowl. Add all the remaining ingredients and toss to mix well. Cover and chill well before serving.

SERVES 6

TUNISIA

MZOURA

Carrot Salad

A dash of fiery harissa *perks up this carrot salad.*

1 lb (500 g) carrots, peeled and thinly sliced or julienned
5 tablespoons (3 fl oz/80 ml) olive oil
2 cloves garlic, finely minced
1 teaspoon *harissa* mixed with 6 tablespoons (3 fl oz/90 ml) water (see glossary)
1 teaspoon ground caraway
1 teaspoon salt
1 teaspoon ground cumin
¼ cup (2 fl oz/60 ml) wine vinegar
chopped fresh flat-leaf (Italian) parsley or fresh cilantro (fresh coriander)

Bring a saucepan three-fourths full of salted water to a boil. Add the carrots and boil until tender, 5–8 minutes. Drain well.

In a sauté pan over low heat, warm the olive oil. Add the garlic, diluted *harissa,* caraway, salt, cumin and vinegar; stir for 2 minutes. Add the drained carrots and cook, stirring occasionally, until most of the liquid is absorbed, 5–8 minutes. Transfer to a serving dish and garnish with parsley or cilantro. Serve at room temperature.

SERVES 4–6

Carrot Salad

Eggs with Peppers, Tomatoes and Eggplant

A L G E R I A

CHAKCHOUKA

Eggs with Peppers, Tomatoes and Eggplant

A chakchouka *is a North African ragout of vegetables, and sometimes* merguez *(a spicy sausage), topped with eggs. It is an ideal dish for entertaining, as the base can be prepared ahead of time and the eggs dropped in and cooked just before serving. The eggs can be cooked on top of the stove or, once added, finished in the oven. This recipe uses the Mediterranean vegetable triumverate of eggplant, peppers and tomatoes, but you can add cauliflower, potatoes, zucchini (courgettes) or artichokes as you like.*

6 tablespoons (3 fl oz/90 ml) olive oil
2 eggplants (aubergines), peeled and cut into 1-in (2.5-cm) pieces
2 red or green sweet peppers (capsicums), seeded, deribbed and cut into long, narrow strips
½ lb (250 g) *merguez,* cut into 1-in (2.5-cm) pieces (recipe on page 182)
3 tomatoes, peeled, seeded and chopped
2 cloves garlic, minced
2–3 tablespoons chopped fresh flat-leaf (Italian) parsley
6 eggs
salt and freshly ground pepper

❀ In a large sauté pan over medium-high heat, warm 4 tablespoons (2 fl oz/6 ml) of the oil. Add the eggplant and fry, tossing and stirring occasionally, until tender, about 10 minutes.

❀ Meanwhile, in another sauté pan, warm the remaining 2 tablespoons oil over medium heat. Add the peppers and sauté for 5 minutes. As soon as they are ready, add the peppers to the eggplant. When the eggplant is tender add the tomatoes, garlic and parsley, stir well, cover and simmer over low heat, until all the vegetables are soft, about 15 minutes longer.

❀ In another sauté pan over medium heat, sauté the *merguez* until browned and add it to the eggplant mixture.

❀ Remove the lid. Using the back of a spoon, make 6 hollows in the vegetable mixture. Break 1 egg into each hollow. Some recipes advise breaking the yolks, but it is not necessary. Cover and cook until the eggs are set, 4–5 minutes. Sprinkle with salt and pepper to taste and serve at once.

SERVES 3–6

TURKEY

PANCAR SALATASI

Beet Salad

In many countries along the Mediterranean, beets are dressed simply with olive oil and vinegar. Sometimes yogurt is mixed with the vinaigrette, which turns a vibrant pink once it is tossed with the beets. The beet greens can be cooked and served along with the beets, and the salad dressed with either olive oil and vinegar or with olive oil and lemon juice. Other versions toss the beets with thinly sliced oranges and red (Spanish) onions. Here, a simple Turkish beet salad is dressed with olive oil, vinegar and garlic. In France, the beets might be dressed with walnut oil and vinegar and topped with chopped toasted walnuts. In Greece, 1 teaspoon ground allspice or cinnamon would be added to the dressing, or the beets would be dressed with skordalia *made with bread and almonds (see page 58). In Spain 1 teaspoon aniseeds would flavor the dressing, while Tunisian cooks add 1 teaspoon caraway seeds.*

1 large or 2 small bunches beets (beetroots), about 1½ lb (750 g)
¼ cup (2 fl oz/60 ml) olive oil
2 tablespoons red wine vinegar
2 cloves garlic, minced
salt and freshly ground pepper

There are two methods for cooking beets, boiling and baking, with some cooks believing that baking them results in a more earthy flavor.

To boil the beets, scrub them but do not peel. Cut off the leaves but leave 1 in (2.5 cm) of the stem and root attached so the beet doesn't bleed its color into the water. Reserve the greens for another use (see greens with lemon–olive oil dressing on page 49). Put the beets into a saucepan and add water to cover. Bring to a boil, reduce the heat to medium, cover partially and simmer until tender, 20–30 minutes. Drain off the cooking water and add a little cold water to the pot to cool the beets. When they can be handled, peel the beets, then slice or quarter, depending upon the size.

To bake the beets, preheat an oven to 350°F (180°C). Prepare the beets as for boiling and place in a baking pan. Add water to a depth of 1 in (2.5 cm). Cover with foil and bake until tender, about 1 hour. Remove from the oven and, when cool enough to handle, peel and slice or quarter, depending upon the size.

Place the cut beets in a serving bowl. In a small bowl whisk together the oil, vinegar, garlic and salt and pepper to taste. Pour over the beets and toss to coat. Serve at room temperature.

SERVES 4–6

TURKEY

ADAS SALATASI

Lentil Salad

Lentil salads are served in every country of the Mediterranean with only slight variations. Green lentils take longer to cook but they hold their shape better than brown ones. Be careful not to overcook them or they will disintegrate into a purée. Dried haricot, fava (broad) or white beans can be used in place of the lentils. These beans will need to be soaked overnight in water to cover in the refrigerator before cooking. They will also require longer cooking times.

2 cups (14 oz/440 g) dried lentils
6 tablespoons (3 fl oz/90 ml) olive oil
3 tablespoons fresh lemon juice
salt and freshly ground pepper
1 onion, finely chopped
1 or 2 cloves garlic, minced
2 teaspoons ground cumin
4 tablespoons chopped fresh mint and/or fresh flat-leaf (Italian) parsley
quartered or sliced tomatoes (optional)
sliced or quartered hard-cooked eggs (optional)
black olives (optional)
crumbled feta or fresh goat cheese (optional)

Rinse the lentils and place in a saucepan. Add cold water to cover and bring to a boil. Reduce the heat to low and simmer gently, uncovered, until the lentils are tender but not falling apart. The timing will depend upon the age of the lentils; begin testing after 15–20 minutes. Some can take as long as 1 hour; others may be tender in 25 minutes. Drain the lentils well and transfer to a bowl.

While the lentils are still warm, dress with 4 tablespoons (2 fl oz/60 ml) of the olive oil and the lemon juice. Season to taste with salt and pepper.

Warm the remaining 2 tablespoons olive oil in a sauté pan over medium heat. Add the onion and cook for 3–4 minutes. Add the garlic and cumin and cook for 2 minutes.

Fold the onion mixture into the lentils, then fold in the parsley or mint. Let stand for 1 hour, then adjust the seasoning. The lentils will have absorbed some of the salt and the dressing.

Garnish with tomatoes, eggs, olives, or crumbled cheese, if desired. Serve at room temperature.

SERVES 6–8

TURKEY

ÇERKEZ TAVUĞU

Circassian Chicken

This chicken salad in walnut sauce is one of the glories of the Turkish table. The recipe was carried there by slaves brought to Turkey from Georgia. It is usually served as a meze, but you can increase the portions and serve it as a main course luncheon or supper. Some versions are quite spicy with hot pepper. Some cooks add almonds along with the walnuts. If you wish to do this, reduce the walnuts to 2 cups (8 oz/250 g) and add ¾ cup (4½ oz/140 g) almonds. The top is usually dusted with paprika and drizzled with olive oil. You can make this with a whole chicken instead of the chicken breasts; increase the cooking time accordingly.

FOR COOKING THE CHICKEN:

3 lb (1.5 kg) chicken breasts
4 cups (32 fl oz/1 l) water
1 onion, chopped
1 carrot, peeled and cut into chunks
1 bay leaf (optional)
1 fresh thyme sprig (optional)
a few whole cloves (optional)

FOR THE SAUCE:

¼ cup (2 oz/60 g) unsalted butter
1 onion, chopped
4 teaspoons finely minced garlic
2 tablespoons sweet paprika
1 teaspoon cayenne pepper
2 slices bread, crusts discarded
3 cups (12 oz/375 g) walnuts
2 cups (16 fl oz/500 ml) reduced chicken stock from cooking chicken
salt and freshly ground black pepper

FOR THE GARNISH:

3 tablespoons walnut oil
2 teaspoons paprika
chopped fresh flat-leaf (Italian) parsley

Top to bottom: Beet Salad, Lentil Salad, Circassian Chicken

To cook the chicken, place it in a saucepan with the water, onion and carrot. Add the bay leaf, thyme, and cloves, if you like. Bring to a boil and reduce the heat to medium. Simmer, uncovered, until the chicken is tender, about 25 minutes.

Remove the chicken from the stock and set aside to cool. Strain the stock and return it to the saucepan. When the chicken is cool enough to handle, bone and skin the pieces and shred the meat. Place the meat in a bowl, cover and set aside. Add the chicken bones and skin to the stock and simmer until the stock is reduced to 2 cups (16 fl oz/500 ml). Remove from heat.

To make the sauce, melt the butter in a sauté pan over medium heat. Add the onion and sauté until tender and translucent, 8–10 minutes. Add the garlic, paprika and cayenne pepper and sauté for 3 minutes. Remove from the heat.

In a bowl soak the bread in water to cover briefly, then squeeze dry and crumble into a food processor fitted with the metal blade or in a blender. Add the walnuts and grind together until fine. Add the onion mixture and pulse to combine. Add the reduced chicken stock and purée to form a smooth sauce. Season to taste with salt and pepper.

Toss half of the sauce with the chicken and then transfer to a serving plate. Top with the remaining sauce.

To make the garnish, warm together the walnut oil and paprika in a small pan. Drizzle this mixture over the walnut sauce. Sprinkle with parsley and serve at room temperature.

SERVES 6–8

Top to bottom: Puréed Yellow Split Peas, Fish Roe Dip

GREECE

FAVA

Puréed Yellow Split Peas

In Turkey, Egypt and North Africa, as well as in Greece, a bean purée is often part of the meze *table. Although in Greece this purée is made with yellow split peas, broad beans are generally used elsewhere. The addition of the dill is common in Turkey. If you do not drizzle lemon juice on the purée, garnish the plate with lemon wedges. Pita bread (recipe on page 82) is the usual accompaniment and, occasionally, feta cheese.*

1⅛ cups (½ lb/250 g) dried yellow split peas or dried fava (broad) beans
1 small onion, chopped
3 tablespoons olive oil
3½ cups (28 fl oz/875 ml) water
1 teaspoon salt, plus salt to taste
2 tablespoons chopped fresh dill, optional
freshly ground pepper

FOR THE TOPPING:

2–4 tablespoons olive oil
2 tablespoons fresh lemon juice, optional

chopped or thinly sliced red (Spanish) onion or green (spring) onion
freshly ground pepper

If using yellow split peas, rinse well under running water. If using fava beans, place in a bowl with water to cover generously. Refrigerate overnight. Drain and rinse well under running water.

In a 2-qt (2-l) saucepan, combine the peas or beans, onion, oil, the water and the 1 teaspoon salt. Bring to a boil over medium heat. Reduce the heat to low, cover and simmer until the peas or beans are so soft they have disintegrated, about 1 hour.

Transfer to a food processor fitted with the metal blade and purée. Alternatively, pass the beans and their liquid through a coarse sieve. Mix in the dill, if using, and salt and pepper to taste. Transfer the purée to a serving dish, cover with plastic wrap and allow to cool and thicken.

To serve, drizzle with the olive oil and the lemon juice, if using. Top with the onion and a grinding of pepper.

SERVES 4–6

GREECE

Taramasalata

Fish Roe Dip

The basis of this dish is tarama, *or mullet roe. It is available in bulk or in jars in stores specializing in foods from the Middle East. Carp or cod can be substituted. Serve with warm crusty bread and trimmed green (spring) onions, radishes, cucumbers and celery.*

5 slices white bread, crusts discarded
5 oz (155 g) *tarama*
1 onion, coarsely chopped
1 cup (8 fl oz/250 ml) olive oil
juice of 2 large lemons (about ½ cup/4 fl oz/125 ml)
2 tablespoons chopped fresh flat-leaf (Italian) parsley or a small handful of sharply flavored black olives

In a shallow bowl combine the bread with just enough water to cover and let soak briefly. Remove the bread, squeeze dry and place in a food processor fitted with the metal blade or in a blender.

Add the *tarama* and onion and process to mix. With the motor running, slowly add the oil and lemon juice, processing until a smooth paste forms.

Transfer to a shallow serving bowl. Cover and chill.

Serve chilled, garnished with parsley or black olives.

SERVES 6

MEDITERRANEAN

Spiced Olives

What could be a simpler or more elegant appetizer than a bowl of marinated olives?

FOR GREEK OLIVES:

1 lb (500 g) Kalamata olives
4 tablespoons dried oregano
1 tablespoon dried rosemary
1 tablespoon dried thyme
2 strips orange zest, each about 2 in (5 cm) long and ¼ in (6 mm) wide
olive oil

FOR SICILIAN OLIVES:

1 lb (500 g) green olives
3–4 cloves garlic, cut into slivers
2 tablespoons dried oregano
1 teaspoon red pepper flakes
olive oil

FOR MOROCCAN OLIVES:

1 lb (500 g) black or green olives
6 tablespoons chopped fresh flat-leaf (Italian) parsley
6 tablespoons chopped fresh cilantro (fresh coriander)
3 cloves garlic, chopped
1 teaspoon red pepper flakes or 2 fresh chili peppers, slivered
½ teaspoon ground cumin
½ cup (4 fl oz/125 ml) olive oil
2 teaspoons fresh lemon juice, a few strips lemon or orange zest or peel and some juice from ½ preserved lemon (see glossary)

Whether preparing Greek, Sicilian or Moroccan olives, drain the brine off the olives and rinse them well.

To make the Greek olives, dry the rinsed olives thoroughly and combine with all the remaining ingredients, including olive oil to cover or coat.

To make the Sicilian olives, dry the rinsed olives thoroughly and then crack or pit them. Combine with all the remaining ingredients, including olive oil to cover or coat.

To make the Moroccan olives, crack the rinsed olives and place in cold water to cover overnight. Drain well and combine with all the remaining ingredients.

Place the olives in a sterilized jar, cover tightly and refrigerate for at least 2 days.

EACH RECIPE YIELDS 1 LB (500 G) OLIVES

Spiced Olives

PROVENCE

TAPÉNADE

Olive Spread

This savory spread will keep in a covered container for about a week in the refrigerator. It is excellent on warm bread, as an addition to chopped hard-cooked egg yolks for stuffed eggs, or spread under the skin of a chicken before roasting or grilling. It can also be diluted with a little olive oil and used as a dressing for grilled peppers (capsicums) or eggplants (aubergines). Some versions include grated lemon or orange zest; others are flavored with chopped fresh basil.

1 cup (5 oz/155 g) Niçoise or oil-cured black olives, pitted
6 anchovy fillets in olive oil, drained and chopped (about 1 tablespoon)
2 tablespoons capers, rinsed and coarsely chopped
2 cloves garlic, finely chopped
juice of 1 lemon
4–6 tablespoons (2–3 fl oz/60–90 ml) virgin olive oil
2 tablespoons Cognac (optional)

In a food processor fitted with the metal blade or in a blender, combine the olives, anchovies, capers, garlic and lemon juice. Process to form a paste. With the motor running, slowly add enough of the oil to form a spoonable mixture. Stir in the Cognac, if using.

Transfer to a small bowl and serve at room temperature.

SERVES 6

PROVENCE

SALADE NIÇOISE

Niçoise Salad

This salad has evolved over time. At first it was a vegetable salad, but gradually anchovies and tuna worked their way onto the plate. It can be an ample first course or be expanded to be a complete meal, depending upon the portion size and the amount of tuna. The tuna is usually canned white meat tuna packed in good olive oil. Purists insist on anchovy or *tuna, and on artichokes* or *fava beans, but with such wonderful ingredients, who needs to be pure! (In Provence, cooks use young artichokes and favas for this salad and add them raw; because such tender vegetables are more difficult to find outside of France, here they have been cooked.) While cooked potatoes and green beans are not part of an authentic* salade niçoise, *they are excellent additions as well.*

If there is salad left over, you can make a sandwich called pan bagnat, *literally, "wet bread." First, cut a round loaf or baguette in half and scoop out some of the white crumb. Rub the inside of the loaf with a cut garlic clove, then sprinkle with a little vinegar and olive oil and some salt and pepper. Put a serving of the salad between the bread halves and press them together firmly. Wrap well and refrigerate for at least an hour or for up to several hours before serving.*

salt
6 tomatoes, quartered
1 cucumber, peeled and sliced
2 green sweet peppers (capsicums), seeded, deribbed and sliced crosswise
2 small bulbs fennel, cored and sliced crosswise (optional)
6 green (spring) onions, trimmed but left whole, or 1 small onion, thinly sliced (optional)
6 small artichokes, trimmed, cooked, and quartered, or 12 tiny artichokes, trimmed and cooked
½ lb (250 g) shelled young, tender fresh fava (broad) or lima beans, cooked briefly
3 hard-cooked eggs, quartered lengthwise
12 anchovy fillets in olive oil, drained and cut into thin strips, or 2 cans (6 oz/185 g each) canned tuna, broken into large flakes
2 cloves garlic, finely minced
¼ cup (2 fl oz/60 ml) red wine vinegar
½ cup (4 fl oz/125 ml) olive oil
12 fresh basil leaves, chopped
freshly ground pepper
¼ cup (1½ oz/45 g) black olives

Salt the tomato quarters. Divide the tomatoes, cucumber, sweet peppers, the fennel and onions (if using), artichokes, beans and eggs evenly among 6 individual plates, arranging them attractively. Distribute the anchovies or tuna among the vegetables. Alternatively, assemble all the ingredients on a large platter or in a large shallow bowl.

In a small bowl crush the garlic with a little salt, then whisk in the vinegar, oil, basil, and ground pepper to taste. Pour the dressing evenly over the salads.

Garnish with the olives and serve.

SERVES 6

PROVENCE

BRANDADE DE MORUE

Salt Cod Mousse

The word brandade *is Provençal dialect for "something that is stirred." Purists would sneer at the use of the food processor to assemble this purée, which is traditionally prepared in a mortar and pestle. But there is no reason to balk at progress when time is valuable and flavor is not sacrificed. Mashed potatoes can be beaten into the purée. You will need 1 pound (500 g) potatoes, peeled, boiled and mashed by hand (do not use a processor for this step or the potatoes will be gluey). If you use the potatoes, you will need to increase the olive oil by about 1 cup (8 fl oz/250 ml) and add it, warmed, to the potatoes as you mash them. The cod is then beaten into the potatoes with a fork. In Valencia, a similar mixture of salt cod and potatoes is prepared. It includes only olive oil, no milk, and a few pine nuts are mashed in with the potatoes. The dish is garnished with toasted walnuts and chopped hard-cooked eggs.*

1½ lb (750 g) boneless salt cod (see glossary)
1½ cups (12 fl oz/375 ml) olive oil
1¼ cups (10 fl oz/310 ml) milk
2 cloves garlic, puréed
juice of 1 lemon
freshly grated nutmeg
freshly ground pepper
grilled or toasted bread slices

In a bowl combine the salt cod and water to cover. Refrigerate for 24–48 hours, changing the water at least 4 times. The amount of soaking necessary will depend upon the saltiness of the cod; thicker pieces may take longer than thinner pieces.

Drain the cod and place in a large pan with water to cover. Bring to a boil, cover, reduce the heat to low and poach gently until just tender, 8–10 minutes. Drain and cool slightly.

Remove all traces of skin and any small bones and flake the cod with your fingers or a fork.

In a small saucepan heat the oil. In another pan, heat the milk. Put the flaked cod into a food processor fitted with the metal blade. Add the garlic and pulse once to combine. Add half of the warm oil, a bit at a time, processing to combine. Then slowly mix in half of the warm milk. Now slowly beat in first the remaining warm oil and then the remaining warm milk. Add only as much of the remaining oil, bit by bit, as is needed to achieve a very pale, thick and smooth mixture. Add the lemon juice and some nutmeg and season to taste with pepper.

Spoon onto a serving dish and serve warm with grilled or toasted bread.

SERVES 6–8

Top to bottom: Niçoise Salad, Salt Cod Mousse, Olive Spread

Clockwise from top: Eggplant Purée with Tahini, Bulgur Salad, Chick-pea Purée with Sesame, Toasted Bread Salad

LEBANON

TABBOULEH

Bulgur Salad

This salad is best in the summer, as it is dependent upon good tomatoes. In Turkey there is a similar salad to which chopped green sweet peppers (capsicums) are added. For an interesting variation, omit the green onions and toss ½ cup (2½ oz/75 g) chopped white onion with ½ teaspoon ground allspice, then add with the parsley.

1 cup (6 oz/185 g) fine bulgur (cracked wheat)
3 cups (4½ oz/140 g) finely chopped fresh flat-leaf (Italian) parsley
½ cup (1½ oz/45 g) chopped green (spring) onions
1½ cups (2½ oz/75 g) chopped fresh mint
2 cups (12 oz/375 g) chopped ripe tomatoes (about 4)
½ cup (4 fl oz/125 ml) fresh lemon juice
½ cup (4 fl oz/125 ml) olive oil
salt and freshly ground pepper
romaine (cos) lettuce leaves

❦ In a bowl soak the bulgur in water to cover for about 20 minutes, then drain well. Transfer to a serving bowl. Add the parsley, green onions, mint and tomatoes and toss to combine.
❦ In a small bowl whisk together the lemon juice and olive oil. Pour over the bulgur mixture and toss well. Season to taste with salt and pepper.
❦ Serve with romaine leaves for scooping up the salad.

SERVES 4–6

LEBANON

FATTOUSH
Toasted Bread Salad

This Lebanese salad replaces the bulgur wheat of the classic tabbouleh with toasted pita bread.

2 large pita bread rounds (recipe on page 82)
1½ cups (9 oz/280 g) chopped ripe tomatoes
1 cup (5 oz/155 g) peeled, seeded and diced cucumber
1 cup (3 oz/90 g) finely chopped green (spring) onions
1 cup (1½ oz/40 g) finely chopped fresh flat-leaf (Italian) parsley
½ cup (¾ oz/20 g) chopped fresh mint, or more to taste
½ cup (¾ oz/20 g) chopped fresh purslane (optional; see glossary)
seeds of 1 large pomegranate (optional; see glossary)
½ cup (4 fl oz/125 ml) olive oil
½ cup (4 fl oz/125 ml) lemon juice
salt and freshly ground pepper
1 teaspoon ground sumac (optional; see glossary)
1 or 2 cloves garlic, finely minced (optional)
6 romaine (cos) leaves, cut into long strips (optional)

❦ Preheat an oven to 350°F (180°C).
❦ Place the pita bread on a baking sheet and bake, turning once until dry, about 5 minutes. Remove from the oven and, when cool enough to handle, break into bite-size pieces. Set aside.
❦ In a salad bowl combine the tomatoes, cucumber, onions, parsley, mint, and the purslane and pomegranate seeds, if using. Toss well.
❦ In a small bowl whisk together the oil, lemon juice, salt and pepper to taste, and, if using, the sumac or the garlic. Pour half of the dressing over the tomato mixture and marinate for about 30 minutes. Fold in the toasted bread and the romaine, if using. Add the remaining dressing and toss well. Serve at once.

SERVES 4

LEBANON

BABA GHANNOUJ
Eggplant Purée with Tahini

Called mutabbal *in Syria, this dip is also popular in Israel and Jordan. Pita bread (recipe on page 82) and raw vegetables are ideal accompaniments.*

2 globe eggplants (aubergines), about 1½ lb (750 g) total weight
2 cloves garlic, very finely minced
¼ cup (2½ oz/75 g) tahini (see glossary)
⅓–½ cup (3–4 fl oz/80–125 ml) fresh lemon juice, or to taste
salt and freshly ground pepper
3 tablespoons pine nuts, toasted
3 tablespoons chopped fresh flat-leaf (Italian) parsley
1 teaspoon ground cumin (optional)
2 tablespoons pomegranate seeds (optional; see glossary)

❦ Preheat a broiler (griller).
❦ Place the eggplants on a baking sheet and slip under the broiler. Broil (grill), turning often, until charred on all sides and quite tender, 20–30 minutes. Remove from the broiler and let cool.
❦ Cut the eggplants in half and scoop the pulp from the skins into a bowl or into a food processor fitted with the metal blade. Mash with a fork or pulse to purée.
❦ Add the garlic, tahini and lemon juice to the eggplant and beat with a fork or process to purée. Add salt and pepper to taste.
❦ Transfer to a plate or shallow bowl. Sprinkle with the pine nuts, parsley, and with the cumin and pomegranate seeds, if using.

SERVES 6–8

LEBANON

HUMMUS BI TAHINI
Chick-pea Purée with Sesame

A classic dip popular in Syria and Israel as well as its native Lebanon. Serve with pita bread (recipe on page 82) or with cucumbers, radishes, carrots, and/or green (spring) onions for dipping.

1 cup (7 oz/220 g) dried chick-peas (garbanzo beans)
4 cups (32 fl oz/1 l) water
¼ cup (2½ oz/75 g) tahini (see glossary)
2 cloves garlic, finely minced
¼ cup (2 fl oz/60 ml) fresh lemon juice, or to taste
salt
pinch of cayenne pepper

FOR THE TOPPING:

2 tablespoons olive oil
3 tablespoons chopped fresh flat-leaf (Italian) parsley
1 teaspoon ground cumin (optional)
½ teaspoon cayenne pepper (optional)
3 tablespoons pomegranate seeds (optional; see glossary)

❦ Place the chick-peas in a bowl with water to cover generously. Refrigerate overnight.
❦ Drain the chick-peas and rinse well under running water. Place in a 2-qt (2-l) saucepan, add the water and bring to a boil. Reduce the heat to low, cover and simmer until very soft, 1 hour or longer.
❦ Drain the chick-peas, reserving any liquid, and transfer to a food processor fitted with the metal blade. Pulse to purée. Add the tahini, garlic, and lemon juice and purée. Add just reserved cooking liquid or enough cold water to achieve a spreadable consistency. Season with salt to taste and the cayenne.
❦ If serving immediately, spoon the purée onto a shallow plate and smooth the top with a spoon or spatula. Drizzle with the olive oil and strew with the parsley. Sprinkle on the cumin, cayenne or pomegranate seeds in a star pattern. Or you can transfer the purée to a bowl, cover and keep at room temperature for up to 6 hours or in the refrigerator for 1–2 days. Bring back to room temperature before serving. The mixture will thicken upon standing; thin with water or reserved cooking liquid.

SERVES 6–8

Clockwise from bottom: Rice Croquettes, Sweet-and-Sour Eggplant, Pumpkin Salad with Mint

SICILY

ARANCINI DI RISO

Rice Croquettes

The name means "little oranges," which these robust, golden rice croquettes resemble. They come with a variety of fillings; the simplest is cheese and prosciutto, but my favorite is meat and little peas in a tomato sauce. The arancini can be formed up to a day or two ahead of time and refrigerated. Bring to room temperature before deep-frying.

6 cups (48 fl oz/1.5 l) water
3 cups (21 oz/660 g) Arborio rice
2 eggs
½ cup (2 oz/60 g) freshly grated Parmesan cheese
salt and freshly ground pepper
2 tablespoons olive oil

1 onion, chopped
½ lb (250 g) ground (minced) veal or beef
2 tablespoons tomato paste
½ cup (4 fl oz/125 ml) dry red wine or stock (see glossary)
1 cup (8 fl oz/250 ml) tomato sauce (see glossary)
1 cup (5 oz/155 g) shelled peas, blanched for 30 seconds and drained
freshly grated nutmeg (optional)
1 cup (5 oz/155 g) all-purpose (plain) flour
3 eggs
2 cups (8 oz/250 g) fine dried bread crumbs
vegetable oil for deep-frying

In a saucepan bring the water to a boil. Add the rice, cover, reduce the heat to low and cook until the water has been absorbed, 15–20 minutes. The rice should be al dente but cooked through and still a little sticky. Mix in the eggs, one at a time, and the cheese. Season to taste with salt and pepper. Spread out on a baking sheet, cover and refrigerate to cool.

Meanwhile, in a sauté pan over medium heat, warm the olive oil. Add the onion and sauté until tender and translucent, 8–10 minutes. Add the meat and stir, breaking it up, until it browns, just a few minutes. Add the tomato paste and wine or stock and simmer for 5 minutes. Then add the tomato sauce and simmer until thickened, about 15 minutes. Remove from the heat and stir in the blanched peas. Season to taste with salt, pepper and with a little nutmeg, if you like. Let cool to room temperature.

To make the rice balls, put the flour in a shallow bowl. Break the eggs into another shallow bowl and beat lightly with a little water. Place the bread crumbs in a third shallow bowl.

You can make the rice balls small or make them the size of 3-in (7.5-cm) oranges. Put a few spoonfuls of rice in the palm of your hand and make an indentation in the center with your finger, to form a pocket. Slip a spoonful of filling into the pocket and then "fold" the rice over the filling. Roll the rice into a nicely shaped ball. Then roll the ball in the flour, dip it in the beaten egg, and then roll it in the bread crumbs. Set on a wire rack. Repeat until you have used up all of the rice and filling.

Pour oil into a deep sauté pan to a depth of 3 in (7.5 cm) and heat to 375°F (190°C), or until a rice ball dropped into the oil begins to color within moments. When the oil is ready, deep-fry the rice balls, a few at a time, until they are golden, 4–5 minutes. Using a slotted spoon remove to paper towels to drain briefly, and repeat until all of the rice balls are cooked.

Arrange on a warmed platter and serve at once.

SERVES 6–8

SICILY

Caponata

Sweet-and-Sour Eggplant

The variations on caponata *are almost as numerous as Sicilian families. This eggplant compote is served at room temperature as part of an antipasto assortment, or by itself with toasted bread. It is best made a day ahead of time so the flavors can marry. Adjust vinegar and salt at serving time.*

2 eggplants (aubergines)
salt
2 tablespoons plus 1½ cups (12 fl oz/375 ml) olive oil
1 cup (5 oz/155 g) diced celery
3 onions, chopped or sliced ¼ in (6 mm) thick
1 cup (8 fl oz/250 ml) tomato purée
3 tablespoons capers, rinsed and drained
12 black and/or green olives, pitted and coarsely chopped
¼ cup (1½ oz/45 g) pine nuts or slivered almonds, toasted
½ cup (4 fl oz/125 ml) red wine vinegar
2 tablespoons sugar
chopped fresh basil or fresh flat-leaf (Italian) parsley (optional)
3 tablespoons raisins, plumped in hot water and drained (optional)
freshly ground pepper

The eggplants can be peeled or left unpeeled. Cut into 1-in (2.5-cm) dice. Sprinkle with salt and place in a colander for about 1 hour to drain. Rinse and pat dry.

In a small sauté pan over medium heat, warm the 2 tablespoons oil. Add the celery and sauté briefly; it should still be crisp. Set aside.

In a wide sauté pan over medium-high heat, warm 1 cup (8 fl oz/250 ml) of the oil. Add the eggplant and sauté, turning often, until golden and cooked through, 15–20 minutes. Do not undercook. Using a slotted spoon, remove to paper towels to drain.

In the same sauté pan, warm the remaining ½ cup (4 fl oz/125 ml) olive oil over medium-high heat. Add the onions and sauté until tender and translucent, about 8–10 minutes. Add the reserved celery and the tomato purée and simmer, stirring occasionally, for 10 minutes. Add the cooked eggplant, capers, olives, nuts, vinegar, sugar and the basil or parsley and/or raisins, if using. Stir well and simmer, uncovered, over low heat for 20 minutes. Season to taste with salt and pepper.

Transfer to a serving bowl and serve at room temperature.

SERVES 6–8

SICILY

Fegato ai Sette Cannoli

Pumpkin Salad with Mint

Years ago, few people in Sicily could afford to eat meat. Since pumpkin is so meaty, they called this dish fegato*—"liver."* Sette Cannoli *is the name of a fountain with seven spouts, situated in a poor neighborhood in Palermo. Use pumpkin, Hubbard, butternut or any other large yellow winter squash for this salad. Some recipes direct cooks to sauté the garlic in the oil and then discard it before adding the squash to the oil. Others omit the vinegar and cinnamon.*

⅓ cup (3 fl oz/80 ml) olive oil
1 piece pumpkin or squash, about 2 lb (1 kg), peeled and cut into slices ½ in (12 mm) thick
½ cup (¾ oz/20 g) coarsely chopped fresh mint
3 garlic cloves, sliced paper-thin
½ cup (4 fl oz/125 ml) vinegar
½ cup (4 oz/125 g) sugar
pinch of ground cinnamon
salt and freshly ground pepper

In a large sauté pan over medium heat, warm the olive oil. Add the squash slices and cook, turning once, until tender and browned on both sides, about 8 minutes, total cooking time. Remove with a slotted spoon to a serving platter. Strew the mint and garlic slivers over the top.

To the oil remaining in the pan, add the vinegar, sugar and cinnamon and cook, stirring, over high heat until the sugar dissolves and the sauce thickens, 5–7 minutes. Season to taste with salt and pepper. Pour over the squash.

Serve the salad at room temperature.

SERVES 6–8

Clockwise from left: Fried Cheese, Savory Meatballs

GREECE/CATALONIA

KEFTEDAKIA/ALBÓNDIGAS

Savory Meatballs

No one can resist small, tasty meatballs as a tapa, meze *or snack. Here are two versions.*

FOR GREEK MEATBALLS:

3 slices bread, soaked in water to cover and then squeezed dry
1 lb (500 g) lean ground (minced) lamb or beef
1 cup (5 oz/155 g) finely minced onion
1 clove garlic, finely minced
3 eggs
4 tablespoons finely minced fresh flat-leaf (Italian) parsley
1 teaspoon dried oregano
½ teaspoon ground cinnamon
salt and freshly ground pepper

FOR CATALONIAN MEATBALLS:

½ lb (250 g) ground (minced) veal or beef
½ lb (250 g) ground (minced) pork
2 cloves garlic, finely minced
3 tablespoons finely minced fresh flat-leaf (Italian) parsley
1 egg
1 slice bread, soaked in water to cover, then squeezed dry
½ teaspoon freshly grated nutmeg
1 teaspoon paprika
salt and freshly ground pepper

FOR COOKING THE MEATBALLS:

1½ cups (7½ oz/235 g) all-purpose (plain) flour for coating
vegetable oil or olive oil for panfrying

To make either one of the meatball mixtures, in a bowl combine all the ingredients, including salt and pepper to taste, and mix well, kneading the mixture with your hands until it is smooth. Cover and chill.

Place the flour in a shallow bowl. Shape the meat mixture into 1-in (2.5-cm) balls and coat evenly with the flour. In a deep sauté pan over medium-high heat, warm a little oil. When the oil is hot, add the meatballs and panfry, turning often, until golden on all sides, 8–10 minutes.

Transfer to a warmed platter and serve at once.

EACH MEATBALL RECIPE SERVES 6–8

GREECE

SAGANAKI

Fried Cheese

This dish takes its name from the two-handled pan in which the cheese is fried. In Sicily, the dish is called formaggio all'argentiera; argentiera *means "silver" and its use is a comment on cheeses being fried in the place of meat, which is expensive. Sicilian cooks use* caciocavallo, *flavor the oil with a smashed garlic clove, and sprinkle the fried cheese with a little vinegar and oregano.*

½ lb (250 g) *haloumi, kefalotiri* or *kasseri* cheese (see glossary)
all-purpose (plain) flour for dredging
olive oil
salt and freshly ground pepper
2 tablespoons chopped fresh flat-leaf (Italian) parsley
lemon wedges

Cut the cheese into slices about ½ in (12 mm) thick, 1½–2 in (4–5 cm) wide and 2–3 in (5–7.5 cm) long. Dredge in flour.

Pour oil into a frying pan to a depth of ¼ in (6 mm) and place over medium heat. When the oil is sizzling hot, slip in the cheese slices, a few at a time, and fry, turning once, until golden, 2–3 minutes on each side. Using a slotted spoon remove to paper towels to drain briefly.

Arrange on a warmed platter. Season to taste with salt and pepper, sprinkle with the parsley and garnish with lemon wedges. Serve at once.

SERVES 4–6

GREECE

HORTA LADOLEMONO

Greens with Lemon–Olive Oil Dressing

Greeks often cook greens, dress them with a classic lemon and olive oil dressing called ladolemono *and then serve them as a salad. Although they commonly gather wild greens in the countryside, cultivated greens are equally delicious prepared this way. This same sauce is good on cooked beets, fennel, fava (broad) beans, white beans and artichokes. As the greens cook down considerably, be sure to allow at least ½ pound (250 g) uncooked greens per person. Some people believe that drinking the cooking juices contributes to long life and good health.*

2 lb (1 kg) mixed young, tender greens such as arugula (rocket), sorrel, dandelion greens, beet (beetroot) greens, escarole, kale, collard greens, curly endive and frisée, in any combination

FOR THE *LADOLEMONO* DRESSING:

½ cup (4 fl oz/125 ml) olive oil
¼ cup (2 fl oz/60 ml) fresh lemon juice
salt and freshly ground pepper

Wash the greens in many changes of water, to rid them of all sand.

Bring a large pot three-fourths full of water to a boil. Add the greens and boil, uncovered, over high heat until tender, just a few minutes. Drain well. (Reserve the cooking juices if you'd like to try drinking them. You might want to add a little salt and fresh lemon juice.) Arrange the greens on a serving dish.

In a small bowl, make the dressing by whisking together the oil, lemon juice, and salt and pepper to taste.

Serve the greens warm or at room temperature. Toss with the *ladolemono* dressing at serving time.

SERVES 4

Greens with Lemon–Olive Oil Dressing

EGYPT

BEID MASLUQ

Hard-Cooked Eggs with Cumin and Coriander

The people of the Middle East love hard-cooked eggs. Here, the eggs are dipped in seasoned salt. Sometimes they are deep-fried and then dipped whole in a mixture of 2 teaspoons ground cinnamon, 2 tablespoons crushed, toasted cumin seeds, 1 teaspoon ground turmeric, 1 tablespoon coarse salt and freshly ground pepper to taste.

1 tablespoon coriander seeds
2 teaspoons cumin seeds
1 tablespoon coarse salt
6 hard-cooked eggs, cut into halves or quarters

In a small, dry pan over medium heat, combine the coriander and cumin seeds and toast, stirring or shaking the pan, until fragrant, just a few minutes. Transfer to a mortar and crush with a pestle, or grind in a spice mill.

Place in a shallow bowl and stir in the salt. Each diner dips the egg pieces into the spiced mixture.

SERVES 6

EGYPT

BEID HAMINE

Long-Cooked Eggs with Onion Skins

Hamin *means "oven," and these eggs can be cooked in a slow oven or on top of the stove. They have a creamy texture following long hours of cooking, and are a rich beige from the onion skins and coffee. In Egypt they are eaten with* ful mudammas *(recipe on page 214). But you might like to try them with a salad.*

6 eggs
skins from 6–10 yellow onions
2 cups (14 oz/440 g) coffee grounds
2 tablespoons olive oil

Place the eggs in a saucepan. Tuck the onion skins around them so that all the surfaces are covered. Add the coffee grounds and then water to cover by 2 in (5 cm) and the oil (the oil prevents the water from evaporating). Cover and simmer over very low heat for 6–8 hours.

SERVES 6

EGYPT

FALAFEL

Chick-pea Croquettes

Street food at its best. Although these crunchy croquettes are Egyptian in origin, they are now equally popular in Syria, Lebanon and Israel. For directions on cooking chick-peas, see hummus bi tahini *(recipe on page 45); use ¾ cup (5 oz/155 g) dried chick-peas for this recipe. The croquettes are delicious tucked into warm pita bread with tomato, cucumber, lettuce and tahini dressing.*

FOR THE CROQUETTES:

2 cups (12 oz/370 g) drained, cooked chick-peas (garbanzo beans)
⅓ cup (3 fl oz/80 ml) water
1 slice firm white bread, crust discarded, torn into pieces
2 tablespoons all-purpose (plain) flour, plus all-purpose flour for cooking
½ teaspoon baking soda (bicarbonate of soda)
3 cloves garlic, finely minced
1 egg, lightly beaten
2 tablespoons chopped fresh flat-leaf (Italian) parsley
½ teaspoon freshly ground black pepper
½ teaspoon cayenne pepper
½ teaspoon ground cumin
½ teaspoon ground turmeric
½ teaspoon ground coriander
1 tablespoon tahini (see glossary)
salt

FOR THE TAHINI DRESSING:

½ cup tahini (see glossary)
½ cup (4 fl oz/125 ml) fresh lemon juice
1 cup (8 fl oz/250 ml) water

Clockwise from top left: Chick-pea Croquettes, Long-Cooked Eggs with Onion Skins, Hard-Cooked Eggs with Cumin and Coriander

2 cloves garlic, finely minced
salt
freshly ground black pepper or cayenne pepper
all-purpose (plain) flour for coating
vegetable oil for deep frying
8 pita bread rounds (recipe on page 82)
chopped tomato, cucumber and lettuce

To make the croquettes, pass the chick-peas through the coarse blade of a meat grinder into a bowl. Alternatively, place in a food processor fitted with the metal blade and pulse briefly to grind coarsely; transfer to a bowl. Add the water, bread, the 2 tablespoons flour, baking soda, garlic, egg, parsley, black and cayenne peppers, cumin, turmeric, coriander, tahini and salt to taste. Mix well and set aside.

To make the dressing, combine all the ingredients, including salt and pepper to taste, in a food processor fitted with the metal blade or in a blender and purée until smooth. Add water as needed to thin to dressing consistency. (This same mixture can be used as a dip, in which case it should be thinned only until a spreadable consistency.)

Form the chick-pea mixture into 1-in (2.5-cm) balls and flatten them slightly between the palms of your hands. You should have 16 balls. Place the flour for coating in a shallow bowl.

Pour oil into a deep sauté pan to a depth of 3 in (7.5 cm) and heat to 375°F (190°C), or until a dab of the chick-pea mixture dropped into the oil begins to color within moments. When the oil is ready, coat the balls with the flour and slip them into the oil; do not crowd the pan. Deep-fry until golden, 3–4 minutes. Using a slotted spoon remove to paper towels to drain briefly, and repeat with the remaining balls.

Tuck the *falafel* into the pita with tomatoes, cucumbers, lettuce and the dressing. Serve at once.

SERVES 8

GREECE

OTAPODI TOURSI

Marinated Octopus Salad

To guard against the octopus being tough, pound it against a hard surface a few times before cooking. Small octopus may be used in place of a single large one; the cooking time will be reduced. If you like, the sliced fennel or celery can be sautéed in a little olive oil rather than added to the octopus raw. The cooked octopus can also be cut up, threaded onto skewers, drizzled with some of the dressing and grilled or broiled. Serve the skewers with more dressing drizzled over the top and lemon wedges on the side. In Spain the cooked octopus is cut up and sautéed briefly with lots of minced garlic, paprika and red pepper flakes for a dynamic warm tapa. Be sure to bring this octopus salad to room temperature before serving.

1 octopus, about 2 lb (1 kg)
⅓ cup (3 fl oz/80 ml) red wine vinegar
⅔ cup (5 fl oz/160 ml) olive oil
2 tablespoons dried oregano
1 tablespoon finely minced garlic
grated zest of 1 lemon or orange (optional)
salt and freshly ground pepper
4 fennel or celery stalks, thinly sliced
green olives (optional)
chopped fennel fronds (optional)
chopped fresh flat-leaf (Italian) parsley

Octopus is often sold already dressed. If it has not been cleaned, invert it and cut away the mouth, pulling out the viscera along with it. Remove the ink sac as well, then rinse the octopus thoroughly.

Put the octopus in a large, heavy pot without any water; the octopus will give off liquid as it cooks. Cover and cook over low heat, making sure there is always a little liquid in the pot. The octopus will turn bright pink and will give off quite a bit of liquid. Test to see if it is tender after about 1 hour; if not, continue cooking over medium heat until tender when pierced. When ready, remove from the pot and let cool.

Cut the octopus into bite-size pieces. Transfer to a bowl or container. In a small bowl whisk together the vinegar, oil, oregano, garlic, citrus zest (if using), and salt and pepper to taste. Pour this dressing over the octopus. Cover and refrigerate for at least 4 hours or for up to 1 week.

Transfer the octopus and its marinade to a serving dish and bring to room temperature. Serve with the fennel or celery. Garnish with green olives and chopped fennel fronds or parsley, if desired.

SERVES 6 *Photograph pages 30–31*

ANDALUSIA

TORTILLITAS DE CAMARONES

Shrimp Fritters

These small, crisp pancakes are a specialty of the city of Cadiz.

1 cup (5 oz/155 g) finely chopped onion
4 tablespoons finely chopped fresh flat-leaf (Italian) parsley
2 tablespoons minced fresh chives
½ lb (250 g) small shrimp (prawns), peeled, deveined and coarsely chopped
grated zest of 1 lemon (optional)
1 cup (5 oz/155 g) all-purpose (plain) flour
⅓ cup (2 oz/60 g) chick-pea (garbanzo bean) flour or additional all-purpose flour
salt and freshly ground pepper
vegetable oil or olive oil for deep-frying
lemon wedges

In a bowl combine the onion, parsley, chives, shrimp, lemon zest (if used), flour(s) and salt and pepper to taste. Stir in just enough water to make a mixture that has the consistency of a thick pancake batter (about 2 cups/16 fl oz/500 ml). Cover and refrigerate for 3 hours.

Pour oil into a deep sauté pan to a depth of ¼–½ in (6–12 mm) and heat to 325°–350°F (165°–180°C), or until a dab of the shrimp mixture sizzles almost immediately upon being dropped into it. When the oil is ready, drop the shrimp mixture by tablespoonfuls into the oil and flatten with a spatula; do not crowd the pan. Fry until golden on the first side, then turn and fry until golden and crisp on the second side, about 3–4 minutes total cooking time. Using a slotted spoon remove to paper towels to drain briefly.

Arrange on a warmed platter and serve at once with lemon wedges.

SERVES 4

ANDALUSIA

ENSALADA DE ARROZ

Rice Salad

Rice salads are served in Spain, Italy and France and are usually embellished with tuna or shellfish. In northern Spain, the Spanish prefer a mayonnaise dressing, but in the south and in southern Italy and France cooks dress the rice with a vinaigrette, which results in a lighter salad. This same salad can be made with ½ pound (250 g) cooked squid, shrimp (prawns) or mussels in place of the tuna. The cooked rice will absorb maximum flavor if tossed with the vinaigrette while still warm.

1 cup (7 oz/220 g) short-grain white rice
1½ cups (12 fl oz/375 ml) water
1 teaspoon salt, plus salt to taste
1 cup (8 fl oz/250 ml) olive oil
½ cup (4 fl oz/125 ml) lemon juice or ⅓ cup (3 fl oz/80 ml) red wine vinegar
2 teaspoons finely minced garlic (optional)
½ cup (2½ oz/75 g) finely minced red (Spanish) onion
¼ cup (1½ oz/45 g) diced pimiento or other red sweet pepper (capsicum)
4 tablespoons chopped fresh flat-leaf (Italian) parsley
1 teaspoon chopped fresh tarragon (optional)
2 teaspoons dried oregano (optional)
freshly ground pepper
1 can (6–7 oz/185–220 g) oil-packed tuna, drained

In a saucepan combine the rice, the water and the 1 teaspoon salt. Bring to a boil, reduce the heat to low, cover and simmer until the rice absorbs the water and is tender, 15–20 minutes. Remove from the heat and transfer to a bowl.

In a small bowl whisk together the oil, lemon juice or vinegar and the garlic, if using. Pour two thirds of the oil mixture over the warm rice and toss to dress evenly. Add the onion, sweet pepper, parsley and the tarragon or oregano, if using. Mix well and season to taste with salt and pepper.

In a bowl combine the tuna and the remaining oil mixture. Toss well and arrange atop the salad. Serve at room temperature.

SERVES 4–6

Top to bottom: Shrimp Fritters, Rice Salad

CATALONIA

BUÑUELOS DE BACALAO

Salt Cod Fritters

The mixture for these tasty fritters can be prepared and refrigerated 4–6 hours in advance. Deep-fry just before serving.

1¼ lb (625 g) boneless salt cod (see glossary)
1 lb (500 g) potatoes, peeled and cut into chunks
1 bay leaf
2 cloves garlic, finely minced
1 cup (8 fl oz/250 ml) water
5 tablespoons (2½ oz/75 g) unsalted butter
1 cup (5 oz/155 g) all-purpose (plain) flour
4 eggs
2 tablespoons chopped fresh flat-leaf (Italian) parsley
salt and freshly ground pepper
vegetable oil or olive oil for deep-frying

In a bowl combine the salt cod and water to cover. Refrigerate for 24–48 hours, changing the water at least 4 times. The amount of soaking necessary will depend upon the saltiness of the cod; thicker pieces may take longer than thinner pieces.

Drain the cod and place in a saucepan with water to cover. Bring to a boil, cover and remove from the heat. Let stand for about 20 minutes, then remove the cod from the water (save the water in the pan) and let cool slightly. Remove all traces of skin and any small bones and shred the cod by hand or with a fork. Set aside.

Add the potatoes and bay leaf to the salt-cod cooking water and bring to a boil. Cook until the potatoes are soft, about 15 minutes. Drain and pass through a ricer or food mill placed over a bowl. Add the salt cod and garlic to the bowl and mix well. Set aside.

In a small saucepan over medium heat, bring the water and butter to a boil. Add the flour all at once and stir well until the mixture forms a ball and pulls away from the sides of the pan, 4–5 minutes.

Transfer the flour mixture to a bowl or to a food processor fitted with the metal blade. Beat in the eggs, one at a time.

Add the egg-flour mixture and parsley to the cod mixture and mix well. Season to taste with salt and pepper.

Clockwise from top: Potato and Onion Omelet, Salt Cod Fritters, Grilled Bread with Tomato

Pour oil into a deep sauté pan to a depth of 3 in (7.5 cm) and heat to 375°F (190°C), or until a dab of the cod mixture sizzles and begins to color immediately upon being dropped into the oil. When the oil is ready, drop the cod mixture by tablespoonfuls into the oil; do not crowd the pan. Deep-fry until golden, 3–4 minutes. Using a slotted spoon remove to paper towels to drain briefly, and repeat until all of the fritters are cooked. Arrange on a warmed platter and serve piping hot.

SERVES 8–10

CATALONIA

PA AMB TOMAQUET

Grilled Bread with Tomato

Bruschetta *is the Italian cousin of this Catalan appetizer. Whatever the country, this dish always starts with good-quality bread that is just grilled and then rubbed with garlic and drizzled with fruity olive oil. In summer a fresh ripe tomato is rubbed into the top, or is very finely chopped almost to a purée and then smeared on the bread. Each slice may also be embellished with chopped anchovy or a paper-thin slice of cured ham.*

6 slices country-style bread, about ⅓ in (9 mm) thick
virgin olive oil
2 cloves garlic
2 very ripe tomatoes, halved or very finely chopped
salt and freshly ground pepper

Preheat the broiler (griller) or make a fire in a charcoal grill. Brush one side of bread slice lightly with a little oil and place on a broiler pan or grill rack, oiled side up. Broil or grill, turning to toast both sides, until golden.

While the bread is still hot, rub oiled side with the garlic cloves and tomato halves or chopped tomato. Drizzle with more oil and season to taste with salt and pepper. Serve at once.

SERVES 6

CATALONIA

TORTILLA ESPAÑOLA

Potato and Onion Omelet

Tortillas *are Spanish omelets. They are thick and firm like an Italian frittata and are served at room temperature, cut into wedges, as part of every tapas selection. This is the classic* tortilla; *you could, if you like, embellish it by mixing 2–4 ounce (60–125 g) diced cured ham into the beaten eggs.*

about ¾ cup (6 fl oz/180 ml) olive oil
4 large baking potatoes, peeled and cut into slices ⅛ in (3 mm) thick
salt and freshly ground pepper
2 onions, thinly sliced
6 eggs

In a large sauté pan over medium heat, warm about 6 tablespoons (3 fl oz/90 ml) of the oil. Add half of the potatoes and cook, turning often, until tender and golden, about 15 minutes. Season to taste with salt and pepper. Using a slotted spatula remove the potatoes to a large bowl. Fry the remaining potatoes in the same manner, season with salt and pepper and remove to the bowl with the first batch.

Add enough oil to any oil remaining in pan to measure about ¼ cup (2 fl oz/60 ml). Add the onions and sauté until they are soft and tender, about 15 minutes. Sprinkle to taste with salt and pepper. Remove with the slotted spatula to the bowl holding the potatoes. Pour off the oil and reserve. Wipe out the pan well. Toss together the onions and potatoes.

Break the eggs into a bowl and beat until blended. Add the eggs to the potatoes. In the same sauté pan over medium heat, warm the reserved oil, adding as much additional oil as needed to measure 3 tablespoons. Pour in the eggs and potatoes. Reduce the heat to low and cook until golden on the bottom, 8–10 minutes. Invert a plate over the pan and, holding the pan and plate together firmly, invert the pan and lift it off. Add 1 or 2 tablespoons oil to the pan and slide the omelet back into the pan, browned side up. Cook until golden brown on the bottom, about 8 minutes.

Slide the omelet out onto a serving platter. Let cool a bit, then cut into wedges to serve.

SERVES 6–8

Marinated Sardines

APULIA

MELANZANE IN INSALATA

Grilled Eggplant Salad

In Calabria, in addition to the mint, the eggplant is sprinkled with minced raw garlic after grilling (do not add any garlic to the oil). If you like, fry the eggplant slices in olive oil rather than grill them.

2 cloves garlic, minced
½ cup (4 fl oz/125 ml) olive oil, or as needed

2 eggplants (aubergines), peeled and cut lengthwise into slices ½–¾ in (12 mm–2 cm) thick
salt and freshly ground pepper
¼ cup (2 fl oz/60 ml) red wine vinegar
chopped fresh mint or fresh flat-leaf (Italian) parsley

Ready a fire in a charcoal grill.

In a small bowl stir the garlic into the oil and brush the eggplant slices on both sides with the oil. Sprinkle on both sides with salt and pepper and then place on the grill rack over medium-hot coals. Grill, turning once, until tender, about 3–5 minutes.

Transfer to a serving platter and sprinkle with the vinegar and the mint or parsley. Serve at room temperature.

SERVES 4

SICILY

CAZZILLI

Potato Croquettes

While these potato balls could be served as an accompaniment to a simple dish of grilled meat, they are more often served as a snack. You can use baked potatoes in place of the boiled potatoes; discard the skins before you put them through the ricer. The croquettes can be formed up to 8 hours in advance and refrigerated, and then fried just before serving. Similar croquettes are made in Greece, mizithra *or* kefalotiri *cheese (see glossary) is used in place of the pecorino or Parmesan. In Turkey no herbs or cheese are used in the croquettes, but allspice is added to the potato mixture and a stuffing of lamb, onion and tomato is sometimes tucked in the center.*

2 lb (1 kg) boiling potatoes, peeled and cut into halves or quarters
2 eggs, separated
3 tablespoons chopped fresh flat-leaf (Italian) parsley
⅓ cup (1⅓ oz/45 g) freshly grated pecorino or Parmesan cheese
3–4 tablespoons chopped fresh mint or dill (optional)
¼ cup (¾ oz/20 g) finely minced green (spring) onions (optional)
1 clove garlic, minced (optional)
¼ cup (1¼ oz/40 g) pine nuts (optional)
2 oz (60 g) prosciutto, finely chopped (optional)
salt and freshly ground black pepper
all-purpose (plain) flour for coating
fine dried bread crumbs for coating
vegetable oil for deep-frying

In a saucepan combine the potatoes with water to cover. Bring to a boil, cover, reduce the heat to medium and simmer until tender, 15–20 minutes. Drain well and pass through a ricer or food mill into a bowl. Add the egg yolks, parsley, cheese, the mint or dill, onions, garlic, pine nuts and prosciutto, if using. Mix well. Season to taste with salt and pepper.

Form the potato mixture into 1-in (2.5-cm) balls. Place the flour and bread crumbs in separate shallow bowls. Place the egg whites in a separate shallow bowl and beat lightly. Dip the balls into the flour, then into the egg whites and finally into the crumbs. Place on a rack until ready to fry.

Pour oil into a deep sauté pan to a depth of 3 in (7.5 cm) and heat to 375°F (190°C), or until a dab of the potatoes dropped into the oil begins to color within moments. When the oil is ready, slip the balls into the oil, a few at a time, and fry until golden, about 3–4 minutes. Using a slotted spoon remove to paper towels to drain briefly, and repeat with the remaining balls.

Arrange on a warmed platter and serve at once.

SERVES 6–8

SICILY

SARDE MARINATI

Marinated Sardines

Sardines are also served for the appetizer course in Spain and France. This same method can be used for marinating anchovies. Sliced tomatoes and cucumbers, crusty bread and chilled white wine are good accompaniments.

1 lb (500 g) fresh sardines or anchovies
1 teaspoon salt
½–⅔ cup (4–5 fl oz/125–160 ml) white wine vinegar
¼ white onion, thinly sliced or chopped
2 cloves garlic, finely minced
¼ cup (2 fl oz/60 ml) olive oil
2 tablespoons fresh lemon juice
freshly ground pepper
chopped fresh flat-leaf (Italian) parsley

Cut the heads off the fish and discard. Gut the fish, cutting the stomach cavity from the top to tail to free the viscera. Now you must fillet the fish and leave them flattened and opened like a book. To do this, first lay each fish on its stomach and press firmly on its middle. Turn the fish over and lift up and pull out the backbone from the head end, cutting it free at the tail end. Place the fish skin side down in a shallow dish or container. Repeat with the remaining fish.

Sprinkle the fish with the salt, then pour on the vinegar and scatter on the onion and garlic. Cover and refrigerate for about 24 hours.

Remove the fish from the marinade, reserving the onion and garlic. Pat the fish dry with paper towels. Arrange the fish on a shallow serving platter. In a small bowl whisk together the olive oil, lemon juice and pepper to taste. Pour the dressing evenly over the fish. Sprinkle with parsley and top with the reserved onion and garlic. Cover and refrigerate a few hours longer before serving. These will keep for a day or so.

SERVES 6–8

Left to right: Potato Croquettes, Grilled Eggplant Salad

GREECE

SKORDALIA

Garlic Sauce

Skordalia, a pleasantly pungent garlic sauce, is a staple of the Greek table. Here are two versions. The first combines the garlic with bread crumbs, ground almonds, and olive oil; the second version is made with potatoes. Both sauces can be used as a dressing on cooked beets, cauliflower, green beans, seafood or other popular meze *offerings. A third garlic sauce, the Sicilian* scurdalia, *is also made with potatoes; it is seasoned with a little hot chili pepper and some poppy seeds.*

FOR *SKORDALIA* MADE WITH BREAD:

3 slices white bread, crusts discarded and bread crumbled (about ½ cup/1 oz/30 g)
1 cup (5½ oz/170 g) almonds, ground
4–6 cloves garlic, minced
salt
¼ cup (2 fl oz/60 ml) red wine vinegar or 3 tablespoons fresh lemon juice
¾–1 cup (6–8 fl oz/180–250 ml) olive oil

In a food processor fitted with the metal blade or in a mortar with a pestle, grind together the bread, almonds, garlic and a little salt until a paste forms. Mix in the vinegar or lemon juice. Then add the oil, a few drops at a time, and process or work by hand until the mixture is thick and creamy and holds its shape when dropped from a spoon. Add only as much oil as is needed to achieve this consistency.

MAKES ABOUT 2½ CUPS (20 FL OZ/625 ML)

FOR *SKORDALIA* MADE WITH POTATOES:

1 lb (500 g) boiling or baking potatoes
4–6 cloves garlic, minced
salt
1 egg yolk (optional)
¼ cup (2 fl oz/60 ml) red wine vinegar
¾–1 cup (6–8 fl oz/180–250 ml) olive oil

If using boiling potatoes, peel them and then boil in water to cover generously until tender; cooking time will depend upon size of potatoes. Drain well. If using baking potatoes, prick the surface with fork tines and then bake in a 400°F (200°C) oven until tender, about 45 minutes. Let cool slightly, then remove the skins. Put the potatoes through a ricer or food mill held over a bowl.

Place the garlic and salt to taste in a mortar and grind with a pestle until a smooth purée forms. Add the garlic paste, the egg yolk, if using, and the vinegar to the potatoes, mixing them thoroughly. Then gradually add the olive oil, a few drops at a time, and beat until thick and creamy. Add only as much oil as is needed to achieve the proper consistency.

MAKES ABOUT 2½ CUPS (20 FL OZ/625 ML)

GREECE

HORIATIKI SALATA

Tomato, Cucumber and Feta Salad

If you've been to Greece, you know this is the one salad that appears on nearly every table. It is simplicity itself and its success is dependent upon sweet, vine-ripened tomatoes, flavorful cucumbers and tangy feta cheese. If you find raw onion too strong for your taste, marinate it in a bit of the dressing for 15 minutes to soften it and temper its bite.

FOR THE DRESSING:

¼ cup (2 fl oz/60 ml) red wine vinegar
½ cup (4 fl oz/125 ml) olive oil
1–2 tablespoons dried oregano
1 clove garlic, finely minced (optional)
salt and freshly ground pepper

FOR THE SALAD:

4 tomatoes, cut into 8 wedges
1 cucumber, peeled and sliced ¼ in (6 mm) thick
2 green sweet peppers (capsicums), seeded, deribbed and thinly sliced crosswise
1 red (Spanish) onion, sliced paper-thin
20 Kalamata olives
½ lb (250 g) feta cheese, coarsely crumbled

About 1 hour before serving the salad, make the dressing. In a small bowl whisk together the vinegar, olive oil, oregano and the garlic, if using. Season to taste with salt and pepper.

Combine all the salad ingredients in a large salad bowl or on individual plates. Drizzle the dressing evenly over the top. Let stand for about 1 hour and then serve.

SERVES 4

Clockwise from top: Tomato, Cucumber and Feta Salad; Garlic Sauce; Pickled Vegetables

GREECE

VEGETABLES À LA GRECQUE

Pickled Vegetables

Why the French title à la grecque *and not the Greek* khoriatiko, *which means "country style"? This cooking term is now known by cooks and diners alike in many countries to mean vegetables—artichokes, carrots, pearl onions, celery, cauliflower, mushrooms—cooked in a fragrant, herb-laced bath of olive oil, wine and water. (If you are cooking trimmed baby artichokes or pared hearts in this fashion, simmer them until the point of a knife pierces them easily, then drain and taste the marinade. If it is bitter, discard it and cover the artichokes with olive oil and lemon juice.) These lightly pickled vegetables are served at room temperature as part of a* meze *assortment or they are served as a side dish.*

¼ cup (2 fl oz/60 ml) olive oil
2 cups (16 fl oz/500 ml) dry white wine or 1 cup (8 fl oz/250 ml) each dry white wine and water
1 heaping tablespoon cracked coriander seeds
3 bay leaves
1 tablespoon peppercorns, bruised
2 fresh thyme sprigs
4 thin lemon slices
1 clove garlic, smashed
salt

ONE OF THE FOLLOWING VEGETABLES:

1 lb (500 g) pearl onions
1 lb (500 g) carrots, peeled, cut in half lengthwise if thick and cut into 2-in (5-cm) lengths
1 large bunch celery, trimmed and cut into 2-in (5-cm) lengths
4–5 cups (about 1 lb/500 g) cauliflower florets
1 lb (500 g) fresh cultivated button mushrooms, stem ends trimmed
chopped fresh flat-leaf (Italian) parsley

In a saucepan combine the oil, wine (or wine and water), coriander seeds, bay leaves, peppercorns, thyme, lemon slices, garlic and salt to taste. Bring to a boil. Reduce the heat to a simmer. Select one of the vegetables, add it to the pan and cook until just tender. Onions and carrots will take about 20 minutes. Celery and cauliflower will take 4–6 minutes. Mushrooms will take about 3 minutes.

Using a slotted spoon remove the vegetables to a serving bowl. Reduce the marinade by half over high heat; if desired, strain and pour over the vegetables. Sprinkle with the parsley.

Let cool to room temperature, then serve.

SERVES 8

TURKEY

MİDYE TAVASI

Fried Mussels with Tarator Sauce

Tarator *is a general name for nut sauces that are thickened with bread crumbs, usually flavored with garlic and thinned with vinegar or lemon juice. The sauces are popular in Syria and Lebanon as well as Turkey, and while walnut sauces are the most common, almonds, hazelnuts (filberts), pine nuts or pistachios can also be used. In general, walnut and hazelnut sauces are thinned with vinegar, and almond and pine nut sauces are thinned with lemon juice.* Teradot *is a* tarator *made with tahini (see glossary) used in place of the bread crumbs (use 3–4 tablespoons tahini in place of the crumbs in the following recipe and increase the lemon juice to taste).* Tarator *is best made a few hours ahead of serving, to allow the flavors to blend. It thickens upon sitting, however; thin to desired consistency with water.* Tarator *is also delicious on cooked vegetables and fried fish.*

FOR THE *TARATOR* SAUCE:

1 cup (4 oz/125 g) walnuts, toasted and then finely ground
1 tablespoon finely minced garlic
1 cup (2 oz/60 g) fresh bread crumbs
½ cup (4 fl oz/125 ml) olive oil
¼ cup (2 fl oz/60 ml) wine vinegar
salt

FOR THE MUSSELS:

36–40 mussels, scrubbed and debearded
2 cups (16 fl oz/500 ml) water
about 2 cups (10 oz/315 g) all-purpose (plain) flour
salt and freshly ground pepper
2 eggs
1½ cups (12 fl oz/375 ml) water
vegetable oil for deep-frying

To make the sauce, combine all the ingredients except the salt in a food processor fitted with the metal blade or in a blender and process until smooth. (Do not be alarmed if the walnuts tint the sauce a pale purple.) The sauce should be the consistency of thick mayonnaise. If it is too thick, thin with a little water. Season to taste with salt. Cover and set aside for a few hours, if possible, to allow the flavors to blend.

To prepare the mussels, soak 12 bamboo skewers in water for 30 minutes, then drain.

Discard any open mussels that do not close when touched, as they are dead. Combine the mussels and water in a large sauté pan. Cover, place over high heat and steam just until the mussels open. Remove the mussels from the steaming liquid and pull off any beards that may have remained. Discard any mussels that did not open.

Thread about 3 or 4 mussels on each skewer. Spread the flour on a shallow plate or baking pan and season to taste with salt and pepper. Beat the eggs and water together in a shallow bowl.

Left to right: Fried Mussels with Tarator Sauce, Stuffed Grapeleaves, Deep-Fried Eggplant Sandwiches

❀ In a deep sauté pan, pour in oil to a depth of 3 in (7.5 cm) and heat to 375°F (190°C), or until a dab of the egg-water mixture sizzles almost immediately upon being dropped in the oil. When the oil is ready, dip each skewer into the seasoned flour, then into the egg mixture, and then again into the flour. Working in batches, slip the skewers into the hot oil and deep-fry until brown and crisp, about 3 minutes. Using tongs, remove to paper towels to drain briefly, and repeat until all of the mussels are fried.
❀ Serve hot with the *tarator* sauce.

SERVES 4–6

TURKEY

DOLMAS

Stuffed Grapeleaves

The Turkish word dolma *means "to stuff," and* dolmas, *or stuffed grapeleaves, come with two types of filling: rice or meat and rice. The meatless* dolmas *are called* yalanci, *or "liar"* dolmas *because they look like the meat-filled grapeleaves. Rice-stuffed grapeleaves are usually served cold as a first course or as part of a* meze *assortment. They can be accompanied with lemon wedges or dollops of yogurt. The same rice mixture can be used to stuff mussels and vegetables such as peppers (capsicums), eggplants (aubergines), tomatoes and zucchini (courgettes). In Greece, grapeleaves or vegetables with a meat-and-rice filling are served cold as an appetizer or hot as a main course; the latter are often accompanied by* avgolemono *sauce (see glossary). To turn this Turkish rice filling into a meat filling to serve for a first or main course, reduce the rice to ½ cup (3½ oz/110 g), omit the tomatoes and mint or dill, and add ½ pound (250 g) ground (minced) lamb. Turkish cooks often serve these* dolmas *with a seasoned yogurt sauce.*

FOR THE RICE FILLING:

1 cup (7 oz/220 g) long-grain rice
3 tablespoons butter or olive oil
2 onions, chopped
3 cloves garlic, finely minced
½ teaspoon ground cinnamon
½ teaspoon ground allspice
⅔ cup (4 oz/125 g) peeled, seeded and diced tomatoes
½ cup (2½ oz/75 g) pine nuts, toasted
½ cup (3 oz/90 g) dried currants, plumped in hot water to cover and drained
2 tablespoons chopped fresh flat-leaf (Italian) parsley
2 tablespoons chopped fresh mint or dill
salt and freshly ground pepper

FOR PREPARING THE *DOLMAS:*

36 bottled grapeleaves, rinsed of brine, well drained and stemmed
1 cup (8 fl oz/250 ml) olive oil
2–3 tablespoons fresh lemon juice

❀ To make the rice filling, in a bowl combine the rice and water to cover. Let stand for 30 minutes. Drain.
❀ In a sauté pan over medium heat, melt the butter or warm the oil. Add the onions and sauté, stirring occasionally, until tender and translucent, about 10 minutes. Add the garlic, cinnamon and allspice and sauté for 3 minutes. Transfer to a bowl.
❀ Add the drained rice, tomatoes, pine nuts, currants, parsley, mint or dill, salt to taste and a nice amount of pepper. Mix well.
❀ To assemble the *dolmas,* place the grapeleaves on a work surface, smooth sides down. Place a teaspoon or so of the filling near the stem end of the leaf. Fold the stem end over the filling, fold in the sides over the filling and then roll up the leaf into a cylinder. Do not roll too tightly, as the rice will expand in cooking.
❀ Arrange the *dolmas,* seam sides down, in a large, wide sauté pan. Pour the olive oil and the lemon juice over the *dolmas.* Add enough hot water to cover by 1 in (2.5 cm). Weight down with 1 or more plates. Bring to a boil, cover, reduce the heat to very low and cook until the filling is cooked, 45–50 minutes.
❀ Alternatively, to bake in an oven, preheat the oven to 300°F (150°C). Prepare the *dolmas* as directed up to the point where they are covered, then place in the oven and bake until the filling is cooked, 45–60 minutes.
❀ Uncover the pan immediately so the *dolmas* cool quickly, then transfer to platters as soon as possible. Cover and refrigerate for up to 3 days before serving. Bring to room temperature at serving time.

MAKES 36 *DOLMAS*

TURKEY

PATLICAN BÖREGI

Deep-Fried Eggplant Sandwiches

Although traditionally served as appetizers, these cheese-filled sandwiches can also be offered as a vegetable accompaniment to a main course. The Italian version of this dish omits the oven step. The slices, which are cut thinner, are salted, drained and filled with slices of prosciutto and provolone before frying. Parmesan cheese is added to the bread-crumb coating.

3 small eggplants (aubergines), about ½ lb (250 g) total weight, peeled and cut crosswise into slices ½ in (12 mm) thick
olive oil
salt and freshly ground pepper
6 oz (185 g) *kasseri* (see glossary) or Monterey jack cheese, grated
6 oz (185 g) feta cheese, crumbled
3 eggs
2 tablespoons chopped fresh flat-leaf (Italian) parsley
1 tablespoon chopped fresh dill
1 cup (5 oz/155 g) all-purpose (plain) flour
1½ cups (6 oz/185 g) fine dried bread crumbs
vegetable oil for deep-frying

❀ Preheat an oven to 400°F (200°C). Place the eggplant slices on oiled baking sheets and brush them with oil. Sprinkle to taste with salt and pepper and bake until almost cooked through, about 15 minutes. Let cool.
❀ In a bowl combine the cheeses, 1 of the eggs, parsley and dill. Place a heaping spoonful of filling on half the eggplant slices. Top with a second slice about the same size, then press together. Place the flour and bread crumbs in separate shallow bowls. Break the remaining 2 eggs into another shallow bowl and beat lightly. Dip the eggplant sandwiches first in the flour, then in the egg, and finally in the bread crumbs, coating evenly. Place on a rack or a baking sheet lined with parchment paper. Let stand for 1 hour. (Or refrigerate for as long as overnight; bring the eggplant sandwiches to room temperature before frying.)
❀ Pour oil into a deep sauté pan to a depth of 3 in (7.5 cm) and heat to 375°F (190°C), or until a bit of bread dropped into the oil begins to color within moments. When the oil is ready, slip in the sandwiches, a few at a time for about 2 minutes. Using a slotted spoon lift out the sandwiches and let them rest for 1 minute to melt the cheese, then return them to the oil, top side down, to fry until golden, about 2 minutes longer. Using a slotted spoon remove to paper towels to drain briefly, and repeat with the remaining sandwiches.
❀ Arrange on a warmed serving platter. Cut in half and serve at once.

SERVES 8

TURKEY

MİDYE DOLMASI

Stuffed Mussels

Essentially, this popular meze *is a type of* dolma, *but instead of stuffing the rice mixture into a vegetable or vine leaf, the filling is put into mussel shells. This same filling can be used for stuffing hollowed-out tomatoes, eggplants (aubergines) and sweet peppers (capsicums); use water or stock in place of the mussel liquid. Most recipes call for prying open raw mussels. It is easier to steam the mussels just until they open and then spoon the rice filling over the barely steamed mussel. Allow about 5 mussels per person as these are rather rich.*

30–40 mussels, scrubbed and debearded
3 or 4 cups (24 or 32 fl oz/750 ml or 1 l) water
1 teaspoon salt

FOR THE FILLING:

¾ cup (6 fl oz/180 ml) olive oil
4 onions, chopped
¼ cup (1¼ oz/40 g) pine nuts, toasted
1 cup (7 oz/220 g) long-grain white rice
2 or 3 small tomatoes, peeled, seeded and diced
¼ cup (1½ oz/45 g) dried currants, plumped in hot water and drained
1 tablespoon sugar (optional)
½ teaspoon ground cinnamon
¼ teaspoon ground allspice
1 cup (8 fl oz/250 ml) liquid from steaming mussels
salt and freshly ground pepper

Discard any open mussels that do not close when touched, as they are dead.

Combine the mussels, 2 cups (16 fl oz/500 ml) of the water and the salt in a large sauté pan. Cover, place over high heat

Clockwise from left: Orange, Onion and Olive Salad, Stuffed Mussels, Pomegranate and Walnut Paste

and steam just until the mussels open. Remove the mussels from the steaming liquid, reserving the liquid. Pull off any beards that may have remained. Discard any mussels that did not open. Strain the steaming liquid through a sieve with cheesecloth (muslin). Set the mussels and liquid aside.

To make the filling, in a large sauté pan over medium heat, warm the oil. Add the onions and sauté until soft, 10–15 minutes. Add the pine nuts and rice and cook for 10 minutes, stirring occasionally. Add the currants, sugar (if using), cinnamon, allspice, the reserved mussel liquid, and salt and pepper to taste. Cover and simmer over low heat for 10 minutes or so, then remove from the heat. Let the mixture stand, covered, for 15 minutes. Mix well, then adjust the seasoning.

Place a spoonful of the filling in each mussel, separating the shells just enough to slip in a small spoon. Do not overstuff the shell as the filling will continue to cook. Place the mussels back in the sauté pan, or in 2 pans, as these mussels cook best in a single layer. If using 1 pan, pour the remaining 1 cup (8 fl oz/250 ml) water into it; if using 2 pans, pour 1 cup (8 fl oz/250 ml) into each pan. Weight the mussels down with a plate or lid, cover and cook over gentle heat until the rice is tender and the flavors have blended, 20–30 minutes.

Remove from the heat and transfer to a serving platter. Serve at room temperature.

SERVES 6–8

TURKEY

MUHAMMARAH

Pomegranate and Walnut Paste

A common dish on the Turkish meze *table, this purée is also a delicious, spicy dip for cooked meats and fish. Syrian cooks prepare a similar dish. If pomegranate syrup is unavailable, substitute lemon juice. Serve with pita bread (recipe on page 82).*

1 tablespoon coarsely ground dried red chili pepper
1 teaspoon ground cumin
1½ cups (6 oz/185 g) walnuts, toasted
½ cup (2 oz/60 g) fine dried bread crumbs
¼ cup (2 fl oz/60 ml) olive oil
2 tablespoons pomegranate syrup (see glossary)
pinch of sugar
salt
¼ cup (2 fl oz/60 ml) tomato purée (optional)
½ teaspoon ground allspice (optional)
2 red sweet peppers (capsicums), roasted, peeled, seeded, and puréed (optional; see glossary)
chopped fresh flat-leaf (Italian) parsley

In a food processor or blender, combine the chili pepper, cumin, nuts, bread crumbs, olive oil, pomegranate syrup, sugar, salt to taste, and the tomato purée, allspice, and sweet peppers, if using. Purée until smooth. Alternatively, pound the walnuts to a paste in a mortar and pestle, then mix in the other ingredients.

Spoon into a small bowl and garnish with parsley. Chill until ready to serve.

SERVES 4–6

TURKEY

PORTOKAL SALATASI

Orange, Onion and Olive Salad

This salad, with minor variations, also appears in Greece, Sicily, Spain and North Africa. Sometimes mint, lemon balm, dill and parsley are chopped and strewn on top at the last minute. A popular Moroccan salad calls for lightly brushing the orange slices with olive oil mixed with fresh lemon juice and then sprinkling them with cinnamon and orange-flower water.

2 large oranges
1 red (Spanish) onion, sliced paper-thin
1 cup (4–5 oz/125–155 g) sharply flavored black olives, pitted
olive oil
pinch of cayenne pepper (optional)

Peel the oranges and remove all the white pith. Slice the oranges crosswise into slices ⅛ in (3 mm) thick. Use a knife tip to remove all seeds.

On a shallow serving dish, layer the orange slices and then top with the onion. Let sit for 30 minutes. Sprinkle with the olives and drizzle on a thin stream of olive oil. If you like, dust lightly with cayenne, then serve.

SERVES 4

AU MAL ASSIS
CHANGE-EXCHANGE
YACHTS
PIZZA
RESTAURANT
NI-30 4081

FRANCE
SHIP STORES
Glacier
La Pizza
Restaurant
NI 304001
304038
NI 304086

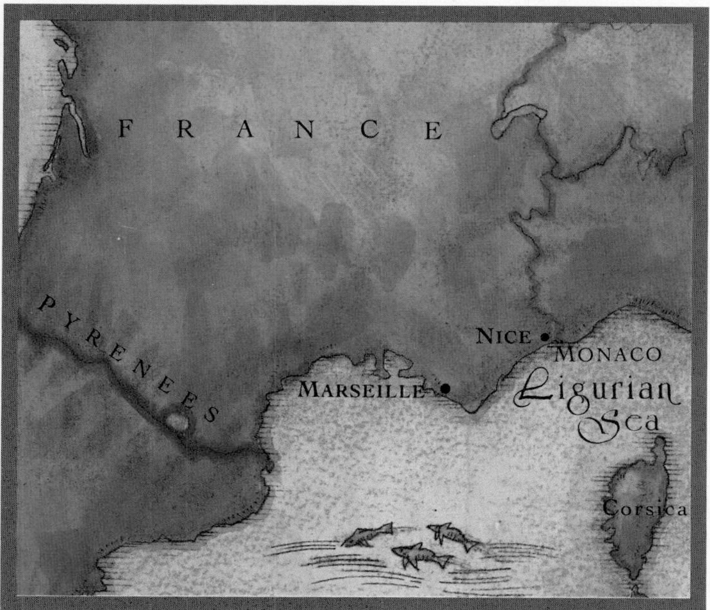

FRANCE

Roussillon, Languedoc, Provence

If national cuisines correspond to languages, regional culinary styles may legitimately be compared to dialects. These two forms of differentiation sometimes coincide completely or overlap; the south of France is a case in point. As every aspiring Francophile is quick to learn, the Languedoc (from *langue d'oc*) is supposedly the region where *yes* is rendered as *oc,* in contrast to the realm of *langue d'oil,* the lands where *oil* signify affirmation. Even when first put forward by Dante, this classification was somewhat imprecise, for reasons that need not detain us here. It is nonetheless true that the historic provinces of Languedoc and Provence speak even today the distinct idiom that is known as Provençal. The domain of Provençal is also home to a cuisine that is more frequently eulogized than any other in the Mediterranean; in 1919, a certain Madame Daudet even suggested that the cooking of Provence is "the best of all cooking." What is certain is that it exhibits in high measure all the main characteristics of Mediterranean cuisine.

The separate identity of the south, in both linguistic and culinary terms, is particularly evident at its western

Previous pages: The picturesque Côte d'Azur, dotted with charming villages, meanders from the mouth of the Rhône to Italy.
Left: The austere simplicity of this facade in St. Cannat is characteristic of the architecture of many villages in southern France.

and eastern extremities. Languedoc was incorporated into France as early as the thirteenth century, but Roussillon, bordering on Catalonia, was acquired from Spain by Louis XIV in 1659; even today it remains resolutely Catalan in speech and cuisine. The county of Nice was joined to France as late as 1860, after five centuries of rule by the House of Savoy; it is not surprising that much Italian is still spoken there and that its version of the Provençal diet includes pasta dishes such as *cannelloni, ravioli* and *gnocchi.*

The ancient trans-Mediterranean connections of the French south have been equally important. The Greeks founded many of its most important cities: in Languedoc, Agde and Nîmes; and in Provence, Marseilles, Nice and Antibes. All except Nîmes were ports (although Agde now lies two and a half miles inland), and the maritime orientation of the south, with all that implied for trade and cuisine, was thus set two and half millennia ago. It was the Greeks, too, who endowed the region with that foremost essential of the Mediterranean diet, the olive, and who must be regarded as the progenitors of the legendary *bouillabaisse.* The Romans were so attached to the area that they regarded it as a province, not a colony—hence the name of Provence—and as a token of their attachment they drained the marshes of the Rhône Valley, making it an important center for cattle breeding

The sweeping field of lavender surrounding an old farm structure known as a mas *is a quintessential Provençal landscape.*

and dairy farming. They also added Narbonne in Languedoc to the complement of the south's ports and introduced apiculture to its hinterland.

After the silting up and gradual inland retreat of its ports, Languedoc was culturally and economically overshadowed by neighboring Provence. But in its heyday, Montpellier, now separated from the Mediterranean by several kilometers of flat land and a saltwater lagoon, was France's chief trader with the East, a role that Marseilles came to inherit. Montpellier was, indeed, purveyor of spices to the whole country, and the centrality of this trade to the city's prosperity is mirrored even in the derivation of its name, from Monspistillarius, Mount of the Spice Merchants. Highly seasoned foods remain popular in Languedoc, not only, perhaps, because of this mercantile past but also thanks to Arab influences emanating from Spain; Charles Martel notwithstanding, the Arabs occupied Narbonne for several decades and used it as a base for raids on Avignon in 734 and Lyons in 743. Significant, too, is that the preoccupation with spices and their properties led, in accordance with Greco-Arab precedent, to the study of medicine and ultimately to the establishment of the University of Montpellier. Aside from spices, there is no trace of possible Arab culinary influence on Languedoc other than its rich, flaky pastries.

Languedoc is less integrally Mediterranean than Provence. It reaches up to Lyons in the north and borders on Gascony in the east; the coastal area represents a fairly small proportion of its total surface. The counts of Toulouse, resident in a thoroughly non-Mediterranean city, seem to have had as much influence on the cuisine of Languedoc as the spice merchants of Montpellier, and it should come as no surprise that butter and animal fat take the place of olive oil throughout the province. The Provençal combination of tomato and eggplant, beloved of almost all Mediterranean cuisines, does not much appeal to the folk of Languedoc, except as an accompaniment to fish.

The pride and joy of Languedoc cuisine is, of course, *cassoulet,* a stew combining various meats—of which pork must always be one—with white beans. The essential varieties of *cassoulet* are reducible to three: that of Castelnaudry, where generous portions of ham are joined to the pork; that of Carcassonne, which favors the inclusion of hunks of mutton; and that of Toulouse, which preaches the compatibility of goose and/or duck with the pork and is also open to the use of mutton. The only historical note relevant here is that fava (broad) beans were used before haricot beans arrived from the New World by way of northern Italy.

After Paris, Provence is perhaps the region of France best known to and beloved of foreigners; for fogbound northern Europeans, the simple phrase "the south of France"—by which they mean Provence—is redolent of bright color, ease and aesthetic enjoyment. This image is not without justification, and it is for good reason that so many painters made their homes in Provence. But the picture should be modified by awareness of the annual hardship induced by the blowing of the fierce, dry northerly mistral, and of the variation of terrain among the coast, the valley of the Rhône, and the area around Aix en Provence. Even the Mediterranean littoral is not a

Annual celebrations in which the residents wear the regional costumes of Arles, in southern France, signify local pride in a long and colorful history.

uniform whole; the lack of a coastal road until comparatively recent times made each major port a world of its own, dependent on shipping for its communications with the outside. The cuisine of Provence is correspondingly more diverse than is sometimes imagined.

The factors of unity within this diversity are easily identified. First comes the combination of olive oil, garlic and tomato into the *sauce provençale,* the mere addition of which to a dish qualifies it for the description *à la provençale.* Highly typical for Provençal cuisine is also the abundant use of herbs; their profusion in the region is mythically ascribed to King Balthazar, one of the Magi, who generously scattered them on the ground as he passed through the region. Ratatouille is but the best-known example of the Provençal fondness for vegetables—tomatoes, artichokes, eggplants and bell peppers, in order of importance. Finally, Provence is noteworthy for the full exploitation of the seafood that still proliferates all along the coast, from Marseilles to Menton.

The most renowned dish of Provence is without doubt *bouillabaisse,* a fish chowder available in numerous local varieties. The comparative merits of these distinct efforts are as hotly disputed as those of the rival versions of *cassoulet* in neighboring Languedoc. The origins of *bouillabaisse* have been credibly ascribed to the Greeks, who typically enough enshrined its genesis in a tale of adultery among the gods: Venus is said to have concocted the first *bouillabaisse,* lacing it generously with supposedly soporific saffron; after her husband Volcan had drunk deeply enough of it, she sneaked off for a rendezvous with Mars. Given the Greek antecedents of the city, *bouillabaisse* supremacy might as well be awarded to Marseilles. The version produced there calls for a combination of soft- and firm-fleshed fish, onions and tomatoes, and a lengthy list of seasonings, which of course includes saffron.

Provence is more distant from Spain than is Languedoc, and Villefranche was the only settlement occupied by the Arabs, and that, quite briefly. One might nonetheless hope to discern an Arab influence on Provençal cuisine corresponding to the inspiration the troubadours derived from the poetry of Muslim Spain. Provence is certainly indebted to the agricultural enterprise of the Muslims for some of the vegetables fundamental to its cuisine, and also for the rice that is still grown in the Rhône Delta region known as the Camargue, but no particular dish seems attributable to an Arab forebear. It is nonetheless curious to note that Rabelais speaks of *coscoton à la moresque* being eaten in sixteenth-century Provence. Were, perhaps, other dishes of Arab origin also once popular? Thanks to the presence of a large community of North African immigrants, couscous is now available anew in Marseilles, but the intermingling of its aromas with the scent of *bouillabaisse* is evidence not so much of culinary continuity as of the unceasing migration of peoples and their cultures that typifies the Mediterranean.

BREADS AND SAVORY PASTRIES

The art of making leavened bread was reputedly discovered in ancient Egypt, where wheat grew in abundance.

BREADS AND SAVORY PASTRIES

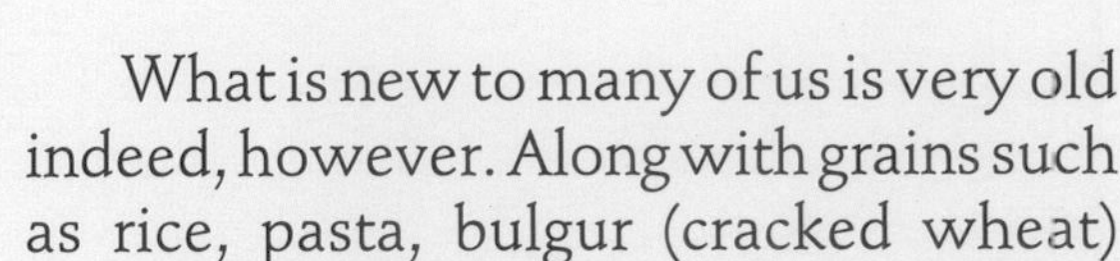

In recent years a greater appreciation for rustic country breads has developed. Their rich flavor, texture and versatility have been discovered and the tasteless white, airy bread that has been the staple at many markets is being passed by. A "bread revolution" is going on and restaurants and small bakeries are feeding the hunger for good bread made with whole grains.

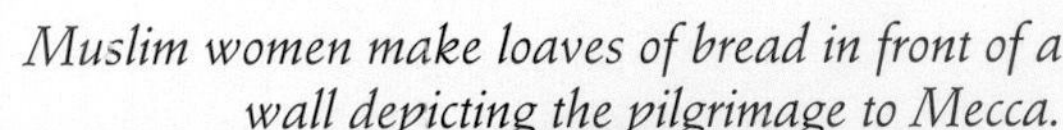

Muslim women make loaves of bread in front of a wall depicting the pilgrimage to Mecca.

What is new to many of us is very old indeed, however. Along with grains such as rice, pasta, bulgur (cracked wheat) and couscous, rustic breads form the basis of the daily Mediterranean diet. There is never a meal without bread. In fact, a meal might be only bread with a little cheese and tomato. Bread is baked fresh daily and because it has no preservatives, must be eaten as quickly as possible. It is made with flavorful unbleached whole-grain flours—wheat, corn, rye—and occasionally embellished with nuts, olives and herbs. Sweetened or egg-enriched breads, such as challah, and those made with refined flours are served on special occasions and are usually associated with holidays.

Butter rarely accompanies bread on the Mediterranean table. Nor is bread commonly served with a dish of olive oil for dipping, as is often the case in restaurants serving Mediterranean cuisine outside the region, unless, of course, one is trying to judge the quality of the oil and bread is the neutral vehicle. Bread is, however, ideal for sopping up oil or pan juices on a dinner plate and occasionally, in the instance of pizza, *pitta, scacciata,* and *focaccia,* it can be the plate.

The stove with oven below is a relatively new appliance in the Mediterranean home. Sometimes families built an outdoor brick beehive oven for bread baking. But more often, people delivered their bread (and casseroles) to the village baker for cooking in the wood-burning oven. In most Moroccan homes, the bread was kneaded

Previous pages: Bread of Apulia (recipe page 77)

Along with olive oil and wine, bread is part of the quintessential Mediterranean trinity.

in a large unglazed red clay pan called a *gsaa* and then sent, usually carried on the head of a child, to the community oven. The loaves of each family were identified with a wooden stamp.

In the eastern Mediterranean, bread is sacred—a gift from God. If one sees a piece of bread lying on the ground, one picks it up, kisses it and puts it in a safe place. The bakers' guilds in Ottoman Turkey had Adam as their patron saint and believed that the Archangel Gabriel taught him how to make dough after the expulsion from the Garden of Eden. To the ancient Greeks it was *artos,* from *artio,* "to flavor." In Greek the word for cook is *mageiras,* which takes its root from *maza,* "that which is kneaded." The goddess of bread was Demeter, goddess of the earth, family and property. In Italy there is the expression *Senza il pane tutta diventa orfano*—"Without bread everyone is an orphan."

Because bread is the staff of life and has sacramental associations, it is never wasted. A few crusts become the thickener for soup; the crumbs become the base for a sauce like *skordalia* or *rouille.* Leftover bread is cut into croutons for soup or salad; in *panzanella* or *fattoush,* bread is the heart of the salad and not just a garnish.

Often bread is grilled, then brushed simply with olive oil and rubbed with a clove of garlic or a cut tomato. Or it might be spread with a paste like *tapénade* or eggplant (aubergine) or bean purée. Bread chunks are threaded onto skewers between pieces of meat to absorb the juices, or small pieces are folded over and used to grasp meat or vegetables off of a plate. Some breads such as Sardinian *carta di musica* are traditionally dried for long-term storage and for carrying on journeys, and later revived, softened by a quick dampening with water.

Another crucial element of the Mediterranean diet is the vast repertoire of traditional savory pastries. These may be made with yeast dough, flaky or short pastry, or *filo* sheets, and they are an important part of the regional menu. The smaller ones like Syrian *sambusak,* Lebanese *fatayeer* and *sbanik bil ajin,* North African *briks;* Greek *tiropetes;* Turkish *böreks;* and Spanish *empanadas* are baked or deep-fried and usually are served as appetizers or snacks. Larger pastries can be meals in themselves, however. The Moroccan *b'stilla,* a sweet and savory pigeon-and-almond pie; the Greek *pitta;* vegetable pies such as *spanokopita* and *prassopita;* chicken-filled *kotopitta;* and various lamb pies are all substantial courses. Similar pies, called *peda* in Albania and *börek* in Turkish cuisine, are filled with meat, eggs, cheese and vegetables and are given the same reverent attention at table.

Mastering the preparation of these pies is an art. Young women learn how to roll out paper-thin dough, *filo* (called *yufka* in Turkey, and *phyllo* in Greece) on a special round table with a thin dowel called an *oklava* in Turkey. To see them roll out a perfect round eighteen to twenty-four inches in diameter every time is a little daunting for those of us who still struggle to turn out a simple nine-inch pie crust. These large pies are baked in special heavy-duty brass pans called *tapsi* in Greece. Cooks not skilled in dough rolling may use packaged *filo* dough to produce a satisfactory interpretation of these pies.

The Greek word *pitta,* for savory pie, carried over into Italian cuisine and eventually it evolved into *pizza,* but in Calabria and Apulia these pies have retained the old name. Other double-crusted pies are made in Sicily. *Cocas* are the Catalan version of the single-crusted Italian pizza and come with a variety of toppings, while the double-crusted pies in Spain are called *empanadas* and can be large or small. They too come with an impressive repertoire of fillings. Although one may try to find a clear cultural connection to link all of these filled pastries, what they mainly have in common is peasant ingenuity and thriftiness: the use of dough to enclose small bits of leftover foods in the case of little pastries, and in the larger versions, making simple and inexpensive dishes seem more festive and special.

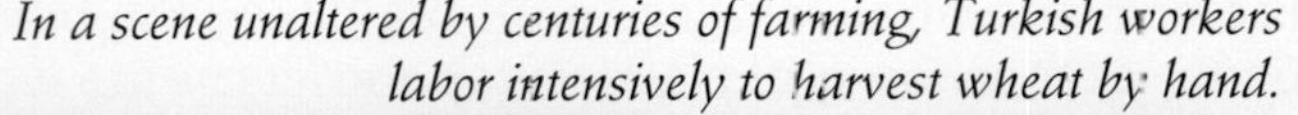

In a scene unaltered by centuries of farming, Turkish workers labor intensively to harvest wheat by hand.

CALABRIA/SICILY/APULIA

SCACCIATA

Double-Crusted Pizza

Apulia, Calabria and Sicily were invaded by the Greeks, who left their culinary imprint on the food. Some of the double-crusted pies served there today are still called by the original Greek name, pitta. *Two fillings are provided here, one a classic tomato, tuna and olive mixture from Calabria and the second a simple blend of fresh and salted ricotta cheeses.*

FOR THE BASIC PIZZA DOUGH:

2½ teaspoons yeast
1¼ cups (10 fl oz/310 ml) warm water (110°F/43°C)
3½ cups (17½ oz/545 g) semolina flour
1 teaspoon salt
3 tablespoons olive oil

FOR THE TOMATO-AND-TUNA FILLING:

5 tablespoons (3 fl oz/80 ml) olive oil
2 lb (1 kg) tomatoes, peeled, seeded and chopped
3 tablespoons chopped garlic
6 anchovy fillets in oil, drained and chopped
3 tablespoons chopped fresh flat-leaf (Italian) parsley
½ cup (2½ oz/75 g) pitted sharply flavored black olives, chopped
1 tablespoon capers, rinsed and drained
5 oz (155 g) oil-packed canned white tuna

FOR THE RICOTTA FILLING:

1 rounded cup (9 oz/280 g) fresh ricotta cheese
½ cup (2 oz/60 g) grated salted ricotta cheese
¼ lb (125 g) salami, chopped
3 hard-cooked eggs, chopped

olive oil for brushing on pizza

To make the dough, in a small bowl, dissolve the yeast in ½ cup (4 fl oz/125 ml) of the warm water and let stand until bubbly, about 5 minutes.

In a large mixing bowl, stir together the flour and salt. Add the yeast mixture, the remaining ¾ cup (6 fl oz/180 ml) warm water and the oil and beat in well. Mix until the dough leaves the sides of the bowl clean. Using an electric mixer fitted with a dough hook, knead at medium speed until the dough is smooth and elastic, about 5 minutes. Alternatively, turn out the dough onto a lightly floured work surface and knead until smooth and elastic, about 10 minutes. Form the dough into a ball and place in an oiled bowl. Turn the ball to coat all surfaces with oil. Cover and let rise in a warm place until doubled in bulk, 45–60 minutes.

Preheat an oven to 450°F (230°C).

Meanwhile, make one of the fillings. To make the tomato-and-tuna filling, in a large sauté pan over medium heat, warm 3 tablespoons of the oil. Add the tomatoes and garlic and cook until thickened and most of the liquid evaporates, about 5 minutes. Set aside to cool. In a small sauté pan over medium heat, warm the remaining 2 tablespoons oil. Add the anchovies and stir for a moment or two. Then add the parsley, olives, capers and tuna fish, stir well and remove from the heat. Set aside.

To make the ricotta filling, assemble all of the ingredients.

Punch down the dough. Divide the dough in half. On a lightly floured surface, roll out half of the dough large enough to line the bottom and sides of a shallow, round 12-in (30-cm) baking pan or a shallow, rectangular 9-by-12-in (23-by-30-cm) baking pan. Carefully transfer the dough to the pan and press it in gently.

If using the tomato-and-tuna filling, spoon the reserved tomato mixture into the dough-lined pan. Top with the tuna mixture. If using the cheese filling, form a layer of the fresh ricotta in the dough-lined pan, then top with layers of the grated ricotta, salami and finally the chopped egg.

Roll out the remaining dough in the same manner and transfer to the top of the pie. Pinch the edges together to seal securely and trim away any excess dough. Brush the top lightly with oil. Bake until the crust is golden, about 15 minutes. Serve hot, cut into squares or wedges.

SERVES 6–8

LEBANON

FATAYEER SBANIKH

Spinach Pies

These savory pastries would make good luncheon "sandwiches" or picnic fare or can be made smaller and served as an hors d'oeuvre. They can be made a few hours ahead of time and reheated in a 350°F (180°C) oven for 5 minutes.

FOR THE DOUGH:

1 tablespoon active dry yeast
¾ cup (6 fl oz/180 ml) warm water (110°F/43°C)
2½ cups (12½ oz/390 g) all-purpose (plain) flour
1½ teaspoons salt
1 tablespoon olive oil

FOR THE FILLING:

1 lb (500 g) spinach
1 teaspoon salt, plus salt to taste
2 tablespoons olive oil
1 cup (5 oz/155 g) finely chopped onion
1 teaspoon ground allspice
6 tablespoons (2 oz/60 g) pine nuts, toasted
¼ cup (2 fl oz/60 ml) fresh lemon juice
3 tablespoons chopped fresh mint
½ teaspoon freshly ground pepper

olive oil for brushing on pies

To make the dough, in a small bowl, dissolve the yeast in the warm water and let stand until bubbly, about 5 minutes.

In a large bowl stir together the flour and salt. Add the yeast mixture and oil, mix well and knead briefly on a lightly floured work surface until smooth and elastic.

Shape the dough into a ball and place in an oiled bowl. Turn the ball to coat all surfaces with oil. Cover the bowl with a damp kitchen towel or plastic wrap and let rise in a warm place until almost doubled in bulk, about 1½ hours.

Meanwhile, make the filling. Stem the spinach, chop coarsely, and wash well to remove all traces of sand. Drain well, place in a colander and sprinkle with 1 teaspoon of salt. Let stand for 1 hour. Squeeze all moisture out of the spinach and then chop finely.

In a large sauté pan over medium heat, warm the oil. Add the onion and sauté until tender and translucent, 8–10 minutes. Add the allspice, stir well and cook for 1 minute longer. Stir in the chopped spinach and cook, stirring occasionally, until the spinach wilts, a few minutes. Stir in the pine nuts, lemon juice, mint, salt to taste and pepper. Remove from the heat.

Preheat an oven to 400°F (200°C). Lightly oil a baking sheet.

Punch down the dough and divide it into 12 equal portions. On a lightly floured work surface, roll out each portion into a 6-in (15-cm) round. Spoon about ⅓ cup (2½ oz/75 g) of the spinach mixture into the center of each round. Bring up the three edges of the round to meet in the center and press together to seal. The pastries will be triangular.

Place on the prepared baking sheet. Brush the pastries with oil. Bake until golden, 15–20 minutes. Remove from the oven and brush the tops with olive oil. Serve warm.

MAKES 12 PIES

Photograph pages 8–9

Double Crusted Pizza

about 10 minutes. Stir in the flour and cook, stirring, for a few minutes. Gradually add 2½ cups (20 fl oz/625 ml) of the reserved stock, stirring well, and simmer, stirring occasionally, until thick, 8–10 minutes. Remove from the heat and let cool slightly.

❀ Add the sauce to the chicken. Then stir in the eggs, feta, nutmeg, dill, parsley and the mint (if using). Season to taste with salt and pepper.

❀ Preheat an oven to 350° F (180°C).

❀ Butter a 9-by-12-by-3-in (23-by-30-by-7.5-cm) square or 9-in (23-cm) baking pan. Lay 6 or 7 *filo* sheets in the pan, lightly brushing each one with melted butter before adding the next. Spoon the chicken mixture atop the *filo* and spread it evenly. Lay the remaining *filo* sheets on top, brushing each one with butter before adding the next.

❀ Using a sharp knife, score the top few sheets into large squares. Bake until golden, 40–45 minutes. Let rest for 5 minutes, then cut into squares and serve very warm.

SERVES 6–8

GREECE

SPANOKOPITTA

Spinach and Feta Pie

Everyone knows and loves this rich pie. The same spinach mixture can be used for filling pastry triangles for serving as appetizers. Simply cut the filo sheets into long strips 3 inches (7.5 cm) wide. For

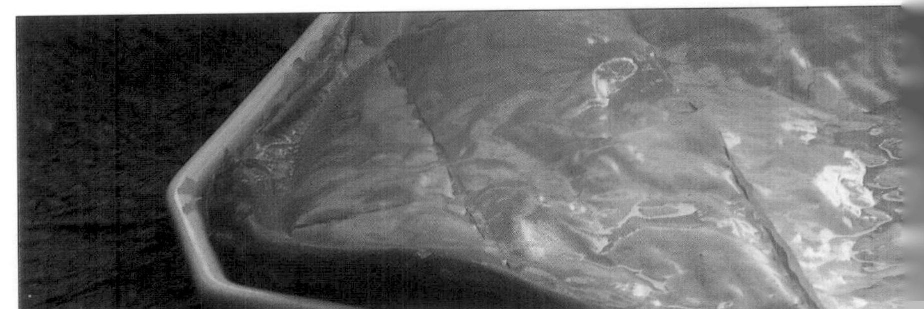

MEDITERRANEAN THE BEAUTIFUL COOKBOOK

Clockwise from top left: Onion and Anchovy Pizza (recipe page 82), Savory Pies with Tomato and Pine Nut Topping, Turnovers with Meat or Spinach Filling

CATALONIA

EMPANADAS

Turnovers with Meat or Spinach Filling

While these little turnovers are primarily found in Galicia, they are now ubiquitous at tapas bars all over Spain. The two fillings given here are typically Catalan. In fact, the spinach filling is decidedly Arabic in flavor and resembles a Lebanese spinach pie (recipe on page 74).

FOR THE DOUGH:

1 tablespoon active dry yeast
¼ cup (2 fl oz/60 ml) warm water (110°F/43°C)
½ cup (4 fl oz/125 ml) milk
3 tablespoons lard or vegetable shortening
3½ cups (17½ oz/545 g) all-purpose (plain) flour
1½ teaspoons salt
2 eggs, lightly beaten

FOR THE SPINACH FILLING:

1 lb (500 g) spinach
3 tablespoons olive oil
2 cloves garlic, minced

6 anchovy fillets packed in olive oil, finely chopped
3 tablespoons pine nuts
6 tablespoons (2 oz/60 g) raisins, plumped in hot water to cover for 30 minutes and drained
salt and freshly ground pepper

FOR THE MEAT FILLING:

6 tablespoons (2 oz/60 g) raisins, soaked in hot water to cover for 30 minutes
3 tablespoons olive oil
2 onions, finely chopped
3 cloves garlic, finely minced
1 teaspoon dried oregano
1 teaspoon paprika
1 tablespoon ground cumin
¾ lb (375 g) ground (minced) pork
¾ lb (375 g) ground (minced) veal or beef
3 tablespoons chopped fresh flat-leaf (Italian) parsley
2 hard-cooked eggs, coarsely chopped
salt and freshly ground pepper

In a small bowl, dissolve the yeast in the warm water and let stand until bubbly, about 5 minutes. Meanwhile, in a saucepan heat the milk with the lard or shortening just until the lard or shortening melts. Cool to lukewarm.

In a large bowl stir together the flour and salt. Add the eggs, cooled milk, and yeast mixture and beat until incorporated and the dough leaves the sides of the bowls. Turn out the dough onto a lightly floured work surface and knead until smooth and elastic, 3–5 minutes.

Form the dough into a ball and place in an oiled bowl. Turn the ball to coat all surfaces with oil. Cover the bowl with a damp kitchen towel or plastic wrap and place in a warm place until doubled in bulk, about 1½ hours.

Punch down the dough and turn out onto a lightly floured work surface. Knead for a few minutes, then reshape into a ball. Cover and let rise again until doubled in bulk, about 1 hour.

While the dough is rising the second time, prepare one of the fillings. To make the spinach filling, stem the spinach and wash well to remove all traces of sand. In a large sauté pan over high heat, place the spinach with the washing water still clinging to its leaves. Cook, turning often, until wilted, just a few minutes. Transfer to a colander, drain and chop coarsely. Drain again, pressing out excess liquid. Place in a bowl.

In a small sauté pan over medium heat, warm the oil. Add the garlic, anchovies and pine nuts and warm through. Add to the spinach along with the raisins. Mix well and season to taste with salt and pepper. Set aside.

To make the meat filling, drain the raisins and reserve ¼ cup (2 fl oz/60 ml) of the soaking liquid, set aside. In a large sauté pan over medium heat, warm the oil. Add the onion and sauté until tender and translucent, 8–10 minutes. Add the garlic, oregano, paprika and cumin and sauté for a few minutes longer. Add the meats, breaking them up with a fork, and cook over high heat until they lose their red color, about 8 minutes. Add the reserved raisin liquid and cook for 5 minutes longer. Transfer to a bowl and fold in the eggs, raisins and parsley. Season to taste with salt and pepper.

Preheat an oven to 350°F (180°C).

Punch down the dough again. Divide in half. On a lightly floured board roll out half of the dough into a circle about ⅛ in (3 cm) thick. Using a cookie cutter or a glass, cut out 3-in (7.5-cm) rounds; you should have about 20 rounds in all.

Place about 2 teaspoons of filling in the center of the round and fold the round in half to form a half-moon. Using the tines of a fork, seal the edges securely. Arrange on an ungreased baking sheet.

Roll out the remaining dough and fill with the remaining filling in the same manner. Arrange on a second baking sheet.

Bake until golden, about 20 minutes. Serve very warm.

MAKES 40 SMALL TURNOVERS

CATALONIA

Cocas

Savory Pies with Tomato and Pine Nut Topping

A coca is a Catalan version of what most people think of as a Neapolitan pizza. These pies are most often topped with tomatoes, peppers (capsicums) and sausage, with tomatoes, pine nuts and anchovies, or with cooked Swiss chard (silverbeet), diced tomatoes and chopped ham. Catalan cooks also make sweet cocas.

FOR THE DOUGH:

1 tablespoon active dry yeast
1¼ cups (10 fl oz/310 ml) warm water (110°F/43°C)
3½ cups (17½ oz/545 g) all-purpose (plain) flour
2 teaspoons salt
2 tablespoons olive oil

FOR THE TOPPING:

olive oil
2 onions, thinly sliced
4–6 cloves garlic, finely chopped
2 green or red sweet peppers (capsicums), seeded, deribbed and thinly sliced
2 lb (1 kg) tomatoes, peeled, seeded and chopped
¼ cup (1½ oz/45 g) pine nuts, lightly toasted
salt and freshly ground pepper
½ lb (250 g) *butifarra* sausage, thinly sliced (optional; see glossary)
½ lb (250 g) bacon, cut into cubes and half-cooked (optional)
thinly sliced fresh mushrooms (optional)
chopped anchovy fillets (optional)
cornmeal for dusting baking sheet(s)

To make the dough, in a small bowl, dissolve the yeast in ¼ cup (2 fl oz/60 ml) of the warm water and let stand until bubbly, about 5 minutes.

In a large bowl, stir together the flour and salt. Add the yeast mixture, the remaining 1 cup (8 fl oz/250 ml) warm water and the oil and beat in well until the dough leaves the sides of the bowl. Using an electric mixer fitted with a dough hook, knead at medium speed until the dough is smooth and elastic, about 5 minutes. Alternatively, turn out the dough onto a floured work surface and knead until smooth and elastic, about 10 minutes.

Form the dough into a ball and place in an oiled bowl. Turn the ball to coat all surfaces with oil. Cover the bowl with a damp kitchen towel or plastic wrap and let rise in a warm place until doubled in bulk, about 1 hour.

Preheat an oven to 450°F (230°C).

Meanwhile, make the topping. In large sauté pan over medium heat, warm enough oil to form a film on the pan bottom. Add the onions and garlic and cook, stirring often, until tender and translucent, 8–10 minutes. Add the sweet peppers and tomatoes and cook until softened and most of the liquid evaporates, about 10 minutes. Transfer to a sieve and drain well. Place in a bowl and season to taste with salt and pepper.

Punch down the dough. Divide the dough in half, if you like. On a lightly floured work surface, roll or pat out into 1 or 2 rounds or ovals. They should be about ¼ in (6 mm) thick. Transfer to cornmeal-dusted baking sheet(s).

Spoon the drained tomato mixture evenly atop the dough. Scatter on the pine nuts and the sausage, bacon, mushrooms or anchovies (if using).

Bake until the crust is golden, about 15 minutes. Serve hot, cut into wedges.

SERVES 8

PROVENCE

PISSALADIÈRE

Onion and Anchovy Pizza

The name of this pie comes from pissala, *which is a salted fish paste. Recipes for this onion pie vary widely. Some call for 2 pounds (1 kg) onions and others call for as much as 6 pounds (3 kg). More important than the amount, however, is how you cook the onions. They must be cooked on low heat for a long time until almost a purée. The Italian Riviera version of this pie, called* pizza all' Andrea, *has a little tomato purée spread beneath the layer of onion. Some recipes include minced garlic and others do not. And the amount of anchovy can vary from a timid few fillets to a robust dozen.*

basic pizza dough (recipe on page 74)

For the filling:
¼ cup (2 fl oz/60 ml) olive oil, plus olive oil for mixing with anchovy fillets (optional)
3 lb (1.5 kg) onions, thinly sliced
salt
2 or 3 cloves garlic, minced (optional)
1 fresh thyme sprig (optional)
freshly ground pepper
6–10 anchovy fillets in oil
¼ cup (1½ oz/45 g) niçoise olives

Prepare the pizza dough as directed and set aside to rise.

To make the filling, in a large, heavy sauté pan over medium heat, warm the ¼ cup (2 fl oz/60 ml) oil. Add the onions, sprinkle to taste with salt, cover and simmer over low heat, stirring occasionally, until the onions have cooked down into a thick purée, 45–60 minutes. The onions should not take on any color. Add the garlic and thyme sprig halfway through cooking (if using). When the onions are ready, remove and discard the thyme sprig, if used, and season to taste with pepper.

Preheat an oven to 375°F (190°C).

Punch down the dough. On a lightly floured surface roll out the dough large enough to line a rectangular baking pan measuring 12-by-15-in (30-by-37.5-cm) or a round 15-in (37.5-cm) pizza pan.

The topping can be added in one of two ways. Chop the anchovy fillets, mix them with a little olive oil and then spread them over the dough. Top with the onions, spreading them in a thick layer. Or spread the onions on first, cut the anchovy fillets into long strips and arrange them decoratively on top. Dot with the olives.

Bake until golden, 35–40 minutes. Alternatively, begin baking the pie at 400°F (200°C); after 15–20 minutes, reduce the heat to 350°F (180°C) and continue to bake for 15–20 minutes. Serve warm, cut into squares or wedges.

SERVES 8 *Photograph page 80*

LEBANON

KHUBZ ARABI

Pita Bread

The classic pita bread, sometimes called pocket bread, is easy to make. It is known as pita *or* pitta *in Greece,* pita *in Israel, and many other Middle Eastern countries and* pide *in Turkey. You may use up to 2 cups (10 oz/315 g) fine whole-wheat (wholemeal) flour, if desired. The breads freeze well. Pack in tightly closed bags and freeze for 2–3 weeks.*

1 tablespoon active dry yeast
1 teaspoon sugar
2 cups (16 fl oz/500 ml) warm water (110°F/43°C)
about 6 cups (30 oz/940 g) unbleached all-purpose (plain) flour
2 teaspoons salt
3 tablespoons olive oil

In a small bowl dissolve the yeast and sugar in ½ cup (4 fl oz/125 ml) of the warm water and let stand until bubbly, about 5 minutes. Place 2 cups (10 oz/315 g) of the flour in a large bowl and add the yeast mixture and the remaining warm water. Beat with a wooden spoon until well blended. Cover with a kitchen towel or plastic wrap and let stand in a warm place until frothy, about 30 minutes.

Add 3 cups (15 oz/470 g) of the flour, the salt and olive oil. Using an electric mixer fitted with the dough hook, beat on low speed until mixed, about 5 minutes. Alternatively, beat by hand for 10 minutes.

Sprinkle a little of the remaining 1 cup (5 oz/155 g) flour onto a work surface. Turn the dough out onto the surface and knead, adding more of the flour as needed to reduce stickiness, until the dough is smooth and elastic, about 5 minutes.

Form the dough into a ball and place in a lightly oiled bowl. Turn the ball to coat all surfaces with oil. Cover the bowl with a damp kitchen towel or plastic wrap and let rise in a warm place until doubled in bulk, about 1½ hours.

Punch down the dough. Divide it into 12 equal balls and place them on a floured work surface. Cover with a kitchen towel and let rise again until doubled in bulk, about 30 minutes.

On a lightly floured surface roll out each ball into a 6-in (15-cm) round. Be careful not to make any breaks in the surface of the rounds or the breads may not form a pocket when baked. Place on a lightly floured work surface or baking sheets, cover with kitchen towels and let rise for 20–30 minutes.

Meanwhile, preheat an oven to 475°F (245°C). Lightly oil a heavy baking sheet.

Slide as many bread rounds as will comfortably fit onto the prepared baking sheet. Bake until puffed and golden, about 5 minutes. Turn over and return to oven to brown second side briefly. Alternatively, remove from oven and slip under a preheated broiler (griller) to brown second side. Remove to wire racks to cool. Repeat until all the breads are baked. Cover the breads with a lightly dampened towel or place in a plastic bag to keep flexible.

MAKES ABOUT 1 DOZEN ROUNDS *Photograph pages 8–9*

ISRAEL

CHALLAH

Sabbath Bread

This is the traditional Sabbath night bread. It can be formed as a single braid or as a dramatic triple-braid loaf.

2 tablespoons active dry yeast
2 tablespoons sugar
1 cup (8 fl oz/250 ml) warm water (110°F/43°C)
5 cups (25 oz/780 g) all-purpose (plain) flour
3 eggs, lightly beaten
⅓ cup (3 oz/90 g) margarine, melted, or vegetable oil
2 teaspoons salt
1 egg yolk beaten with 2 tablespoons cold water for glaze
sesame or poppy seeds

In the bowl of an electric mixer fitted with the paddle attachment, dissolve the yeast and sugar in the warm water and let stand until bubbly, about 5 minutes. Add 1 cup (5 oz/155 g) of the flour and beat at medium speed until incorporated. Add the eggs, one at a time, and then the margarine or oil. Add an additional 1 cup (5 oz/155 g) flour and beat on high speed for 3 minutes.

Sabbath Bread

❀ Attach the dough hook and add the salt and the remaining 3 cups (15 oz/470 g) flour. Knead until smooth, about 10 minutes.

❀ Alternatively, combine all the ingredients as directed, but beat them together with a wooden spoon. Once they are fully incorporated, turn the dough out onto a lightly floured work surface and knead until smooth, about 15 minutes.

❀ Form the dough into a ball and place in an oiled bowl. Turn the dough to coat all surfaces with oil. Cover with a damp kitchen towel or plastic wrap and let rise in a warm place until doubled in bulk, about 1½ hours.

❀ Punch down the dough and turn it out onto a floured surface. For a single-braid loaf, divide the dough into 3 equal portions. For 2 single-braid loaves, divide the dough in half and then divide each half into 3 equal portions. For a triple-braid loaf, divide the dough into 3 unequal portions, large, medium and small, and then divide each of those portions into 3 equal portions. In each case, using your palms, roll out each dough portion on a lightly floured surface into a rope no longer than 12 in (30 cm). The size will depend upon which loaf you are making. Braid each set of 3 ropes, pressing the ends together and tucking them under slightly. If making 1 or 2 single-braid loaves, simply place them on an oiled baking sheet once they are formed. If making a triple-braid loaf, place the largest braid on an oiled baking sheet. Lay the medium braid on top and press firmly to attach it. Then top with the littlest braid, again pressing to attach. Cover the bread(s) with a kitchen towel and let rise until doubled in bulk, about 45 minutes.

❀ Meanwhile, preheat an oven to 350°F (180°C). Just before baking brush the loaf or loaves with the egg wash and sprinkle with sesame or poppy seeds. Bake until golden, about 30 minutes for the 2 small loaves, about 40 minutes for the large single-braid loaf and as long as 50 minutes for the triple-braid loaf. Test for doneness by tapping the bottoms of the loaves; they should sound hollow. Let cool on wire racks.

MAKES 1 LARGE OR 2 SMALL LOAVES

TUNISIA

BRIKS Á L'OEUF

Pastries Stuffed with Tuna and Egg

For these traditional Tunisian pastries, spoonfuls of cooked meat, poultry or canned tuna are placed on sheets of ouarka *and a whole egg is nested on the filling. The pastry is then carefully sealed without breaking the egg. The meat is usually lamb seasoned with onion, cumin, paprika, cayenne, and parsley or cilantro. Other fillings include mashed potatoes seasoned with onion, garlic and parsley or chopped cooked chicken and potatoes with onion. Spring roll wrappers, or* filo, *are remarkably good substitutes for the* ouarka. *Be careful when you eat these not to dribble egg yolk down your shirt front.*

1 tablespoon peanut oil, plus oil as needed for *filo* and deep-frying
1 onion, chopped
1 can (6 oz/185 g) oil-packed tuna, drained and mashed
2 tablespoons chopped fresh flat-leaf (Italian) parsley
1–2 tablespoons fresh lemon juice
salt and freshly ground pepper
pinch of cayenne pepper or a little *harissa* (optional; see glossary)
6 Chinese spring roll wrappers or *filo* sheets (see glossary)
6 eggs
1 or 2 egg whites, lightly beaten

In a sauté pan over medium heat, warm the 1 tablespoon oil. Add the onion and sauté until tender and translucent, 8–10 minutes. Transfer the onion to a strainer to drain, then place in a bowl.

Add the tuna, parsley, lemon juice, salt and pepper to taste and cayenne or *harissa* (if using).

If you are using the spring roll wrappers, place an equal amount of the filling on each one. Using the back of a spoon, make a depression in each mound of filling. Break 1 egg into each depression. Brush the edge of each wrapper with egg white, covering a ½-in (12-mm) border. Carefully fold the wrapper in half and press firmly to form a ½-in (12-mm) rim.

If using *filo* sheets, working with 1 sheet at a time, brush the sheet lightly with peanut oil and fold in half from a narrow end. Place one sixth of the filling about 3 in (7.5 cm) in from the top of the folded sheet, leaving a 1-in (2.5-cm) border on either side. Using the back of a spoon, make a depression in the filling. Break 1 egg into the depression. Brush all the edges of the *filo* sheet with egg white. Carefully fold in the left side, then the right side, and finally fold up the bottom third to cover the filling completely. Press edges to seal securely.

Pour oil into a deep sauté pan to a depth of 5 in (7.5 cm) and heat to 375°F (190°C), or until a bit of pastry dropped in the oil begins to color within moments. When the oil is ready, add the pastries, 2 or 3 at a time, and deep-fry until golden, about 4–5 minutes. Using a slotted spoon, remove to paper towels to drain briefly, and repeat with the remaining pastries. Serve hot.

MAKES 6 PASTRIES

TUNISIA

KHUBZ MBASSIS

SEMOLINA BREAD

Many Mediterranean breads are made with a sourdough starter. For example, the starter used here will work for Italian breads as well, such as pane pugliese *(recipe on page 77). It is difficult to make starter in small batches, but as it is just flour and water, you can afford to discard it if it becomes too sour or goes bad before you can use it. This recipe was given to me by Baroui Karoui.*

FOR THE SOURDOUGH STARTER:

1 cup (8 fl oz/250 ml) warm water (110°F/43°C)
⅛ teaspoon active dry yeast
2 cups (10 oz/315 g) all-purpose (plain) flour

FOR THE BREAD:

1 tablespoon active dry yeast
1 tablespoon sugar
2 cups (16 fl oz/500 ml) warm water (110°F/43°C)
½ cup (4 oz/125 g) sourdough starter
¼ cup (2 fl oz/60 ml) olive oil
4 tablespoons seeds of paradise (see glossary)
3 cups (15 oz/470 g) semolina flour
2 cups (10 oz/315 g) all-purpose (plain) flour
1 tablespoon salt

To make the starter, place the warm water, yeast and flour in the bowl of an electric mixer fitted with the paddle attachment and beat at medium speed until the mixture pulls away from the sides of the bowl, about 3 minutes. Alternatively, beat the ingredients together with a wooden spoon.

Place the starter in a 2-qt (2-l) plastic container or any container large enough for the starter to triple in size. Cover

Left to right: Pastries Stuffed with Tuna and Egg, Semolina Bread

and let sit at room temperature overnight. The starter may be used the next day, but if at all possible refrigerate it for a few days to develop its flavor. You will need only a small amount of the starter for this recipe; reserve the remainder in the refrigerator for up to 3 days to use in making other loaves.

To make the bread, in the bowl of an electric mixer fitted with the paddle attachment, dissolve the yeast and sugar in the warm water. Add the starter and mix with the paddle until it is incorporated and the water is foamy.

Attach the dough hook and add the olive oil, 2 tablespoons of the seeds of paradise, both flours and the salt. Knead on medium speed until the dough is smooth, elastic and pulls away from the sides of the bowl, about 10 minutes.

Alternatively, combine all the ingredients as directed, but beat them together with a wooden spoon. Once they are fully incorporated, turn out the dough onto a floured work surface and knead until smooth and elastic, about 15 minutes.

Form the dough into a ball and place in a lightly oiled bowl. Turn the ball to coat all surfaces with oil. Cover the bowl with a damp kitchen towel or plastic wrap and let rise in a warm place until doubled in bulk, 1½–2 hours. Punch down the dough, re-cover and let rise a second time until doubled in bulk, about 1 hour.

Punch down the dough and divide into 2 equal portions. On a floured work surface, roll out each portion into a round 12 in (30 cm) in diameter. Working with 1 round, lightly brush the outer edge with water. At 1-in (2.5-cm) intervals, pull up the edge of the dough and press it firmly onto the moistened top, about 1 in (2.5 cm) from the edge. The dough will have a fluted appearance, much like a pie crust. Repeat with the second round.

Place the breads on 1 or 2 baking sheets. Lightly sprinkle the tops with the remaining seeds of paradise. Cover them with a kitchen towel and let rise until they are half again as high, about 45 minutes.

While the loaves are rising, preheat an oven to 425°F (220°C). If you have a large pizza stone, place it in the oven to preheat at the same time.

Place the baking sheet(s) in the oven or slip the loaves onto the pizza stone. During the first 15 minutes of baking, lightly spray the loaves with a water mister 3 or 4 times; this will give them nice crisp crusts.

Bake until the loaves are pale gold and sound hollow when the bottoms are tapped, about 45 minutes. Remove to wire racks to cool.

MAKES 2 ROUND LOAVES

SYRIA

SANBUSAK

Cheese or Meat Pastries

Savory filled pastries are a staple in the Middle East. Here are two fillings that are enclosed in a rich short crust rather than a yeast dough.

FOR THE CHEESE FILLING:

1 lb (500 g) feta cheese
2 eggs
4 tablespoons chopped fresh mint or 2 tablespoons dried mint
white pepper

FOR THE MEAT FILLING:

2 tablespoons olive oil
2 onions, finely chopped
1 teaspoon ground cinnamon
½ teaspoon ground allspice
1 lb (500 g) ground (minced) lamb
¼ cup (1½ oz/45 g) pine nuts, toasted
salt and freshly ground pepper

FOR THE DOUGH:

½ cup (4 oz/125 g) unsalted butter
½ cup (4 fl oz/125 ml) olive oil
½ cup (4 fl oz/125 ml) warm water (110°F/43°C)
1 teaspoon salt
3 cups (15 oz/470 g) all-purpose (plain) flour

FOR COOKING THE PASTRIES:

1 egg, lightly beaten, if baking the pastries
6 tablespoons (2 oz/60 g) sesame seeds, for cheese-filled pastries
mild olive oil or vegetable oil, if deep-frying

Choose one of the fillings. To make the cheese filling, crumble the cheese into a bowl or mash with a fork. Add the eggs and mint and mix well. Season to taste with pepper.

To make the meat filling, in a large sauté pan over medium heat, warm the oil. Add the onion and sauté until tender and translucent, 8–10 minutes. Add the cinnamon and allspice and cook for 2 minutes longer. Add the lamb, break it up, and cook until it colors, about 5 minutes. Stir in the pine nuts and season to taste with salt and pepper. Simmer until the meat is juicy but has not released too much liquid. Remove from the heat and let cool completely before stuffing the pastries.

To make the dough, in a small saucepan over low heat, melt the butter; do not let it bubble. Remove from the heat and add the oil, warm water and salt. Transfer to a food processor and pulse once to combine. Gradually add the flour, pulsing after each addition. The dough will be very soft and should not stick to the sides of the bowl.

Alternatively, make the dough by hand, proceeding as directed but gradually beating in the flour with a wooden spoon. Do not overmix the dough; it should just come together in a rough mass.

Transfer the dough to a lightly floured surface. Divide the dough into 8 equal portions. Roll out each portion into a thin sheet and cut out 3-in (7.5-cm) rounds. You will have about 36 rounds in all.

Place a heaping teaspoonful of filling in the center of each round and fold the round in half, forming a half-moon. Using the tines of a fork, seal the edges securely.

To bake the pastries, preheat an oven to 350°F (180°C). Place the pastries on ungreased baking sheets and brush them with the beaten egg. If the pastries are stuffed with the cheese filling, sprinkle them with the sesame seeds. Bake until golden, about 30 minutes. Serve warm.

To deep-fry the pastries, pour oil into a deep sauté pan to a depth of 2–3 in (5–7.5 cm) and heat to 375°F (190°C), or until a bit of pastry dropped into the oil begins to color within moments. If the pastries are stuffed with the cheese filling, dip them into the sesame seeds and then slip them into the hot oil; do not crowd the pan. If they are filled with meat, simply slip them into the oil. Deep-fry until golden, 3–5 minutes. Using a slotted spoon remove the pastries to paper towels to drain briefly, and repeat with the remaining pastries. Serve hot.

MAKES ABOUT 3 DOZEN PASTRIES

EGYPT

SEMIT

Sesame Bread Rings

In Egypt, street vendors display these bread rings on long poles. Semit *can be eaten for breakfast or as a snack with some cheese. The savory rings are popular in Greece and Turkey as well. Seeds of paradise (see glossary) or equal parts sesame seeds and poppy seeds can be substituted for the sesame seeds.*

4 cups (1¼ lb/625 g) all-purpose (plain) flour
1 teaspoon salt
⅔ cup (5 fl oz/160 ml) milk
2 tablespoons unsalted butter
4 teaspoons active dry yeast
2 tablespoons sugar
½ cup (4 fl oz/125 ml) warm water (110°F/43°C)
1 egg
½ cup (4 oz/125 g) sesame seeds

Sift together the flour and salt into a large bowl. In a saucepan over medium heat, scald the milk. Remove from the heat, add the butter and let cool to lukewarm.

While the milk is cooling, in a small bowl dissolve the yeast and sugar in the warm water and let stand until bubbly, about 5 minutes.

Add the yeast mixture to the cooled milk. Then gradually add the milk mixture to the flour, stirring with a wooden spoon until a soft dough forms that does not stick to the sides of the bowl. Then, using an electric mixer fitted with the dough hook, knead the dough until it is smooth and elastic, about 8 minutes. Alternatively, turn out the dough onto a lightly floured work surface and knead until smooth and elastic, about 15 minutes.

Form the dough into a ball and place in an oiled bowl. Turn the ball to coat all surfaces with oil. Cover the bowl with a damp kitchen towel or plastic wrap and let rise in a warm place until doubled in bulk, 1½–2 hours.

Punch down the dough and divide it into 16 equal portions. Flour your hands. On a lightly floured work surface, use your palms to roll each portion into a long, thin rope. Then join together the ends of the rope to form a ring. Each ring should be 6–7 in (15–18 cm) in diameter. Place on oiled baking sheets or sheets lined with parchment paper, allowing 2 in (5 cm) space between the rings. In a small bowl beat the egg with a little water. Brush each ring with a little of this mixture. Sprinkle the rings with the sesame seeds. Let rise in a warm place until doubled in bulk, about 30 minutes.

Meanwhile, preheat an oven to 425°F (220°C).

Bake the bread rings for 7–10 minutes. Lower the oven temperature to 325°F (165°C) and continue to bake until golden brown, about 20 minutes longer or until the bottoms sound hollow when tapped. Let cool on wire racks.

MAKES ABOUT 16 RINGS

Left to right: Sesame Bread Rings, Cheese or Meat Pastries

1 tablespoon active dry yeast
½ cup (4 fl oz/125 ml) warm water (110°F/43°C)
3⅓ cups (17 oz/530 g) all-purpose (plain) flour
¼ cup (2 fl oz/60 ml) unsalted butter, at room temperature

Using a slotted spoon remove to paper towels to drain briefly, and repeat with the remaining strips. Arrange on a warmed platter, sprinkle with salt and pepper and serve hot.

SERVES 8

ITALY

ITALY

The South, Sicily, and Sardinia

Italian unity is a relatively recent and still fragile phenomenon, not much more than a hundred years having passed since the foundation of the Italian state. This is not to deny the existence of a shared Italian ethos. Indeed, this ethos assumes what geography and history confirm: a fairly sharp dichotomy between north and south. There is, of course, no fixed line on the map precisely separating them from each other, but the south may be thought of as beginning somewhere below Tuscany, where the Apennines and their foothills swell out to fill the remainder of the Italian peninsula. In pre-Roman times, Etruscan power prevailed to the north of this invisible line, and Greek to its south.

This political division even today has its culinary reflection: Polenta, an originally Etruscan preparation, remains far more common in the north than the south. The divisive effects of geography on the cuisine are more numerous and significant, however. The terrain of the south makes it inhospitable to the cow, resulting in a general absence from its cuisine of the dairy products, especially butter, that are routine in the north. By way of compensation, the sun-baked, unpromising soil of the south is ideal for the cultivation of the olive, and olive oil is used unsparingly. The north-south dichotomy is also one of economics. The pasta of the affluent north is soft, flat and limp, made with eggs and dough, while that of the

Previous pages: The picturesque village of Positano, near Naples, was most likely founded by refugees from Paestum who were forced to flee the Saracens in the Middle Ages. Left: The Mediterranean pines of Fregene, near Rome, assume an ethereal charm as the sun begins to rise.

SOUPS

Legumes are the base of many hearty Mediterranean soups and stews.

Soups

The word *supper* comes from the French *souper,* literally "soup." In the Mediterranean, a robust soup is often the whole meal. Rather than serving a broth or simple purée, the thrifty Mediterranean cook adds beans, rice, pasta, bread, meat or fish to the pot, making the soup a filling and nourishing repast. Such a practice offers a more practical way to eat as well: It is more healthful to eat a large lunch that one can burn up and digest during the day and then enjoy a soup for supper. This prescription is not always possible, of course, given the increasing demands of the modern life for a quick lunch and a big dinner, but the concept is a creditable one.

Most of the soups in this chapter are hearty. Legumes are popular in the Mediterranean and many of the recipes are what are called the "bean and green" soups. The Syrian *shouraba il addis* combines lentils and greens and may be thickened with egg and lemon or served with a dollop of yogurt. Some families add rhubarb for tartness, which is an interesting use of a stalk many think of as a fruit but that is really a vegetable. (It is used in Greece and Turkey as well, in combination with tomato for a sweet-and-sour sauce for fish.) Wild fennel and bitter greens are added to the Sicilian *maccu,* a fava (broad) bean soup, which sometimes incorporates pasta as well.

White, or *borlotti,* beans are essential to *soupe au pistou* or a good minestrone. Sometimes all of the beans are puréed; other times, only a portion of them are puréed to thicken the broth and the rest are left whole for texture and contrast. An assortment of beans forms the base for *harira,* the Moroccan soup that is the traditional meal eaten to break the fast during Ramadan. In the most elaborate versions of this soup, lamb, rice, chick-peas (garbanzos) and lentils are combined, and eggs and lemon are swirled in at the end of cooking for added body. Simpler versions call for only lentils and noodles. In the Valencian *olla gitana,* or "gypsy pot," chick-peas are part of an unusual mélange of pumpkin, green beans, pears and tomatoes, and the soup is thickened with a classic *picada* of almonds, garlic and fried bread.

Egyptians still employ traditional methods in the cultivation and transportation of their crops.

Previous pages: clockwise from top left; Valencian Gypsy Soup (recipe page 108), Cádiz Fish Soup with Bitter Orange (recipe page 114), Almond Soup from Granada (recipe page 114), Cold Tomato Soup (recipe page 114)

In marketplaces throughout Morocco, everything from pottery and clothing to a surprising variety of fresh fruits and vegetables is for sale.

Those soups that are not thickened by beans are often given body by the addition of bread. *L'aïgo bouido,* the aromatic Provençal garlic soup, stirs in pasta or bread. A Sardinian fennel soup is baked in a casserole with layers of bread and cheese. The Andalusian *gazpacho* takes its name from the Arabic for "soaked bread," even though garlicky croutons sometimes replace the bread crumbs. And bread is combined with almonds in *sopa de almendras* from Granada.

Pasta is the other common soup ingredient in the Mediterranean, and not only in Italian soups. Provence is connected to the Italian Riviera both by its geography and its love of pasta. So *aïgo bouido* will often have vermicelli, as will a *soupe de poisson*. Noodles are often added to Middle Eastern soups, including noodles made from flour and fermented milk. This pasta pellet is called *trahana* in Greece, *tarhana* in Turkish and *kishk* in Arabic. In Sardinia they use another tiny pasta made from semolina called *fregula.* Not unlike couscous in texture, it enriches *minestra con le vongole,* clam soup with sun-dried tomatoes. Rice is also used for body, in *harira,* the Egyptian *melokhia,* and in some of the egg-and-lemon-based *avgolemono* soups.

Although the liquid that forms the base for many Mediterranean soups is water, when cooked with fresh vegetables it becomes a flavorful vegetable stock. Chicken and meat stocks are also used for soups, but less often. Trimmings from prosciutto and its precious bone, *pancetta* ends, lamb bones and scraps, and chicken bones and feet are treasures saved for adding to various cooking waters. Occasionally, lemon juice is used to enhance the flavor of a particularly mild stock.

When vegetables are in abundance, they are puréed for soup. Tomatoes, carrots, fennel, potatoes or pumpkins are often handled this way and then garnished simply with a splash of virgin olive oil, a dollop of yogurt or a smattering of chopped fresh herbs. Meatballs are the guest stars of vegetable soups in Sicily and Apulia, in Greek egg-and-lemon soup, in Turkish yogurt soup and in the Catalan *sopa de albóndigas.* Meat-based soups are often reserved for special occasions, where they make a festive and filling repast.

Complex fish and shellfish soups are found in the Mediterranean. As they often contain considerable seafood and are then meals in themselves, most of them can be found in the fish and shellfish chapter. Included here, however, are three simple seafood soups: the Valencian *caldo de perro gaditano* (recipe on page 114), a light broth flavored with bitter oranges and afloat with a few small pieces of fish; a clam soup from Sardinia; and the estimable Provençal *soupe de poisson* (recipe on page 108), in which fish and fish stock are puréed together.

SICILY

MACCU

Fava Bean Soup

Here is the quintessential peasant soup, a thick bean purée that can be enriched with tomatoes, wild or cultivated fennel fronds, chicory, Swiss chard, beet greens and/or mustard greens. Dried favas can usually be purchased already peeled. If you cannot find them peeled, buy about 1¼ pounds (625 g), soak as directed, drop into boiling water for 30 seconds, drain and then peel and proceed with the recipe. If you prefer, sauté only the onion and garlic and boil the greens before adding them to the soup. Cooked small pasta shapes also make a good addition.

2¼ cups (1 lb/500 g) dried fava (broad) beans
8 cups (64 fl oz/2 l) water
1 cup (1 oz/30 g) finely chopped fennel fronds
5 tablespoons (3 fl oz/80 ml) fruity olive oil, plus olive oil for garnish
1 cup (4 oz/125 g) diced onion
2 cloves garlic, finely minced
2 cups (12 oz/375 g) peeled, seeded and chopped tomatoes (optional)
8 cups (1 lb/480 g) greens such as Swiss chard (silverbeet), beet (beetroot) greens, chicory (curly endive), mustard or escarole, or a mixture, well washed and coarsely chopped
salt and freshly ground pepper
freshly grated pecorino cheese for serving (optional)

Place the beans in a bowl with water to cover generously and refrigerate overnight. Drain and rinse well. Put the beans and fennel fronds in a heavy soup pot with the water. Bring to a boil, reduce the heat to low and simmer, uncovered, until the beans are very soft and can be mashed with a spoon in the pot, 1–2 hours. Add water if the beans start to dry out before they are cooked and stir occasionally to prevent sticking and/or scorching. Stir in 3 tablespoons of the oil.

In a wide sauté pan over medium heat, warm the remaining 2 tablespoons oil. Add the onion and garlic and sauté for a few minutes. Add the tomatoes (if using) and greens. Stir to wilt the greens. The washing water clinging to the leaves should be enough moisture; if not, add about 1 cup (8 fl oz/250 ml) water to make the steam to wilt them.

Add the wilted greens mixture to the bean purée and, if necessary, thin the soup with water. (It thickens upon sitting.) Simmer for 10 minutes.

Season to taste with salt and pepper. Serve with a splash of olive oil and with a sprinkling of grated cheese, if desired.

SERVES 6

SARDINIA

MINESTRA CON LE VONGOLE

Clam Soup with Fregula and Sun-dried Tomatoes

Fregula *is a tiny semolina pasta not unlike couscous. As couscous is more readily available at most markets, you may use it in this soup. If you are using sun-dried tomatoes that have not been packed in oil, reconstitute them in water to cover and then add the soaking water to the saucepan with the clam liquid.*

3 lb (1.5 kg) clams in the shell, well scrubbed
4 cups (32 fl oz/1 l) water
2 tablespoons olive oil

1 large onion, chopped
1 clove garlic, crushed
6 whole sun-dried tomatoes in olive oil, drained and finely minced
½ cup (2½ oz/75 g) *fregula* or couscous
salt and freshly ground pepper

chopped fresh flat-leaf (Italian) parsley or mint

Discard any clams that do not close at the touch. In a wide saucepan bring the water to a boil. Add the clams and steam until they open, 3–5 minutes. Using a slotted spoon transfer the clams to a bowl; discard any that did not open. Pour the cooking liquid through a sieve lined with cheesecloth (muslin). Set the liquid aside. Remove the clams from their shells and discard the shells. Set the clams aside.

In a 1½-qt (1.5-l) saucepan over medium heat, warm the oil. Add the onion and garlic and sauté until tender and translucent, 8–10 minutes. Add the tomatoes and the reserved clam liquid and simmer for 10 minutes. Add the clams and *fregula* or couscous and simmer until the pasta is done, about 5–7 minutes. Season to taste with salt and pepper.

Serve hot, garnished with parsley or mint.

SERVES 4–6

Clockwise from top: Wild Fennel Soup, Clam Soup with Fregula and Sun-dried Tomatoes, Fava Bean Soup

SARDINIA

Minestra di Finocchi Selvatici

Wild Fennel Soup

It's unlikely that most people will find wild fennel where they live, but cultivated fennel, also called anise, is available at many markets. This soup is simple to prepare and can be a meal in a bowl if lots of bread and cheese are added.

2 lb (1 kg) wild or cultivated fennel bulbs
6 cups (48 fl oz/1.5 l) salted water or stock (see glossary), or as needed to cover
salt and freshly ground pepper
6 tablespoons (3 oz/90 g) unsalted butter
2 tablespoons olive oil
8–12 slices coarse country-style bread
⅓ lb (5 oz/155 g) fresh white cheese such as ricotta

Cut the fronds and stems from the fennel bulbs. Reserve the fronds for garnish, if desired. Cut fennel bulbs in half lengthwise, remove the tough core and peel off any discolored outer leaves. Slice the fennel coarsely crosswise. In a large saucepan bring the salted water or stock to a boil. Add the fennel, reduce the heat to low and simmer, uncovered, until tender, 15–20 minutes. Remove from the heat. Season to taste with salt and pepper. Set the fennel aside in the broth.

In a large sauté pan over medium heat, melt 2 tablespoons of the butter with 1 tablespoon of the oil. Add half of the bread slices and fry, turning once, until golden on both sides, about 3 minutes on each side. Drain on paper towels. Repeat with the remaining bread and oil and half of the remaining butter. Cut each slice into 2-in (5-cm) pieces.

Preheat an oven to 350°F (180°C). In a large, ovenproof earthenware casserole or individual soup ramekins, arrange a layer of bread and a layer of cheese. Using a slotted spoon remove some of the fennel from the broth and layer it on the cheese. Drizzle some of the fennel broth over the top. Repeat the layers until all the bread, cheese, fennel and broth are used.

Arrange the remaining 2 tablespoons butter in thin slivers over the top.

Place in the oven and bake until golden, about 20 minutes. Serve very hot. If you like, chop the fennel fronds and use them to garnish the soup.

SERVES 4

TURKEY / PROVENCE

SOUPE DE POISSON

Fish Soup

This classic soup of Nice, a purée of mild white fish, is usually eaten with toasted bread and rouille, *a garlicky sauce tinted with sweet pepper (capsicum) or tomato. Some versions of the soup add pasta and a little saffron, as does this one, although both ingredients can be omitted and the soup will still be delectable.*

4–6 tablespoons (2–3 fl oz/60–90 ml) olive oil
2 fish heads
2 fish frames
2 lb (1 kg) small mild white fish
3 onions, sliced
3 or 4 cloves garlic, chopped
¼ cup (2 fl oz/60 ml) Cognac
2 lb (1 kg) tomatoes, peeled, seeded and diced
1 fresh thyme sprig
1 bay leaf
3-in (7.5-cm) strip orange zest (optional)
7 cups (56 fl oz/1.75 l) water
½ teaspoon saffron threads, steeped in ¼ cup (2 fl oz/60 ml) dry white wine

FOR THE *ROUILLE:*

4 cloves garlic, finely minced
salt
2 slices white bread, crusts discarded, soaked in water to cover and squeezed dry
1 teaspoon cayenne pepper, or to taste
2 tablespoons tomato paste (optional)
1 sweet red pepper (capsicum), roasted, seeded, deribbed and chopped (see glossary)
6 tablespoons (3 oz/90 ml) olive oil
fresh lemon juice to taste (optional)
salt and freshly ground pepper

salt and freshly ground pepper
pinch of cayenne pepper
3 oz (90 g) dried pasta such as spaghetti or angel hair, broken
½ cup (2 oz/60 g) freshly grated Parmesan cheese

18–24 slices baguette, toasted and rubbed with garlic

In a large sauté pan over medium heat, warm 2 tablespoons of the olive oil. Add the fish heads and frames and sauté them until they start to give off some liquid, about 10 minutes. Transfer to a stockpot.

Add 2 more tablespoons of the oil to the sauté pan over medium heat and add the fish. Toss in the oil until lightly golden, about 8 minutes. Add to the stockpot.

To the oil in the pan add the onions and garlic and sauté over medium heat, adding more oil as needed to prevent sticking, until pale gold, about 15 minutes. Add the onions and garlic to the stockpot. Pour the Cognac into the sauté pan and deglaze over high heat, scraping up any browned bits. Add to the stockpot along with the tomatoes, thyme, bay, orange zest (if using) and the water. Bring to a boil, reduce the heat to low, cover and simmer until the fish is falling apart, about 30 minutes. Add the saffron and wine and simmer for 5 minutes longer.

Meanwhile, make the *rouille*. In a mortar with a pestle, grind the garlic with salt to taste to a paste. Add the bread and mix in, then add the cayenne, tomato paste (if using) and sweet pepper, mixing in well. Slowly add the olive oil, a few drops at a time, working it in steadily with the pestle. Season to taste with salt and pepper and with the lemon juice (if using). Alternatively, make this sauce in a blender, adding the olive oil gradually after the other ingredients have been puréed. Transfer to a bowl and set aside.

Remove the soup from the heat and remove the large bones, then purée it, a few ladlefuls at a time, in a blender or by passing it through a food mill. Then, in both cases, push it through a fine-mesh sieve to remove the small bones.

Put the puréed soup in a saucepan and bring to a boil. Thin with additional stock or water if desired, and season to taste with salt, pepper and cayenne. Do not be alarmed if the soup takes a lot of salt. It needs it!

Add the pasta and cook over low heat until tender, about 20 minutes.

Ladle the soup into individual bowls. Pass the *rouille,* Parmesan and toasted bread at table.

SERVES 6–8

PROVENCE

SOUPE POTIRON

Pumpkin Squash Soup

Pumpkin squash is the basis for many Mediterranean soups and vegetable stews. In Morocco, cooked chick-peas (garbanzo beans) or rice may be added. Cooked rice is sometimes added in France as well. In Greece, the soup is commonly thickened with semolina and garnished with sautéed thinly sliced onions, chopped fresh parsley and olive oil. In Italy, it is topped with chopped fresh sage or croutons and Parmesan or pecorino cheese. Chopped cooked greens can be added as well.

3 tablespoons olive oil
2 onions, sliced or diced
¼ teaspoon ground coriander (optional)
¼ teaspoon ground cinnamon (optional)
1 piece pumpkin squash, about 2½ lb (1.25 kg), peeled and diced
6–8 cups (48–64 fl oz/1.5–2 l) chicken stock (see glossary) or water, or as needed
1 cup (8 fl oz/250 ml) light (single) cream or milk
salt and freshly ground pepper
croutons and freshly grated Parmesan cheese for garnish

In a large saucepan over medium heat, warm the oil. Add the onion and sauté until tender and translucent, 8–10 minutes. Add the coriander and cinnamon, if using, and sauté a few minutes longer. Add the squash cubes and the stock or water and bring to a boil. Reduce the heat to low, cover and simmer until the squash is tender, 15–20 minutes.

Working in batches, transfer to a blender or a food processor fitted with the metal blade and purée until smooth. Return the soup to the pan.

Add the cream or milk and season to taste with salt and pepper. Reheat gently.

Ladle into individual bowls and garnish with croutons and Parmesan.

SERVES 6

ANDALUSIA

OLLA GITANA

Valencian Gypsy Soup

Provençal cooks prepare soupe à la citrouille, *which is very similar to this soup in that it contains a combination of white beans, pumpkin squash, onion, diced ham, garlic, croutons and chopped mint. This Spanish pumpkin and bean soup, however, is made a bit more interesting with the addition of diced pears and a* picada, *a flavorful paste, of garlic, almonds and bread.*

1 cup (7 oz/220 g) dried chick-peas (garbanzo beans)
2 qt (2 l) plus 3 cups (24 fl oz/750 ml) water

Top to bottom: Pumpkin Squash Soup, Fish Soup

FOR THE *PICADA:*

½ cup (4 fl oz/125 ml) olive oil
10 blanched almonds, toasted
1 slice course country-style bread, cut into finger-sized strips
1 clove garlic
2 tablespoons wine vinegar (optional)

1 onion, diced
1 tablespoon sweet paprika
2 tomatoes, peeled, seeded and diced
pinch of saffron threads steeped in ¼ cup (2 fl oz/60 ml) hot chicken stock (see glossary)
½ lb (250 g) green beans, cut into 2-in (5-cm) lengths
1½ cups (8 oz/250 g) diced or coarsely chopped, peeled pumpkin squash
3 firm pears, peeled, cored and cut into chunks
salt and freshly ground pepper

In a bowl combine the chick-peas with water to cover and let soak in the refrigerator overnight. Drain and rinse well.

Place the chick-peas in a large saucepan and add the water. Bring to a boil, reduce the heat to low and simmer, partially covered, until tender, about 1 hour.

While the soup is simmering, make the *picada.* In a sauté pan over medium heat, warm the oil. Add the almonds, bread and garlic and sauté until golden, about 8 minutes. Using a slotted spoon transfer to a mortar; reserve the oil in the pan. Using a pestle crush the almond mixture to a paste and then work in the vinegar (if using).

To the oil in the pan, add the onion and sauté over medium heat until pale gold, about 15 minutes. Stir in the paprika and then the tomatoes and cook, stirring occasionally, for 10 minutes. Add the saffron and stock and stir well.

Add the green beans, squash and pears to the chick-peas and simmer for 10 minutes.

Add the *picada* and the tomato mixture to the soup and stir to combine. Simmer for 10 minutes. Season to taste with salt and pepper. Serve hot.

SERVES 6–8 *Photograph on pages 100–101*

Top to bottom: Lentil Soup, Lamb and Bean Soup, Melokhia Leaf Soup

SYRIA

SHOURABA IL ADDIS

Lentil Soup

Lentil soups are popular throughout the Mediterranean. Most are puréed; some include greens or rice. In Turkey lentil soup is garnished with mint and cayenne pepper warmed in butter, or with fried onions and fried bread croutons. Elsewhere, minced garlic sautéed in oil with ground coriander is strewn on the soup.

3 tablespoons unsalted butter or olive oil
1 large onion, chopped (about 1½ cups/6 oz/185 g)
1 carrot, peeled and chopped
1 celery stalk with leaves, chopped
8 cups (64 fl oz/2 l) lamb stock or water
1¾ cups (14 oz/440 g) dried red, green or brown lentils
1 cracked marrow bone (optional)
1 teaspoon ground cumin
pinch of ground allspice
2 small rhubarb stalks, trimmed and cut into 1-in (2.5-cm) pieces (optional)
1–2 tablespoons fresh lemon juice
salt and freshly ground pepper

❀ In a heavy saucepan over medium heat, melt the butter or warm the oil. Add the onion, carrot and celery and sauté until tender and lightly golden, about 15 minutes. Add the stock, lentils and the bone, if using, and bring to a boil. Reduce the heat to low, cover and simmer until the lentils are very soft, about 45 minutes.
❀ Remove the bone. Add the cumin, allspice and the rhubarb, if using. Simmer 15–20 minutes longer, to cook the rhubarb and blend the flavors.
❀ Working in batches, purée the soup in a blender, then return it to the pan. Reheat gently and season to taste with lemon juice, salt and pepper. Serve hot.

SERVES 6

MOROCCO

HARIRA

Lamb and Bean Soup

Muslims serve this hearty soup to break the fast at the end of Ramadan. There are many variations on this recipe. All of them are lemony, some omit the eggs, some have only lentils, and still others add noodles or orzo *(ricelike pasta).*

½ cup (3½ oz/105 g) dried chick-peas (garbanzo beans)
salt
9 cups (72 fl oz/2.1 l) water
⅔ cup (5 oz/155 g) lentils
3 tablespoons white rice
3 tablespoons all-purpose (plain) flour mixed with ½ cup (4 fl oz/125 ml) water
2 tablespoons unsalted butter
1 tablespoon olive oil
½ lb (250 g) lamb, cut into ½-in (12-mm) cubes
2 onions, chopped (about 3 cups/12 oz/375 g)
2 cloves garlic, finely minced
½ teaspoon ground ginger
1 teaspoon ground cinnamon
½ teaspoon ground turmeric
2 cups (16 fl oz/500 ml) puréed canned plum (Roma) tomatoes or 1½ lb (750 g) peeled, seeded and chopped fresh plum tomatoes
½ cup (¾ oz/20 g) chopped fresh flat-leaf (Italian) parsley
¼ cup (⅓ oz/10 g) chopped fresh cilantro (fresh coriander)
2 teaspoons freshly ground pepper, or to taste
2 eggs
¼ cup (2 fl oz/60 ml) fresh lemon juice

❀ Place the chick-peas in a bowl with water to cover generously. Refrigerate overnight. Drain and rinse well.
❀ Transfer the chick-peas to a 1-qt (1-l) saucepan and add 3 cups (24 fl oz/750 ml) of the water. Bring to a boil, reduce the heat to low, cover and simmer until cooked through but not falling apart, about 1 hour. Remove from the heat and salt lightly. Drain the chick-peas, reserving the cooking liquid. You will have about 1½ cups (9 oz/280 g) chick-peas. Set the chick-peas and liquid aside.
❀ Pour another 3 cups (24 fl oz/750 ml) of the water into a 3-qt (3-l) saucepan and bring to a boil. Add the lentils and rice and simmer for 20 minutes. Add the flour-water paste, stirring in well.
❀ While the lentils are simmering, in a large sauté pan over high heat, melt the butter with the oil. Add the lamb and brown well on all sides, about 5 minutes. Add the onions, garlic, ginger, cinnamon and turmeric and sauté for a few minutes. Add the remaining 3 cups (24 fl oz/750 ml) water and simmer, uncovered, over low heat for 30 minutes.
❀ Add the meat-onion mixture, drained chick-peas, tomatoes, parsley and cilantro to the lentils and simmer for 15 minutes. Add salt to taste and the pepper; the soup should be peppery. If it seems too thick, thin it with a little of the reserved cooking liquid. Remove the soup from the heat.
❀ In a small bowl whisk together the eggs and lemon juice. Stir into the soup. Serve at once.

SERVES 6

EGYPT

MELOKHIA

Melokhia Leaf Soup

The melokhia *is a leaf of a species of mallow plant. The leaves resemble mint or small spinach and they form the basis of a classic and ancient Egyptian soup. They have an undistinguished taste but contribute an interesting texture to a soup. It is almost impossible to buy fresh* melokhia *outside its world of use, but you can find dried* melokhia *in stores that specialize in Middle Eastern foods. This soup is traditionally flavored with* taklia *(also called* ta'leya*), a mixture of garlic, coriander and cayenne pepper sautéed in clarified butter. Cooked rice or diced bread is also sometimes added to the soup.*

1½ cups (4 oz/125 g) dried *melokhia* leaves
6 cups (48 fl oz/1.5 l) meat or chicken stock (see glossary)

FOR THE *TAKLIA:*

2 tablespoons clarified butter (see glossary)
4 cloves garlic, finely minced
1 tablespoon ground coriander
½ teaspoon cayenne pepper
chopped onion marinated in fresh lemon juice or distilled white vinegar for garnish (optional)

❀ In a blender or a food processor fitted with the metal blade, crush the dried *melokhia* leaves. You'll have about 1¼–1½ cups (4 oz/125 g) powder. In a bowl soak this powder in a little of the cold stock for about 20 minutes, to soften it. In a saucepan bring the remaining stock to a boil. Stir in the soaked *melokhia,* reduce the heat to low and simmer uncovered, stirring often to prevent *melokhia* from sinking to the bottom, until thickened, about 20 minutes.
❀ While the soup is simmering, make the *taklia.* In a sauté pan over medium heat, melt the butter. Add the garlic and sauté for a few minutes. Stir in the coriander and cayenne and cook for 2–3 minutes longer.
❀ When the soup is ready, stir in the *taklia* and simmer for 2 minutes. Ladle into individual bowls and pass the marinated onions, if desired, for diners to garnish the soup to taste.

SERVES 6

GREECE

and the Balkans

Whether or not the present-day inhabitants of Greece are, to any degree at all, the lineal descendants of the ancient Greeks is a matter of scholarly dispute. None will deny, however, that a devotion to gastronomy and the anchoring of food in social and ritual life combine to provide an element of continuity between ancient and modern Greece.

Food, including the quintessential Mediterranean trinity of olive oil, bread and wine, figures prominently in Greek mythology, which is not surprising, considering the Greek gods had desires and appetites at least as voracious as those of mortals. The trouble seems to have started with Zeus, who, finding his father Kronos asleep after eating too much honey—obviously the primordial food—chained him and transported him to the end of the world. He then went on to disguise himself as a snake and ungallantly to seduce his sister Demeter, the earth mother. The result of this liaison was Persephone, goddess of harvests, whose annual parole from bondage in the underworld—the unfortunate consequence of ingesting a pomegranate seed at the wrong time—was appropriately fixed for harvest time. Distraught at the loss of Persephone, Demeter was consoled by a family of herdsmen, and as a token of her gratitude gave them some ears of corn she happened to be carrying. Triptolemus, the youngest son

Previous pages: Mykonos is quickly becoming the St. Tropez of the Cycládes Islands, where the chic descend in large numbers during the summer months. Left: Dubrovnik, founded some 1300 years ago, was considered one of the most important medieval city states on the Adriatic.

Fish and Shellfish

The most popular Mediterranean method for cooking fish is grilling over an open wood fire.

FISH AND SHELLFISH

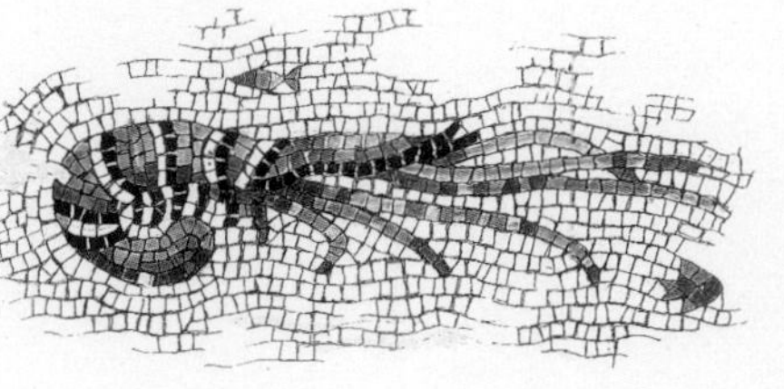

Fish is arguably the most common form of animal protein on the Mediterranean menu. Local fish markets are busy, noisy, exciting places; their numerous stalls are filled with glistening creatures from the sea. To those of us accustomed to a limited selection at our markets, much of it "fresh frozen," the variety is overwhelming.

Throughout the Mediterranean, but especially in Greece and Turkey, the red mullet is prized and is usually served pan-fried. Sea bass, called *levrek* in Turkey, *rofos* in Greece and *spigola* in Italy, can be grilled or baked. Swordfish—*kiliç* in Turkey, *pesce spada* in Italy and *xifias* in Greece—can be baked or grilled and is most popular in Turkey and Sicily. In Sicily, tuna is grilled, stewed or baked as well as added to pasta. Along with these Mediterranean favorites are John Dory, turbot, angler (monkfish), mackerel, grouper, sea bream, cod, sole, porgy, perch, sardines, anchovies, snapper, trout, pike, skate, eel, octopus, squid, scallops, a variety of shrimp and prawns, clams, mussels, lobsters, crabs and other delicacies. One never tires of the treasures of the sea or the rivers.

However plentiful and varied the fish and shellfish may be, most are prepared with a minimum of fanfare—a drop or two of fragrant olive oil, a spritz of fresh lemon or orange juice, a dash of vinegar, some slivers of garlic, a few sprigs of rosemary or marjoram, a bay leaf or two, a sprinkling of cumin, paprika or coriander. And, of course, there is always a good dusting with salt. Sometimes fish is put into a flavorful marinade for a few hours before cooking, with the Moroccan *chermoula* the pinnacle of the marinade family.

By far the most popular method for cooking fish in the Mediterranean countries is grilling over a wood fire. Sometimes herbs are thrown onto the fire to add another flavor dimension. Fish can be grilled whole, sliced into steaks or cut into cubes and threaded onto skewers. It can be wrapped in grapeleaves to prevent it from sticking to the grill and to impart a subtle flavor. When fish is cooked over a wood fire, the slightly smoky scent perfumes the delicate flesh, so only a light sauce is required. Lemon and olive oil with or without herbs is the usual marinade or sauce.

Second only to grilling is frying. Fish and shellfish can be pan-fried without a coating, as in Greek sautéed sea bass with vinegar and rosemary or the Catalan *gambas al ajillo,* shrimp with garlic and lemon. Or they are deep-fried, first cloaked in a covering that may be as simple as a quick dip in flour and then quickly immersed in hot oil, drained, and served piping hot, doused with a squeeze of fresh lemon. The fish emerge crisp on the outside, tender and succulent on the inside, and not cooked a moment longer than necessary. Tiny fish or combinations of fish and shellfish—the ubiquitous local *fritto misto* of southern Italy—are piled high on a platter and served along with a dish of cut lemons or sometimes a dipping sauce such as the Turkish walnut or hazelnut *tarator,* the Catalan *romesco,* the Provençal aioli.

Previous pages: left to right; Grilled Swordfish (recipe page 131), Stuffed Mackerel (recipe page 131)

The repertoire of baked fish and shellfish recipes has increased as the oven has appeared in more and more homes. These recipes are generally simple to prepare. Dishes such as Greek *garides youvetsi,* shrimp with feta cheese and tomato sauce; *coquilles St.-Jacques à la provençale;* Moroccan *al toune bil tomatich,* tuna with tomato sauce and preserved lemon; Sicilian *triglie in cartoccio,* red mullet in parchment; or Provençal eel with leeks, olives and wine can be assembled ahead of time and then slipped into a hot oven just before serving.

Sometimes fish is roasted as if it were meat. *Gigot de mer*—"leg of lamb of the sea"—finds monkfish (angler fish) studded with garlic and baked atop a bed of *ratatouille.* In the Sicilian *alalungo al ragu,* tuna is studded with garlic and mint, fried, and then braised either in the oven or atop the stove.

Many of the baked or braised fish dishes are served at room temperature, as in the past they were baked in the town oven and then carried home to be eaten later. In the Mediterranean, people are accustomed to room-temperature foods and find that the flavors develop as the dish rests. *Sarde a beccaficu,* Sicilian stuffed sardines, are good hot but perhaps even better cold. The Lebanese *samak bi tahini,* a whole fish coated with a rich sesame sauce, surrounded by sliced cucumbers and radishes, topped with toasted pine nuts and pomegranate seeds and served cold, is one of the most spectacular dishes of the region. Boned whole Turkish mackerel stuffed with a fragrant rice pilaf, baked and served hot or at room temperature is carefully carved at the table.

The Mediterranean is also home to what is probably the largest array of fish stews and soups. They can be simple: fish balls braised in a savory tomato sauce, mussels steamed in wine and garlic, or squid simmered in a simple tomato sauce with peas. In some stews, shellfish and fish are combined in an opulent medley to show off the day's catch. Because of the great variety offered at fish markets, an elaborate fish stew such as peppery *bourthéto* of Corfu; Sardinian *cassola,* a relative of the Spanish *zarzuela;* Provençal *bourride* or *bouillabaisse;* Tunisian fish couscous; or the pan-Italian *zuppa di pesce* can be prepared easily and without having to pray for fair weather and calm seas.

When dogfish or goby or turbot or John Dory are mentioned in a recipe but are not to be found at your local fish market, substitutes are suggested. Your fishmonger may have some excellent suggestions for you as well. Be sure the fish you buy smells sweet and is firm to the touch and glistening. Cook it the day you bring it home. Remember, unlike wine, it does not improve with age. And be careful not to overcook fish; it is best when still moist.

A Greek fishmonger proudly displays the morning's fresh lobster catch.

From ancient times, fishing has played a vital role in the economic activity of the Mediterranean basin.

Top to bottom: Shrimp with Feta Cheese, Baked Fish with Bread Crumbs and Tomatoes

GREECE

PSARI SPÉTSIOTIKA

Baked Fish with Bread Crumbs and Tomatoes

Named for the island of Spétsai, this dish is very easy to prepare and very tasty. The elements are simple: impeccably fresh fish, flavorful vine-ripened tomatoes and good-quality bread crumbs. You may serve it hot or cold.

2 lb (1 kg) firm white fish fillets or steaks
6 tablespoons (3 fl oz/90 ml) olive oil
1 tablespoon fresh lemon juice
salt and freshly ground pepper
2 cups (12 oz/375 g) peeled, seeded and chopped tomatoes
4 cloves garlic, finely minced
½ cup (4 fl oz/125 ml) dry white wine
1 tablespoon sugar or honey
4 tablespoons chopped fresh flat-leaf (Italian) parsley
1 teaspoon dried oregano or ground cinnamon (optional)
1 cup (4 oz/125 g) fine dried bread crumbs

Arrange the fish in a baking dish in which it fits in a single layer. In a small bowl whisk together 2 tablespoons of the oil, lemon juice, salt and pepper to taste and pour over the fish. Let stand for about 30 minutes at room temperature.

Meanwhile, preheat an oven to 400°F (200°C).

In a saucepan over medium heat, combine the tomatoes, garlic, wine, sugar or honey, parsley and the oregano or cinnamon, if using. Bring to a simmer and cook for about 10 minutes. Season to taste with salt and pepper.

Pour the tomato sauce evenly over the fish. Scatter the bread crumbs evenly over the top, then drizzle with the remaining 4 tablespoons (2 fl oz/60 ml) oil. Bake until the fish is cooked through and bread crumbs are golden brown, about 15 minutes.

Serve immediately.

SERVES 4

GREECE

GARIDES YOUVETSI

Shrimp with Feta Cheese

Although this dish is a specialty of Salonika, it is served all over Greece. It can be prepared a few hours ahead of time and then baked in ramekins just before serving.

1½ lb (750 g) shrimp (prawns), peeled and deveined
salt and freshly ground pepper to taste, plus 2 teaspoons pepper
½ cup (4 fl oz/125 ml) olive oil
1 yellow onion, chopped
1 bunch green (spring) onions, including tender green tops, minced
2 cloves garlic, finely minced
1 tablespoon dried oregano
3 tablespoons chopped fresh basil or dill (optional)
4 tomatoes, peeled, seeded and chopped
1 teaspoon honey or sugar
½ cup (4 fl oz/125 ml) dry white wine
½ lb (250 g) feta cheese, crumbled
4 tablespoons chopped fresh flat-leaf (Italian) parsley

Sprinkle the shrimp with salt and pepper. In a large sauté pan over high heat, warm ¼ cup (2 fl oz/60 ml) of the oil. Add the shrimp and sear quickly on both sides. Remove from the pan and set aside. (Refrigerate if not cooking within the next 15 minutes.)

In the same pan over medium heat, warm the remaining ¼ cup (2 fl oz/60 ml) oil. Add the yellow onion and sauté until tender and translucent, 8–10 minutes. Add the green onions, garlic, oregano and the basil or dill, if using, and cook for 5 minutes longer. Add the tomatoes, honey or sugar and wine and simmer briskly to thicken the mixture, 8–10 minutes. Season with the 2 teaspoons pepper; do not add too much salt as the feta will be salty.

Meanwhile, preheat an oven to 400°F (200°C). Divide half of the tomato sauce among 4 ramekins. Divide the shrimp evenly among the ramekins. Spoon the remaining tomato sauce over the shrimp. Top each portion with an equal amount of the cheese. Bake until the shrimp are cooked and the cheese melts, about 10 minutes.

Alternatively, cook the tomato sauce as directed. Return the seared shrimp to the tomato sauce, sprinkle the feta on top, cover and simmer until the cheese melts, about 7 minutes.

Serve hot, sprinkled with the parsley.

SERVES 4

MOROCCO

HUT B'NOUA

Fish with Almond Paste

An exotic and unusual dish that is not too sweet. If you want to make this dish with fish fillets, place the fillets atop a bed of the saffroned onions and spread a layer of the almond paste on the fillets. Bake, basting with a little melted butter, for 10–12 minutes.

1 whole snapper, salmon or other whole mild fish, about 3½ lb (1.75 kg), cleaned
salt for rubbing on fish, plus 1 teaspoon salt
2 cups (11 oz/345 g) almonds, toasted
½ cup (4 oz/125 g) sugar
1 teaspoon ground cinnamon
1 tablespoon orange-flower water
2 tablespoons water
2 tablespoons olive oil

1 large onion, finely chopped
½ teaspoon saffron threads steeped in ¼ cup (2 fl oz/60 ml) hot water
½ teaspoon freshly ground pepper
¼ cup (2 oz/60 g) unsalted butter, melted

Rub the fish with salt, inside and out, then rinse. Cut 3 or 4 shallow diagonal slits on each side of the body. Set aside.

Put the almonds and sugar in a blender or in a processor fitted with the metal blade and grind. Add the cinnamon, orange-flower water and the water and pulse briefly to combine. Pack half of this mixture into the fish and skewer closed. Place the fish in an oiled baking pan or ovenproof baking dish. Set aside.

Preheat an oven to 400°F (200°C). In a small sauté pan over medium heat, warm the oil. Add the onion and sauté until tender and translucent, 8–10 minutes. Add the saffron and its soaking water, the 1 teaspoon salt and the pepper. Place the saffroned onions around the fish. Rub the remaining almond paste atop the fish (not on the head or tail) and evenly drizzle on the melted butter. Bake until the fish tests done when pierced with a knife, about 30 minutes.

Transfer the fish and onions to a warmed serving platter and serve at once.

SERVES 6

MOROCCO

CHERMOULA

Spicy Marinade for Fish

Chermoula *is the classic Moroccan marinade for fish. Whether you plan to bake, grill, fry or steam the fish, marinating it in* chermoula *will enhance its flavor. Allow the fish to remain in the marinade for 2–6 hours, or preferably overnight for whole fish. Once the fish is cooked, spoon a little additional* chermoula *over the fish before serving.*

There are many versions of chermoula. *Basically, the variables are whether onion, cayenne pepper or lemon are added. Here are four recipes for* chermoula; *they can also be used for preparing shellfish, chicken, squab (pigeon) and lamb.*

FOR *CHERMOULA* I:

1 onion, finely chopped
4 cloves garlic, finely minced
2 teaspoons ground cumin
1 teaspoon paprika
½ teaspoon saffron threads steeped in 2 tablespoons water
½ cup (¾ oz/20 g) chopped fresh flat-leaf (Italian) parsley
½ cup (¾ oz/20 g) chopped fresh cilantro (fresh coriander)
6 tablespoons (3 fl oz/90 ml) olive oil
¼ cup (2 fl oz/60 ml) fresh lemon juice
salt

FOR *CHERMOULA* II:

4 tablespoons chopped fresh cilantro (fresh coriander)
3 cloves garlic, finely minced
2 teaspoons paprika
2 teaspoons ground cumin
½ teaspoon cayenne pepper
½ teaspoon saffron threads steeped in 2 tablespoons water
3 tablespoons fresh lemon juice
6 tablespoons (3 fl oz/90 ml) olive oil
salt

FOR *CHERMOULA* III:

3 cloves garlic, finely minced
peel of 1 preserved lemon, rinsed and finely minced (see glossary)
½ cup (¾ oz/20 g) chopped fresh cilantro (fresh coriander)
½ cup (¾ oz/20 g) chopped fresh flat-leaf (Italian) parsley
½ teaspoon cayenne pepper
½ teaspoon saffron threads steeped in 2 tablespoons water
1 teaspoon paprika
6 tablespoons (3 fl oz/90 ml) olive oil
3 tablespoons fresh lemon juice

FOR *CHERMOULA* IV:

2 cloves garlic, finely minced
½ cup (¾ oz/20 g) chopped fresh cilantro (fresh coriander)
½ cup (¾ oz/20 g) chopped fresh flat-leaf (Italian) parsley
1 teaspoon freshly ground pepper
½ teaspoon ground cinnamon
½ teaspoon ground ginger
½ teaspoon saffron threads steeped in ¼ cup (2 fl oz/60 ml) water
2 teaspoons ground cumin
1 teaspoon paprika
1½ teaspoons salt
6 tablespoons (3 fl oz/90 ml) olive oil

To make each recipe, in a bowl whisk together all the ingredients. Then arrange the fish in a nonreactive container and pour the marinade over the top. Marinade as directed in introduction.

Each recipe yields enough marinade for about 2 lb (1 kg) whole fish or fish fillets.

Top to bottom: Spicy Marinade for Fish, Fish with Almond Paste

LEBANON

Samak bi Tahini

Fish with Tahini Sauce

This is an Arab classic, served in Syria as well as Lebanon. The fish is baked, cooled to room temperature, coated with a tahini sauce and then decorated with parsley and pine nuts. Cucumber and radish slices and pomegranate seeds (see glossary) also make good garnishes. You can add 1 cup (4 oz/125 g) chopped walnuts to the sauce. Or add ½ teaspoon cayenne pepper and ½ cup (¾ oz/20 g) chopped fresh cilantro (fresh coriander) to the tahini mixture when puréeing it, spread it on the fish when it is half-cooked and return the fish to the oven for an additional 15 minutes; serve hot or at room temperature.

salt
1 whole fish such as snapper or sea bass, 2½–3 lb (1.25–1.5 kg)
3 tablespoons olive oil
2 tablespoons fresh lemon juice
freshly ground pepper

FOR THE TAHINI SAUCE:

3 or 4 cloves garlic, finely minced
1 teaspoon salt
1 cup (8 oz/250 g) tahini (see glossary)
4–6 tablespoons (2–3 fl oz/60–90 ml) fresh lemon juice
6–8 tablespoons (3–4 fl oz/90–125 ml) water, or as needed

¼ cup (1¼ oz/40 g) pine nuts, toasted
3 tablespoons chopped fresh flat-leaf (Italian) parsley

Preheat an oven to 400°F (200°C). Sprinkle salt over the fish, then rinse. Cut 3 or 4 shallow diagonal slits on each side of the body. In a small bowl whisk together the oil, lemon juice, and salt and pepper to taste and rub this mixture over the fish. Place in a baking pan.

Bake, basting occasionally with the pan juices, until the fish tests done when pierced with a knife, 25–35 minutes. Carefully lift the fish onto a serving platter and let cool.

To make the sauce, in a blender or a processor fitted with the metal blade, combine the garlic, salt, tahini and lemon juice. Purée, adding enough of the water to achieve a fluffy mixture.

Remove and discard the skin from the fish. Spread the tahini sauce on the fish. Decorate with the pine nuts and parsley, and serve.

SERVES 6

TUNISIA

Kes Kow bil Hout

Fish with Couscous

Fish couscous is served all over North Africa, but is at its best in Tunisia. It was brought to Sicily by the Arabs, probably during the twelfth or thirteenth century, where today it is known as cuscusù trapanese. *The mystique of preparing the semolina grain more or less vanished with the advent of instant couscous. And after making the basic couscous you may wonder what all the fuss was about. Some insist that cooking the couscous by the long method is best, but if you hold the grains warm atop the stew pot in a colander lined with cheesecloth (muslin) to absorb more of the aroma and taste, and drizzle them with a little fish broth from time to time, you'll have a wonderful dish.*

This couscous can be as simple or as elaborate as you like. Sea bass, mullet and cod are good choices for the fish. Chick-peas and assorted vegetables such as carrots, potatoes, turnips and cabbage can be added. In Tunisia the harissa *is stirred into the stew and served on the side as a condiment. In Sicily* cuscusù *is made with fish, a little onion, garlic and tomatoes, and is scented with a pinch of cinnamon. Red pepper flakes are stirred into 1 cup (8 fl oz/250 ml) of the broth, which is then served as a hot sauce on the side.*

salt
2–3 lb (1–1.5 kg) mixed fish for soup, cut into thick pieces (see introduction)
couscous made with water or part fish stock and seasoned with 1 teaspoon ground cinnamon and a little olive oil or butter (recipe on page 204)
¼ cup (2 fl oz/60 ml) olive oil
2 onions, chopped
2 cloves garlic, minced
1 teaspoon *harissa* (see glossary) or ½ teaspoon cayenne pepper
1 teaspoon ground cumin
½ teaspoon freshly ground black pepper
4–5 cups (32–40 fl oz/1–1.1 l) water or fish stock (see glossary)
2 or 3 tomatoes, peeled, seeded and chopped
3 carrots, peeled and sliced 1 in (2.5 cm) thick
2 turnips, peeled and cut into 2-in (5-cm) pieces
1 cup (6 oz/185 g) cooked chick-peas (garbanzo beans), optional
8 small new potatoes, halved (optional)

Lightly salt the fish and refrigerate it while you make the soup base. Also, begin cooking the couscous.

In a large, heavy saucepan or soup pot over medium heat, warm the oil. Add the onions and garlic and sauté for 5 minutes. Stir in the *harissa* or cayenne, cumin and black pepper. Cook for about 2 minutes, then add the water or stock, tomatoes, carrots and turnips. Simmer for 15 minutes. Add the fish and chick-peas or potatoes (if using) and simmer until the fish and potatoes are done, about 20 minutes.

To serve, spoon some couscous into individual soup bowls. Ladle the fish and vegetables around the couscous and then spoon on some of the broth. Or pile the couscous on a large platter, make a well in the center and put the fish in the middle and the vegetables around the edges. Ladle some of the broth over the top and serve the remaining broth in a bowl on the side.

SERVES 6–8

EGYPT

Samak Magli Kousbariyeh

Fried Fish with Tomatoes and Nuts

In the Middle East fish is usually grilled or fried. Small fish are fried whole; large fish are cut into steaks or chunks. Plain fried fish can be served with tarator *sauce (recipe on page 60),* romesco *sauce (recipe on page 134) or lemon wedges. In this recipe the fish is fried and then topped with a sauce of tomatoes, onions and nuts.*

1½ cups (7½ oz/235 g) all-purpose (plain) flour
2 teaspoons salt, plus salt to taste
½ teaspoon freshly ground pepper
1 teaspoon paprika (optional)
1 teaspoon ground coriander
2 lb (1 kg) mild white fish (see note)
safflower oil, or other vegetable oil for frying

FOR THE SAUCE:

2 tablespoons olive oil
2–3 cups (7–10½ oz/210–315 g) thinly sliced onion
2 cups (12 oz/375 g) peeled, seeded and coarsely chopped tomatoes (about 3 large)

Clockwise from top left: Fish with Couscous, Fish with Tahini Sauce, Fried Fish with Tomatoes and Nuts

1 cup (5 oz/155 g) hazelnuts (filberts) or 1 cup (4 oz/125 g) walnuts, toasted and chopped
⅓ cup (1⅔ oz/50 g) pine nuts, toasted
½ cup (4 fl oz/125 ml) water
4 tablespoons chopped fresh flat-leaf (Italian) parsley
1½ teaspoons salt
½ teaspoon freshly ground pepper
½ teaspoon ground allspice

In a shallow dish stir together the flour, the 2 teaspoons salt, pepper, paprika, and coriander. Dredge the fish in the flour mixture, shaking off any excess.

In a deep sauté pan, pour in oil to a depth of about 2 in (5 cm) and heat to 375°F (190°C), or until a bit of bread dropped into it begins to color within moments. When the oil is ready, slip the fish into it and fry, turning once, until cooked through and golden brown on both sides, about 3 minutes per side. Using a slotted spoon remove to paper towels to drain. Sprinkle with salt and set aside.

To make the sauce, in a large sauté pan over medium heat, warm the oil. Add the onion and sauté until tender and translucent, 8–10 minutes. Add the tomatoes and simmer until soft, about 5 minutes. Add both kinds of nuts and cook for a few minutes longer. Finally, add the water and season with the parsley, salt, pepper and allspice. Simmer for a few minutes to blend the flavors.

Add the fried fish to the sauce. Carefully turn the fish to coat it well and then simmer for 3 minutes to heat through. Alternatively, preheat an oven to 400°F (200°C). Place the fried fish in a baking dish, pour the sauce over the top and bake for 5–8 minutes to heat through.

Arrange the fish and sauce on a warmed deep platter and serve at once.

SERVES 4–6

Clockwise from top left: Braised Albacore Tuna, Red Mullet in Parchment, Stuffed Sardines

SICILY

SARDE A BECCAFICCU

Stuffed Sardines

A beccaficco *is a tiny bird that gets fat from eating figs* (fichi). *This specialty of Palermo takes its name from the fact that the stuffed sardines look like very fat little birds.*

Some recipes suggest slipping bay leaves between the rolled stuffed fish, and some add cheese, capers or olives to the filling. In Catania diced caciocavallo *cheese is added to the bread-crumb mixture and the stuffed sardines are dipped in flour and fried instead of baked. The sardines can be eaten hot or cold, and would make a great addition to an antipasto assortment.*

2½ lb (1.25 kg) fresh sardines (about 24)
6 tablespoons (3 fl oz/90 ml) olive oil
1 cup (4 oz/125 g) fine dried bread crumbs
2 cloves garlic, finely minced
⅓ cup (2 oz/60 g) pine nuts, toasted and chopped
⅓ cup (2 oz/60 g) dried currants, plumped in hot water, drained and chopped
3 tablespoons chopped fresh flat-leaf (Italian) parsley
½ cup (5 oz/155 g) sharply flavored black olives, pitted and chopped (optional)
¼ cup (1 oz/30 g) grated pecorino cheese (optional)
¼ cup (1½ oz/45 g) capers, rinsed, drained and chopped (optional)
about 24 bay leaves (optional)
2–3 tablespoons fresh lemon juice
¼ cup (2 fl oz/60 ml) orange juice (optional)

Clean the sardines by cutting off the head and fins, removing any scales, splitting them open at the belly and removing the guts. Run your finger down the backbone so that the fish opens like a book. Remove the backbone, breaking it off just at the tail.

Preheat an oven to 375°–400°F (190°–200°C).

To make the filling, in a small sauté pan over medium heat, warm 2 tablespoons of the oil. Add the bread crumbs and cook, stirring constantly, for about 3 minutes. Add the garlic and sauté for 2 minutes longer. Remove from the heat and add the pine nuts, currants, parsley and, if desired, the olives, and cheese or capers. Season to taste with salt and pepper.

Open a sardine, skin side down, and place a heaping teaspoonful of the filling near the top. Starting from the head end, roll up the fish toward the tail. Place in a lightly oiled baking dish, tail end up. Stuff and roll the other sardines in the same manner and pack them tightly in the dish so they don't unroll. If you like, slip a bay leaf between the sardines as you fit them into the dish.

In a small bowl whisk together the remaining oil, the lemon juice and the orange juice (if using) and pour over the sardines. Bake until cooked through, about 10 minutes. Transfer to a platter and serve warm or at room temperature.

SERVES 6

SICILY

ALALUNGO AL RAGÙ

Braised Albacore Tuna

Here is a Sicilian recipe for braised tuna that treats the fish somewhat like leg of lamb, in that slivers of garlic and mint are inserted into small incisions in the flesh. The treatment is not unlike that for gigot de mer *(recipe on page 142). Instead of roasting the tuna, however, here it is browned and braised with onions and a scented tomato sauce. Some versions add cinnamon or chili pepper to the sauce. Serve with potatoes.*

2 lb (1 kg) albacore tuna, in one piece, skinned
4 cloves garlic
12 large fresh mint leaves
salt and freshly ground black pepper
½ cup (4 fl oz/120 ml) olive oil
½ cup (4 fl oz/125 ml) dry white wine
1 large onion, chopped
2 cups (12 oz/375 g) peeled, seeded and diced tomatoes
pinch of red pepper flakes (optional)
1 cinnamon stick, about 1 in (2.5 cm) long (optional)

Make 12 incisions about ½ in (12 mm) deep all over the fish. Cut 3 of the garlic cloves into 12 slivers. Insert a garlic sliver and mint leaf into each slit. Sprinkle the fish with salt and pepper. In a heavy saucepan over medium-high heat, warm ¼ cup (2 fl oz/60 ml) of the oil. Add the fish and brown on both sides. Add the white wine and cook until it almost evaporates, just a few minutes.

Meanwhile, mince the remaining garlic clove. In another small pan warm the remaining ¼ cup (2 fl oz/60 ml) oil. Add the onion and minced garlic and sauté until tender and translucent, 8–10 minutes. Add to the tuna along with the tomatoes and, if desired, the cinnamon or pepper flakes. Cover and cook over low heat until the tuna tests done when pierced with a knife, 45–60 minutes. Season to taste with salt and pepper.

Transfer to a warmed dish and serve at once.

SERVES 6

TURKEY

Kiliç Baligi Izgarasi

Grilled Swordfish

Swordfish is greatly esteemed in Turkey. Usually it is marinated and grilled. For this recipe the fish is served as a steak, but it can be cut into cubes and presented as a brochette (kılıç şiş) *as well. If you skewer the swordfish, tuck bay leaves between the cubes. While more moist when eaten hot, this swordfish can be quite tasty as a room-temperature appetizer.* Tarator *sauce (recipe on page 60) can be served as a condiment.*

6 swordfish steaks, each about 6 oz (185 g) and ¾ in (2 cm) thick
1 onion, grated
2–3 tablespoons fresh lemon juice, plus lemon juice for serving (optional)
2 cloves garlic, finely minced
2 tablespoons ground coriander
pinch of cayenne pepper
1 teaspoon paprika
¼ cup (2 fl oz/60 ml) olive oil, plus oil for brushing on fish and serving (optional)
6 bay leaves
salt and freshly ground black pepper

Place the swordfish in a shallow nonreactive container. In a bowl whisk together the onion, lemon juice, garlic, coriander, cayenne, paprika and the ¼ cup (2 fl oz/60 ml) oil. Alternatively, whirl in a blender or a food processor fitted with a metal blade. Pour over the fish. Add the bay leaves. Cover and marinate in the refrigerator, turning the fish a few times in the marinade to coat well, for 5–6 hours.

Preheat a broiler (griller) or prepare a fire in a charcoal grill. Remove the fish from the marinade. Brush both sides of each steak lightly with oil and sprinkle with salt and black pepper. Place on broiler pan or on grill rack and broil or grill, turning once, until done when tested with a knife, 4–5 minutes on each side.

Transfer to a serving platter. If you like, whisk together a little oil and lemon juice to taste and spoon over the fish. Serve at once or at room temperature.

SERVES 6 *Photograph pages 122–123*

TURKEY

Uskumru Dolmasi

Stuffed Mackerel

Here fish is treated as a dolma, *filled with a savory herb, nut and raisin stuffing, then fried, broiled (grilled), cooked over a charcoal fire or baked, and served hot or at room temperature. (If you are grilling or broiling the fish, brush it with olive oil before you begin cooking it and then cook it for about 4 minutes on each side.) Traditionally, the fish bones and meat are removed, leaving only the skin of the fish intact. Then the fish flesh is mixed with the filling ingredients and the mixture spooned back inside the skin. This delicate procedure requires practice and patience. It is far simpler to put the filling in the boned fish and sew or skewer it closed.*

2 tablespoons olive oil, plus olive oil for frying
2 onions, chopped
½ teaspoon ground allspice
1 teaspoon ground cinnamon
½ teaspoon ground cloves
3 tablespoons pine nuts, toasted
3 tablespoons chopped, toasted hazelnuts (filberts) or walnuts
¼ cup (1½ oz/45 g) raisins or dried currants, plumped in hot water and drained
4 tablespoons chopped fresh dill
4 tablespoons chopped fresh flat-leaf (Italian) parsley
1 cup (2 oz/60 g) fresh bread crumbs (optional)
salt and freshly ground pepper
4 whole mackerel, Coho salmon or salmon trout, 10–12 oz (315–375 g) each, cleaned
all-purpose (plain) flour for coating
lemon wedges

In a large sauté pan over medium heat, warm the oil. Add the onions and sauté until tender and translucent, 8–10 minutes. Add the allspice, cinnamon and cloves and sauté for 2 minutes longer. Remove from the heat and add both kinds of nuts, the raisins or currants, dill, parsley and bread crumbs (if using). Season to taste with salt and pepper. Let cool to room temperature.

Divide the filling evenly among the fish and stuff it into the cavities. Sew or skewer closed. Put flour in a large, shallow bowl and season to taste with salt and pepper. Dredge the fish in the flour and shake off the excess.

In a large sauté pan over medium heat, pour in oil to a depth of ½ in (6 mm). When the oil is hot, add the fish (do not crowd the pan) and fry until golden, turning once, about 4 minutes on each side.

Transfer to a serving platter. Serve hot or at room temperature with lemon wedges.

SERVES 4 *Photograph pages 122–123*

SICILY

Triglie in Cartoccio

Red Mullet in Parchment

Since not everyone can find red mullet, trout or other small whole fish will work well for this dish. And you may use aluminum foil instead of parchment paper to wrap the fish. The stuffing is more like a pesto or paste than a filling. You may grill the fish, if you like, in which case you can wrap them in aluminum foil or grapeleaves (see method on page 141).

4 tablespoons finely chopped fresh mint leaves
2 cloves garlic, finely minced
4 anchovy fillets in olive oil, drained and finely minced
¼ cup (1 oz/30 g) fine dried bread crumbs
about ¼ cup (2 fl oz/60 ml) olive oil

4 trout or large red mullet, cleaned and heads and fins removed (6–8 oz/185–250 g each after cleaning)
salt
2 teaspoons chopped fresh marjoram

Preheat an oven to 450°F (230°C). In a mortar with a pestle, pound together the mint, garlic and anchovies to form a paste. Add the bread crumbs and enough oil to form a spreadable paste.

Lay each fish on a sheet of aluminum foil or parchment paper large enough to form a loose envelope that will enclose it completely. Open the fish up and sprinkle the insides with salt. Then spread each cavity with about one-fourth of the paste. Fold the fish closed, drizzle with oil and sprinkle with ½ teaspoon of the marjoram. Fold the foil or paper over the fish and pinch edges together well to seal. Repeat with the remaining fish and filling. Bake until the fish is cooked through, 10–15 minutes. Unwrap, transfer to a platter and serve at once.

SERVES 4

SARDINIA

CASSOLA

Fish Soup

This fish soup takes its name from the cazuela, *or dish, in which it is traditionally cooked. The name seems Spanish and it is, because Sardinia was under Spanish rule for many years (1297–1714). Catalan dialect is still spoken in Cagliari, Sardinia's principal city, where this soup is a specialty. Other food terms that show Spanish influence are* impanadas *for* impanata *(a stuffed pastry),* ghisau *for* guisado *(meat braised in tomato sauce), and* lepudrida *for* l'olla podrida *(a stew of meat and vegetables). This* zuppa di pesce *is quite spicy with hot pepper, but you can temper the fire if you like. You can add crab, eel, octopus and/or squid in place of some of the fish. Or about 1½ pounds (750 g) fish fillets can replace the whole fish, and you can use already made fish stock (such as the stock for the* bourride *on page 144) instead of making the stock from the fish heads.*

2 lb (1 kg) assorted whole firm white fish, such as bass, mullet or scorpion fish
4 cups (32 fl oz/1 l) water or dry white wine
¼ cup (2 fl oz/60 ml) olive oil
2 onions, diced
2 cloves garlic, finely minced
6 fresh basil leaves
red pepper flakes or whole dried chili peppers
1 lb (500 g) tomatoes, peeled, seeded and diced
2 lb (1 kg) clams in the shell, well scrubbed
salt and freshly ground black pepper
12 slices baguette, each about ½ in (12 mm) thick, fried in olive oil

Clean the fish and remove and reserve the heads. Cut the fish into serving pieces, rinse well in salted water, drain and pat dry. Set aside. Place the heads in a saucepan, add the water or wine and bring to a gentle boil. Reduce the heat to low and simmer for 20 minutes, to create a flavorful broth. Strain and set aside.

In a large deep sauté pan over medium heat, warm the oil. Add the onions, garlic, basil and pepper flakes or whole chilies to taste and sauté until the onions are tender and translucent, 8–10 minutes. Add the tomatoes and reserved broth and bring to a boil. Then start adding the fish, slipping in the longest-cooking pieces first. Cook, uncovered, until within 5 minutes of being done, then add the clams (first discarding any that do not close at the touch), and cover to steam them open, 3–5 minutes. Discard any clams that do not open.

Taste and adjust the seasonings with salt and black pepper. Ladle into individual shallow soup plates. Serve with 2 croutons propped up along the sides of each bowl.

SERVES 6

SICILY

PESCESPADA O TONNO ALLA STEMPERATA

Swordfish or Tuna in Melted Sauce

Stemperare *means "to melt," but it also can mean "immoderate" or "excessive." There is nothing excessive about this fragrant sauce, however, except that you might eat too much of it!*

6 thick tuna or swordfish fillets, about ½ lb (250 g) each
salt and freshly ground pepper
olive oil
4 cloves garlic, finely minced
6 celery stalks, chopped
1 cup (4 oz/125 g) green olives, pitted and coarsely chopped
½ cup (3 oz/90 g) raisins, plumped in hot water and drained
¼ cup (1½ oz/45 g) capers, rinsed and drained
⅓ cup (3 fl oz/80 ml) white wine vinegar

Sprinkle the fish with salt and pepper. In 1 or 2 large sauté pans over medium-high heat, warm 2–3 tablespoons oil. Add the fish and sauté 1–2 minutes on each side until lightly colored. Using a slotted spatula, remove to a platter.

Add another 2 tablespoons oil to the pan over medium heat. Add the garlic and celery and sauté, stirring often, until golden, about 10 minutes. Add the olives, raisins and capers and simmer for 2–3 minutes longer. Pour the sauce into a bowl.

Return the fish to the pan (or pans), pour the sauce over the top and sprinkle on the vinegar. Cook for 1–2 minutes over high heat to evaporate the vinegar, then simmer until the fish is done, 3–5 minutes longer.

Transfer to a warm platter and serve immediately.

SERVES 6

SICILY

CALAMARI RIPIENI

Stuffed Squid

All of the Mediterranean countries have recipes for stuffed squid. Rice is the basis of the filling in Greece and Turkey. In France and Italy, bread crumbs bind the filling and sometimes cheese or sausage are added. Here the squid is grilled. If you have not added tomatoes to the filling, you can make a light tomato sauce for spooning over the squid when serving. Or you can stuff the squid and then braise them in a light tomato sauce (see glossary) for 30 minutes; or place them in a well-oiled baking dish, cover the dish and then bake them in a 400°F (200°C) oven for about 25 minutes, basting them occasionally with wine or olive oil. Allow 3 small or 2 medium squid per person.

8 medium or 12 small squid, cleaned with the bodies left whole and the tentacles dropped (see glossary)
1½ cups (3 oz/90 g) fresh bread crumbs
6 tablespoons (3 fl oz/90 ml) olive oil, plus additional olive oil for grilling and serving
salt and freshly ground pepper
1 large onion, chopped
2 cloves garlic, finely chopped
3 tablespoons chopped fresh flat-leaf (Italian) parsley, plus additional parsley for garnish
2 teaspoons dried oregano (optional)
1 tablespoon chopped fresh dill (optional)
2 tablespoons chopped fresh mint (optional)
1 cup (6 oz/185 g) peeled, seeded, diced and drained tomatoes (optional)
1 teaspoon fennel seeds, toasted and ground (optional)
¼ cup (1 oz/30 g) grated pecorino cheese (optional)
2 tablespoons finely minced anchovy fillet (optional)
⅓ cup (1 oz/30 g) diced prosciutto (optional)
fresh lemon juice

Preheat an oven to 400°F (200°C). Prepare the squid and set aside.

In a shallow pan toss together the bread crumbs, 4 tablespoons (2 fl oz/60 ml) of the oil and salt and pepper to taste. Bake, stirring occasionally, until crispy and golden, about 15 minutes. Remove from the oven and transfer to a mixing bowl. Set aside.

Top to bottom: Fish Soup, Swordfish or Tuna in Melted Sauce, Stuffed Squid

❀ Prepare a fire in a charcoal grill.

❀ In a sauté pan over medium heat, warm the remaining 2 tablespoons oil. Add the onion and cook until tender and translucent, 8–10 minutes. Stir in the tentacles, garlic, the 3 tablespoons parsley and one of the optional herbs (if using) and sauté for 2 minutes. Add to the bread crumbs along with tomatoes (if using). Then add any one or more of the additional optional ingredients. Mix well and season to taste with salt and pepper. (If you have added pecorino cheese or anchovy, go easy on the salt.)

❀ Stuff this mixture into the squid bodies and skewer closed with toothpicks. Thread onto skewers. Brush the squid with oil and sprinkle with salt and pepper. Place on the grill rack and grill quickly for a few minutes on each side.

❀ Transfer to a platter and serve with a drizzle of oil and lemon juice and a little chopped parsley.

SERVES 4

CATALONIA

Salsa Romesco

Sauce for Grilled Shellfish

This is Catalan "ketchup," a sauce that accompanies not only grilled shellfish, but also roast lamb, pork or chicken; salads; and grilled vegetables. There are countless variations on this recipe. Some are quite spicy, while others are mild. You can make this sauce with 2 or 3 dried ancho chilies*: Immerse them in water to cover over low heat for 10 minutes, then allow to steep for 20 minutes. Drain and remove the stems and seeds. Omit the roasted red pepper and the red pepper flakes and add cayenne, if necessary, to balance the heat. Also, although not usually made with an egg emulsion such as for aioli, you can add cayenne pepper, puréed roasted red (sweet) pepper and tomatoes, and ground toasted almonds to aioli (recipe on page 144) to create a similar sauce. Some recipes call for adding ground, peeled hazelnuts (filberts) in addition to the almonds. It is easiest to make the sauce in a blender or food processor, so the mixture will emulsify and thicken.*

¾ cup (6 fl oz/180 ml) olive oil
1 large slice white bread, about 1 oz (30 g)
½–¾ cup (3–4 oz/90–125 g) almonds, toasted
½–1 teaspoon red pepper flakes, finely ground
2–3 teaspoons finely minced garlic
1 large red sweet pepper (capsicum), roasted, seeded and deribbed (see glossary)
1 large ripe tomato, peeled, seeded and diced (about ½ cup/3 oz/90 g)
1 teaspoon paprika
salt and freshly ground black pepper
¼ cup (2 fl oz/60 ml) red wine vinegar, or as needed

In a sauté pan over medium heat, warm 3 tablespoons of the oil. Add the bread and fry, turning once, until golden on both sides, about 3 minutes on each side. Break up the bread and place in a blender or in a processor fitted with the metal blade along with the almonds, pepper flakes and garlic. Pulse briefly. Add the roasted pepper, tomato, paprika, and salt and pepper to taste and purée to form a chunky paste. Add the vinegar and pulse once. With the motor running, add the remaining oil in a very slow, thin stream and continue to process until the mixture emulsifies. Taste and adjust the seasonings.

Transfer to a bowl and serve.

MAKES 1½ CUPS (12 FL OZ/375 ML); SERVES 6

CATALONIA

Zarzuela de Mariscos

Shellfish Stew

This little "operetta" of shellfish is so festive that it calls for at least six people to dine together. Keeping the lobster in the shell and the tails on the shrimp makes for somewhat messy eating, but the shells add additional flavor to the dish and ensure a more dramatic presentation. Some versions of this recipe have crushed toasted almonds added; others call for a hint of chili pepper. Another option would be to omit both the almonds and the cayenne pepper from the stew and serve the dish with salsa romesco *(recipe above) as a condiment. Offer grilled bread at the table for sopping up the delicious juices.*

¼ cup (2 fl oz/60 ml) olive oil
1½ cups (6 oz/185 g) chopped onion
1–2 tablespoons finely minced garlic
2 red or green sweet peppers (capsicums), seeded, deribbed and finely diced
3 cups (18 oz/560 g) peeled, seeded and diced tomatoes
1 bay leaf, torn into strips
¼ teaspoon saffron threads steeped in ¼ cup (2 fl oz/60 ml) dry white wine
salt and freshly ground pepper
½ cup (3 oz/90 g) almonds, toasted and ground (optional)
pinch of cayenne pepper (optional)
1½ cups (12 fl oz/375 ml) dry white wine
2 small or medium lobsters, boiled in water to cover for 5 minutes, cleaned and cut into serving-sized chunks
12–18 mussels in the shell, well scrubbed and debearded
12–18 clams in the shell, well scrubbed
12–18 large shrimp (prawns), peeled, with tail piece intact, and deveined
½–¾ lb (500–750 g) scallops, cut in half if large
1–2 tablespoons fresh lemon juice (optional)

In a large heavy pot over medium heat, warm the oil. Add the onion and sauté for 5 minutes. Add the garlic and sweet peppers and cook until the vegetables are soft but not browned, about 5 minutes longer. Add the tomatoes, bay leaf, saffron and its soaking liquid, salt and black pepper to taste, and the almonds and cayenne pepper, if using. Bring to a boil. Reduce the heat to medium and cook, stirring occasionally, until thickened, about 10 minutes.

Add the wine and bring to a boil. Add the lobsters, mussels and clams (first discarding any that do not close at the touch), cover and cook for about 5 minutes. Reduce the heat to medium, add the shrimp and scallops and cook until the lobster, shrimp and scallops are cooked and the clams and mussels have opened, 3–5 minutes longer. Discard any clams or mussels that do not open. Taste and adjust the seasoning. Add the lemon juice, if desired, for flavor balance.

Transfer to a warmed deep serving dish. Serve immediately.

SERVES 6–8

CATALONIA

Gazpacho de Mero

Grouper Gazpacho

The similarities between this fish stew and the soup known as gazpacho are that they are both served in a bowl, include tomatoes and garlic, and are thickened with bread.

4 small dried chili peppers
9 cups (72 fl oz/2.1 l) water
½ cup (4 fl oz/125 ml) olive oil
8 cloves garlic
2 lb (1 kg) onions, thinly sliced
2 lb (1 kg) tomatoes, peeled and finely chopped
2 bay leaves
salt and freshly ground pepper
head and frame from one 2 lb (1 kg) grouper or sea bass, coarsely chopped
2 lb (1 kg) grouper or sea bass fillets, cut into 1-in (2.5-cm) chunks
1 cup (5½ oz/170 g) almonds, toasted
2 slices stale bread, finely crumbled

Remove and discard the seeds from the chili peppers. Place the pepper in a small bowl with about ½ cup (4 fl oz/125 ml) of the water.

In a stockpot or saucepan, bring the remaining water to a boil. Meanwhile, in a sauté pan over medium heat, warm ¼ cup (2 fl oz/60 ml) of the oil. Add 4 of the garlic cloves and sauté until pale gold, about 5 minutes. Add half of the onions and cook for about 5 minutes. Add the tomatoes and cook for 5 minutes longer. Transfer this mixture to the boiling water and add the bay leaves and salt and pepper to taste.

Return to the boil and simmer, uncovered, for 30 minutes. Add the fish head and frame and cook for 20 minutes longer.

Top to bottom: Sauce for Grilled Shellfish, Grouper Gazpacho, Shellfish Stew

Strain and reserve the stock. Pick off any flesh from the fish head and reserve it as well.

❀ Drain the chili peppers. Finely mince 2 of the remaining garlic cloves. In a large saucepan over medium heat, warm the remaining ¼ cup (2 fl oz/60 ml) oil. Add the finely minced garlic and the rest of the onions and sauté for 5 minutes. Add the fish pieces and the flesh from the fish head and cook over low heat, stirring occasionally, for 5 minutes. Add the stock and bring to a boil. Reduce the heat to a simmer.

❀ In a mortar with a pestle pound together the almonds, the remaining 2 garlic cloves and a pinch of salt until a paste forms. Add to the fish soup and simmer until the fish is tender, about 5 minutes. Add the crumbled bread and simmer for another 5 minutes.

❀ Ladle into individual bowls and serve hot.

SERVES 4–6

CATALONIA

Romesco

Stewed Fish with Beans

This fish dish is not to be confused with Catalonia's spicy tomato and almond ali-oli. *It does, however, have tomatoes, almonds and hot pepper in the sauce. Cooked haricot (white) beans are added to the completed fish stew.*

1½ lb (750 g) monkfish (anglerfish) fillets, sliced about 1 in (2.5 cm) thick
1½ lb (750 g) sea bass fillets, cut into 1-in (2.5-cm) chunks
1½ lb (750 g) sole fillets, cut into wide strips (optional)
8 shrimp (prawns), peeled and deveined
1 lb (500 g) squid, cleaned and cut into wide rings (see glossary)
salt
4–5 (2–2½ fl oz/60–75 ml) tablespoons olive oil
4 cloves garlic, finely minced
2 ripe tomatoes, peeled, seeded and sliced
1 green sweet pepper (capsicum), seeded, deribbed and sliced crosswise
1 onion, thinly sliced
½ cup (2½ oz/80 g) almonds, toasted and finely chopped
pinch of saffron threads steeped in ¼ cup (2 fl oz/60 ml) dry white wine
½ teaspoon coarsely ground black pepper
1 fresh chili pepper, chopped
3 tablespoons chopped fresh flat-leaf (Italian) parsley
2 cups (12 oz/375 g) cooked white beans

Lightly sprinkle all the fish and shellfish with salt. Place in the refrigerator until needed.

In a sauté pan over medium heat, warm 4 tablespoons (2 fl oz/60 ml) oil. Add the garlic, tomatoes and sweet pepper and sauté until the pepper is tender, about 10 minutes. Using a slotted spoon, remove to a bowl. Add the onion to the oil remaining in the pan and sauté until golden, 12–15 minutes.

Return the tomato-pepper mixture to the pan and add the almonds, saffron and its soaking liquid, black pepper, chili pepper and parsley. Stir well and add water to cover the vegetables by about ½ in (12 mm). Bring to a boil, add the fish and reduce the heat to a simmer. Cover and simmer for about 10 minutes, then add the shrimp and squid and cook for 2 minutes longer. Stir in the cooked white beans and heat through. Taste and adjust the seasoning.

Transfer to a warmed serving dish and serve at once.

SERVES 6

CATALONIA

Gambas al Ajillo

Shrimp with Garlic

While this is usually served as a tapa, it is too good not to eat as a main course. The same dish can be made with squid, cut into rings, or scallops. Serve with lots of bread to sop up the sauce.

¼ cup (2 fl oz/60 ml) olive oil
¼ cup (2 oz/60 g) unsalted butter
1½ lb (750 g) shrimp (prawns), peeled and deveined
4–6 cloves garlic, finely chopped or thinly sliced
¼ cup (2 fl oz/60 ml) fresh lemon juice
1 teaspoon paprika
½ teaspoon red pepper flakes
salt and freshly ground black pepper
4 tablespoons chopped fresh flat-leaf (Italian) parsley

In a wide, shallow sauté pan or casserole over high heat, warm the oil and butter. Add the shrimp and garlic and sauté quickly for about 2 minutes. Add the lemon juice, paprika, pepper flakes and salt and black pepper to taste.

Transfer to a warmed serving dish, sprinkle with the parsley and serve at once.

SERVES 4

CATALONIA

Calamares con Guisantes

Squid with Garlic and Peas

In Spain there are also versions of this pea-and-mint stew with clams or cuttlefish, but the squid variation is especially appealing. If you wish to substitute clams for the squid, steam open 4 pounds (2 kg) clams, well scrubbed, in 1 cup (8 fl oz/250 ml) white wine, then shell them. Strain the cooking liquid through a sieve lined with cheesecloth (muslin). Add the peas to the puréed and reheated sauce and then add the clams and strained sauce. Heat through and garnish as directed. A large quantity of garlic is used in this recipe, but you can add less. Romans cook a popular calamari-and-peas dish as well, but the garlic is reduced greatly and there are no tomatoes or mint.

4 lb (2 kg) peas, shelled (about 4 cups/1¼ lb/625 g shelled)
salt
½ cup (4 fl oz/125 ml) olive oil
2 heads garlic, cloves separated and peeled
2 slices coarse country-style bread, crusts discarded
1 tablespoon all-purpose (plain) flour
3 tomatoes, peeled, seeded and chopped
½ cup (4 fl oz/125 ml) dry white wine
4 tablespoons chopped fresh mint
4 tablespoons chopped fresh flat-leaf (Italian) parsley
2 lb (1 kg) squid, cleaned and cut into rings 1 in (2.5 cm) wide (see glossary)

Bring a saucepan three-fourths full of water to a boil. Add the peas and salt to taste and boil until tender, 3–5 minutes. Drain and refresh under cold running water. Drain again and set aside.

In a large sauté pan over medium heat, warm the oil. Add the garlic and sauté until golden, about 4 minutes. Using a slotted spoon, remove to paper towels to drain. Add the bread to the same oil and fry, turning once, until golden, about 3 minutes on each side. Again, remove with a slotted utensil to paper towels to drain.

In a mortar with a pestle, pound together the garlic and bread until it forms a paste. (Or purée them in a blender or a food processor fitted with the metal blade.) Set aside.

Add the flour to the oil remaining in the pan and stir over medium heat until it starts to color. Then add the tomatoes, wine, the bread-garlic mixture and 2 tablespoons each of the mint and parsley. Simmer for 15 minutes. If the sauce is too thick, add a little water. It needs to be spoonable and liquid in consistency.

Transfer the sauce to a blender or to a processor fitted with the metal blade and purée. If it is too thick, thin it with water as necessary. Return the sauce to the pan and bring to a boil. Add the squid and stir well. Cook for 1–2 minutes. Stir in the peas and heat for 1 minute longer.

Transfer to a warmed serving dish and serve at once. Top with the remaining 2 tablespoons each mint and parsley.

SERVES 6

Top to bottom: Stewed Fish with Beans, Shrimp with Garlic, Squid with Garlic and Peas

Fish Ball Tagine

TUNISIA

Tagine Kefta Mn Hoot

Fish Ball Tagine

These lightly spicy Tunisian fish balls should be served with couscous (recipe on page 204). In Turkey, similar fish balls are seasoned with dill and green (spring) onions, dredged in flour, fried until golden and served without any sauce as an appetizer with lemon wedges. In Spain, they are seasoned with parsley and a little cheese and then fried and served with tomato sauce.

FOR THE FISH BALLS:

1½ lb (750 g) white fish fillets such as cod, sole, snapper, bass
4 tablespoons chopped fresh flat-leaf (Italian) parsley
3 cloves garlic, finely minced
2 onions, finely chopped
1½ teaspoons salt
½ teaspoon *harissa* (see glossary)
¼ lb (125 g) stale bread, sliced, crusts discarded, soaked in water to cover and squeezed dry, or 1½ cups (3 oz/90 g) fresh bread crumbs
1 egg
olive oil for frying

FOR THE SAUCE:

3 tablespoons olive oil
2 cloves garlic, minced
6 tablespoons (3 fl oz/90 ml) tomato purée
2 cups (16 fl oz/500 ml) fish stock (see glossary) or water
salt and freshly ground pepper

chopped fresh flat-leaf (Italian) parsley

To make the balls, remove any bones in the fish and chop finely. Place in a bowl. Add all the remaining ingredients except the egg and oil. Mix well. Add the egg and knead until smooth. (This mixture may instead be mixed in a food processor fitted with the metal blade.) Dip a spoon and your fingers into cold water, then remove a heaping tablespoonful of fish paste and roll it into a 1-in (2.5-cm) ball. Place on a baking sheet lined with parchment paper. Form balls from the remaining fish mixture in the same way. (If not cooking immediately, refrigerate until ready to cook.)

In a large frying pan over medium heat, pour in oil to a depth of 2 in (5 cm). When the oil is hot, add a few fish balls at a time and fry, turning, to brown lightly on all sides. Using a slotted spoon remove to paper towels to drain. To make the sauce, in a large saucepan over medium heat, warm the oil. Add all the remaining ingredients and bring to a boil, stirring to combine. Add the fish balls, reduce the heat to low and simmer, uncovered, until fish balls are cooked through and the sauce has reduced slightly, about 15 minutes.

Transfer to a warmed serving dish, sprinkle with parsley and serve.

SERVES 4

MOROCCO

Al Toune bil Tomatich

Tuna in Tomato Sauce with Preserved Lemon

Cod, snapper or another firm white fish can be used in place of the tuna here. For more flavor, add 1 teaspoon ground ginger and a pinch of saffron threads to the tomatoes while they are simmering, or add 1 teaspoon ground ginger; 1 clove garlic, finely minced; and ¼ teaspoon cayenne pepper.

A related dish is made without the tomatoes or any marinating time: Make a bed of thinly sliced preserved lemon peel in a baking dish, arrange fish slices on top, drizzle with olive oil or chermoula, *and bake as directed. Sprinkle with olives and chopped parsley just before serving.*

6 thick tuna fillets or firm fish fillets, about ½ lb (250 g) each (see introduction)
½ cup (4 fl oz/125 ml) *chermoula* marinade (recipe on page 127)
4 cups (1½ lb/750 g) peeled, seeded and diced tomatoes
4 tablespoons chopped fresh flat-leaf (Italian) parsley
peel of 1 preserved lemon, cut into thin slivers (see glossary)
18 sharply flavored black olives
2 tablespoons capers, rinsed and drained (optional)

Put the fish in a large nonreactive baking dish, pour the *chermoula* evenly over the top, cover with aluminum foil and marinate for 4 hours in the refrigerator.

Meanwhile, put the tomatoes in a saucepan over medium heat. Cook, stirring often, until they have been reduced to a thick purée, 10–15 minutes. Stir in the parsley, lemon peel, olives and capers (if using) and simmer for 5 minutes longer.

Preheat an oven to 400°F (200°C). Remove the fish from the refrigerator and pour the tomato sauce over it. Re-cover with the foil and bake until the fish is cooked, about 25 minutes.

Transfer to a serving dish or serve directly from the baking dish. Serve hot or at room temperature.

SERVES 6

Tuna in Tomato Sauce with Preserved Lemon

Clockwise from top left: Fish in Grapeleaves, Peppery Fish Stew from Corfu, Sea Bass with Vinegar and Rosemary

GREECE

Psari se Ambelofilla

Fish in Grapeleaves

This dish is not just Greek—it is pan-Mediterranean. The fish can be small like sardines or red mullet, flat like sole or meaty like shark, swordfish or tuna. They can be cooked over a charcoal fire or in a broiler (griller) rather than baked. Brush the oil-lemon mixture on both sides of each packet, sprinkle with salt and pepper and then grill or broil, turning once, 4–6 minutes on each side. The leaves keep the fish moist and add a certain fragrance and elegance of presentation. Thyme, oregano, toasted pine nuts, olives, capers, diced tomatoes or plumped currants may be added to the oil-lemon mixture for baking or spooning over the grilled fish.

2 lb (1 kg) large sardines, cleaned, or sole, swordfish or bass fillets
8 tablespoons (4 fl oz/125 ml) olive oil
4 tablespoons (2 fl oz/60 ml) fresh lemon juice
4 teaspoons chopped fresh thyme (optional)
2 tablespoons dried oregano (optional)
salt and freshly ground pepper
bottled grapeleaves, rinsed of brine and stemmed

Place the fish in a shallow nonreactive dish. In a small bowl whisk together 3 tablespoons of the oil, 2 tablespoons of the lemon juice and the thyme and oregano, if using. Pour over the fish to coat evenly, then sprinkle with salt and pepper. Marinate for about 1 hour at room temperature.

Preheat an oven to 400°F (200°C). Remove the fish from the marinade. Wrap the whole fish or fish fillets individually in grapeleaves. Oil a baking pan large enough to hold the fish in a single layer and arrange a few leaves in the bottom of the pan. Place the fish packets, seam sides down, in the pan. In a small dish whisk together 2 tablespoons of the oil and 1 tablespoon lemon juice. Drizzle over the fish packets. Bake for 10–18 minutes, depending upon the size and thickness of the fish.

Transfer to a warmed platter. Whisk together the remaining 3 tablespoons oil and 1 tablespoon lemon juice and spoon over the fish. Serve at once.

SERVES 4–6

GREECE

Psari Bourtheto

Peppery Fish Stew from Corfu

An assortment of meaty fish or a single variety will work for this recipe. You may marinate the fish in olive oil and lemon juice for 30 minutes before cooking if you have the time, but this step is not essential. The dish can also be baked in a 400°F (200°C) oven for 10–15 minutes. Serve this stew with roasted potatoes.

¼ cup (2 fl oz/60 ml) olive oil
2 onions, halved and thinly sliced
1 clove garlic, finely minced
1 bay leaf, torn into strips
½ teaspoon cayenne pepper, or to taste
1 teaspoon freshly ground black pepper, plus black pepper to taste
2 teaspoons chopped fresh thyme
1 teaspoon finely chopped fresh rosemary (optional)
¼ cup (2 fl oz/60 ml) red wine vinegar
½ cup (4 fl oz/125 ml) dry red or white wine
2 cups (12 oz/375 g) peeled, seeded and diced tomatoes (optional)

salt
2 lb (1 kg) firm white fish fillets, cut into 2-in (5-cm) chunks
3 tablespoons fresh lemon juice
1 teaspoon paprika
4 tablespoons chopped fresh flat-leaf (Italian) parsley

In a large, deep sauté pan or a wide saucepan over medium heat, warm the oil. Add the onions, garlic and bay leaf and sauté until the onions are tender and translucent, 8–10 minutes. Add the cayenne pepper, the 1 teaspoon black pepper, thyme and rosemary (if using) and sauté for 2 minutes. Add the vinegar, wine and tomatoes (if using) and bring to a boil. Sprinkle the fish chunks with salt and pepper and add them to the pan. Reduce the heat, cover partially and simmer until the fish is almost done, about 8 minutes.

Add the lemon juice and paprika and simmer for 2 minutes. Taste and adjust the seasoning. Transfer to a warmed serving dish, sprinkle with the parsley and serve at once.

SERVES 4

GREECE

Levrakia Marinata

Sea Bass with Vinegar and Rosemary

This dish could be prepared with any mild firm fish, whole or cut into fillets: red mullet, sardines, trout, monkfish (anglerfish) or sea bass. It can be served hot or at room temperature. Some versions add a little diced tomato to the sauce.

4 sea bass fillets, about 6 oz (185 g) each
salt and freshly ground pepper
2 tablespoons fresh lemon juice
all-purpose (plain) flour for coating
olive oil for frying

FOR THE SAUCE:

¼ cup (2 fl oz/60 ml) olive oil
2 tablespoons all-purpose (plain) flour
⅓ cup (3 fl oz/80 ml) red wine vinegar
¼ cup (2 fl oz/60 ml) water
1 or 2 cloves garlic, finely chopped
2 tablespoons chopped fresh rosemary
2 bay leaves
1 cup (6 oz/185 g) chopped, peeled tomato (optional)
salt and freshly ground pepper

additional olive oil, if serving at room temperature

Sprinkle the fish with salt and pepper to taste and the lemon juice. Place flour in a shallow dish and dredge the fish in it, shaking off the excess. In a large frying pan over medium heat, pour in oil to a depth of ¼ in (6 mm). Add the fish and fry, turning once, until cooked and golden brown, about 4 minutes on each side. Using a slotted spatula, remove the fish to paper towels to drain. Cover with aluminum foil to keep warm.

To make the sauce, drain off the oil from the frying pan and wipe it out with paper towels. Add the oil and place over medium heat. Add the flour and stir until the flour is golden, about 3–5 minutes. Add the vinegar, water, garlic, rosemary, bay leaves and tomatoes (if using). Reduce the heat to low and simmer until thickened, 3–6 minutes. Season to taste with salt and pepper.

If serving the fish hot, transfer it to a warmed platter, spoon the sauce over the top and serve immediately. If serving the fish at room temperature, arrange it on a platter, spoon the sauce over the top and let cool to room temperature. Or, if you like, cover and refrigerate overnight, then serve the next day. Bring the fish to room temperature, then drizzle a little good olive oil over the top before bringing the fish to the table.

SERVES 4

TURKEY

TURKEY

Some time toward the middle of the eleventh century, a Turkish army broke through to the Mediterranean coast of Anatolia and claimed the city of Antalya on behalf of their ruler, Sulayman Shah the Seljuk. The capture of Antalya, known now for its flourishing orange groves and as a center of Turkey's burgeoning tourist industry, does not conventionally rank among the turning points of Turkish history; it is certainly not on the order of the Battle of Malazgird in 1071, which sealed the fate of Byzantine rule in most of Anatolia, or the conquest of Istanbul in 1453, which consecrated the rise of the Ottomans as a leading power of the day. A mention of this event may serve to remind us, however, that the Turks have been a Mediterranean people for more than nine centuries, vigorously participating in the affairs of the region—cultural as well as military and political—throughout this period and one of the major players for a considerable part of it.

This general preeminence of the Turks was reflected in cuisine; the last of the great culinary traditions to crystallize in the Mediterranean basin, Turkish cuisine has also been among the richest and most influential. The Turks were destined to advance still farther to the west, all the way, in fact, to the walls of Vienna. Their arrival on the shores of the Mediterranean can nonetheless be regarded as the culmination of a migratory process that

Previous pages: The construction of the Blue Mosque in Istanbul was controversial because it was thought unholy to rival the six minarets of the mosque at Mecca. Left: While only one-third of Turkey's land is dedicated to agriculture, it employs well over half of the labor force.

Copperware, no longer hammered out by hand, is sold in souvenir shops, which play an important role in Istanbul's commercial life.

had begun on the borders of China, in the landlocked vastness of Central Asia. This circumstance, too, has found expression in the kitchen, for there are elements in Turkish cuisine that were acquired or developed at virtually every stage in this long progress across Asia.

Culinary traces of the earliest period in Turkish history are meager. *Mantı,* a kind of dumpling still eaten today, was no doubt acquired by the Uighurs, the earliest settled Turkish people of note, from their Chinese neighbors, for the word is of Chinese origin and the dish itself is highly reminiscent of wonton. A delight in stuffing not only pasta but also intestines and vegetables is, however, so constant and widespread in Turkish cuisine that it must be thought of as a primordial feature of the tradition, not something passively received from the Chinese.

Turkish cooking is the only Mediterranean cuisine to have such demonstrable East Asiatic antecedents. Progressive incorporation into the world of Islam, from the tenth century onward, detached the Turks quite early from the cultural sphere of East Asia, and thereby also their cuisine. Their initiation into the classical civilization of Islam came at the hands of the Persians. Persian historians of nationalist bent are, therefore, in the habit of affirming that the succession of Turkish peoples that conquered the Persian-speaking lands as they migrated westward succumbed unquestioningly to the superior cultural models they encountered. Their judgment needs to be modified, especially in the sphere of cuisine.

One of the earliest literary monuments of Turkish Islamic culture, an eleventh-century Turkish-Arabic dictionary, shows clearly that Turkish cuisine was no tabula rasa before contact was made with the Persians. It lists, for example, numerous terms relating to bread and its preparation, many of which, in an adapted form, are still used in present-day Turkish; these terms point to the existence of a rich and indigenous Turkish baking tradition that later merged quite naturally with the bread culture of the Mediterranean. The same source also shows that the early Turks were fond of milk products, including yogurt and its by-products and various types of cheese. Yogurt has been known to the Middle East since antiquity, but there can be no doubting the role played by the Turks in popularizing its consumption, both in the Mediterranean world and beyond. Francis I of France was cured of intestinal disease by a diet of yogurt prescribed by a courtier who had spent some time in Turkey; this is the first evidence of the consumption of yogurt in postmedieval Europe. And the word *yogurt,* which has passed uncontested into all European languages, is itself Turkish. Finally, we find in our dictionary mention of particular dishes, such as *tutmaç* and *börek.* The former, a kind of thick stew made with lentils and noodles, is now virtually unknown, although it was extremely popular for centuries and survived in some parts of Anatolia until the nineteenth century. As for the *börek* mentioned in the dictionary, it is difficult to be sure that it was identical with the influential and popular dish (or rather category of dishes) we now know by that name; the compiler of the dictionary was, after all, a lexicographer, not a cook.

Persian cuisine was indeed highly developed, and it had already exercised a determining influence on the genesis of Arab cuisine two centuries before the Turks joined the realm of Islam. The Turks were by no means immune to the appeal of Persian food. They appreciated the same fruit-and-meat stews the Arabs carried all the way to Morocco and Spain, and a few dishes of this type survive even today in Turkey, although only as archaic and provincial specialties. Vegetable stews known as *yakhni* were also absorbed from Persian into Turkish cuisine.

But the Turks seem to have given the Persians at least as much as they received from them. *Kebab,* the generic name for all kinds of grilled meat, is Persian, but our eleventh-century dictionary proves that the Turks had been acquainted with the art of grilling meat since very early times. Moreover, the range of kebabs developed by the Turks was—and still is—much wider than those known to the Persians. Similar remarks apply to *pilav,* cooked rice or a dish based on cooked rice. The word itself is the Turkicized version of Persian *pulau,* and rice was used, albeit on a limited scale, in Persia before the arrival of the Turks, to whom rice had been unknown in their original homeland; it was after all from Persia that the Arabs disseminated rice throughout the eastern Mediterranean. But the emergence of pilaf dishes, in all their rich variety, ran parallel to the Turkish ascent in the Islamic world, and even in Persia many rice dishes came to be known by Turkish names. Pilaf in general came everywhere to be seen as quintessentially Turkish. It was for good reason that Norman Douglas once posed the rhetorical question, "Is there anything better than a genuine Turkish pilaf?"

A number of purely Turkish dishes found great favor among the Persians as well. *Tutmaç* was eulogized by a thirteenth-century Persian poet as "the caliph of the world of appetite," and *buğra,* probably the ancestor of some varieties of present-day *börek,* held the same culinary peak in Persia that was later conquered by pilaf. A general prevalence of dishes relying on flour, dough and noodles may also be ascribed to Turkish influence.

Given all this, it seems advisable to speak of a joint Turco-Persian cuisine, in the elaboration of which a dominant role cannot be attributed to either party. It was this composite cuisine that the Turks first brought with them to Anatolia; the Seljuks who conquered and ruled much of Anatolia, had after all originated as the offshoot of a dynasty whose rule over vast areas of the Middle East was based in Persia. The content of Seljuk cuisine can be judged from the menu for a royal banquet held in 1237 in Konya: a variety of kebabs including duck and chicken broiled on spits; pepper-seasoned pilaf; a number of vegetable dishes, both fried and stewed; and as dessert *zerde,* a Persian saffron-flavored rice pudding. Information on the diet of Seljuk Anatolia is to be found also, perhaps surprisingly, in the works of the great mystical poet Rumi. A figure often sentimentalized beyond recognition, Rumi in fact took an enthusiastic interest in food, and he lovingly evokes foods that cover the whole spectrum, from vegetables, pulses, fruits and breads to pastries, milk products and even pickles.

The transformation of Anatolia into a Turkish homeland was not a swift, clear-cut process of exclusion. Numerous Greeks were progressively integrated into Turkish society through conversion to Islam. Many others who retained their Christian affiliation became neighbors of the Turks, a situation that continued in western Anatolia until the exchange of populations that took place between Turkey and Greece in 1923. There were, then, many channels and opportunities for the exchange of culinary influence. We have already suggested, while discussing Greece, that the Turks were the more influential partners in this traffic. A Greek contribution is, however, visible in at least three areas. Half a dozen Greek loanwords relating to the preparation of bread—none of them current today—point to a Greek influence in the bakery; the gradual displacement of the elongated flaps of bread still favored in Persia and Central Asia by round loaves is probably also due to Greek example. Second, although the Turks swiftly became proficient sailors and established one of the most powerful fleets in the Mediterranean, the great preponderance of Greek-derived names for all kinds of fish and seafood demonstrates that it was the Greeks who introduced the

Ölüdeniz is a popular beach along the aptly named Turquoise Coast.

Meat, Poultry and Game

Clockwise from top left: Roast Chicken with Oregano and Lemon, Roast Chicken with Rice Stuffing, Quail Stuffed Into Eggplants

TURKEY

Patlicanli Bildircin

Quail Stuffed into Eggplants

This Turkish dish is also popular on the islands of the eastern Aegean and on Cyprus, where it is known as klephtic style, named after the Klephts, guerrilla soldiers who fought in the mountains during the Greek War of Independence and often had to cook underground, to conceal their presence. Here quail are concealed in whole eggplants and baked in the oven. The use of the grated cheese and white wine reflect the Greek variation. Greek cooks also use green (spring) onions in place of the globe onion.

4 eggplants (aubergines), about 8 oz (250 g) each
salt
½ cup (4 fl oz/125 ml) olive oil, or as needed
4 quail, preferably boneless
1 onion, chopped
2 cloves garlic, minced
½ lb (250 g) tomatoes, peeled, seeded and chopped
salt and freshly ground pepper
pinch of ground allspice or cloves
½ cup (4 fl oz/125 ml) water, boiling, or dry white wine
¾ cup (3 oz/90 g) grated *kefalotiri* (see glossary) or Parmesan cheese (optional)

Peel the eggplants lengthwise in a striped pattern. Cut in half lengthwise. Carefully hollow out as much pulp as possible and reserve it for another dish. Sprinkle the eggplant cases with salt and let stand for 30 minutes. Rinse, drain well and squeeze dry.

In a large sauté pan over medium heat, warm the oil. Add the eggplant cases and fry on all sides until lightly browned, 3–5 minutes. Using a slotted spatula remove to paper towels to drain.

Preheat an oven to 375°F (190°C).

In the oil remaining in the pan, sauté the quails over high heat, turning to brown on all sides, about 8 minutes. Remove to a platter. Add the onion to the oil remaining in the pan and sauté over high heat until golden, 8–10 minutes. Then add the tomatoes, salt and pepper to taste and the allspice or cloves. Simmer for 3 minutes.

Spoon most of the tomato sauce into a baking dish large enough to hold the 4 eggplant halves, hollow sides up. If you like, sprinkle a little grated cheese into each of the halves. Place a quail in each half, then top with a dollop of the remaining tomato sauce and grated cheese. Cap with the matching eggplant halves. Pour in the boiling water or wine and cover the dish. Bake until the eggplants and quail are tender, about 40 minutes.

Transfer to a warmed platter or serve directly from the baking dish.

SERVES 4

GREECE

Kotopolo Riganato

Roast Chicken with Oregano and Lemon

You could use rosemary instead of oregano for this savory roast chicken. Potatoes can be roasted along with the chicken. Peel 2 pounds (1 kg) new potatoes, cut into quarters and place in the roasting pan along with about a dozen garlic cloves. Add 1 cup (8 fl oz/250 ml) water or chicken stock to the pan for needed moisture. Once the chicken is ready, remove it from the pan and raise the oven temperature to 450°F (230°C) for several minutes to color the potatoes. Serve the potatoes on the side with the pan juices.

1 roasting chicken, 4–5 lb (2–2.5 kg)
salt and coarsely ground pepper
1 lemon, quartered
6 cloves garlic, crushed
¼ cup (1 oz/30 g) dried oregano
½ cup (4 fl oz/125 ml) olive oil
¼ cup (2 fl oz/60 ml) lemon juice, or to taste

Preheat an oven to 375°F (190°C).

Pat the chicken dry and sprinkle inside and out with salt and pepper. Place the lemon quarters, a few garlic cloves and a little of the oregano in the cavity.

In a small saucepan over medium heat, warm the oil. Add the remaining garlic and the remaining oregano and warm through. Add the lemon juice and season to taste with salt and pepper. Remove from the heat and set aside.

Place the chicken, breast side up, on a rack in a roasting pan. Brush once with some of the oil-lemon mixture and place in the oven. Roast, basting often with more of the lemon-oil mixture, until golden brown and tender and the juices run clear when the chicken is pierced at the thigh joint, about 1½ hours.

Transfer to a warmed platter, let rest for several minutes, then carve and serve.

SERVES 4

LEBANON

Djaj al Timman

Roast Chicken with Rice Stuffing

Seasoned rice pilafs punctuated with dried fruits and nuts are typical stuffings for roast chicken in the Middle East and North Africa. You can substitute about 1½ cups (7 oz/220 g) cooked couscous for the rice and use toasted pine nuts or hazelnuts (filberts) in place of the almonds.

¼ cup (2 oz/60 g) unsalted butter, plus 6 tablespoons (3 oz/90 g) unsalted butter, melted
1 onion, finely chopped
scant ½ cup (3 oz/90 g) long-grain white rice
¼ cup (1 oz/30 g) blanched slivered almonds, toasted
3 tablespoons raisins, plumped in hot water and drained
½ teaspoon ground allspice
1 cup (8 fl oz/250 ml) water
salt and freshly ground pepper

1 roasting chicken, about 4 lb (2 kg)
honey or ground cinnamon or allspice (optional)

In a saucepan over medium heat, melt the ¼ cup (2 oz/60 g) butter. Add the onion and sauté until tender and translucent, 8–10 minutes. Add the rice and almonds and sauté for about 3 minutes. Add the raisins, allspice and the water and bring to a boil. Cover, reduce the heat to low and cook until the water is absorbed, about 15 minutes. Season to taste with salt and pepper and let cool to room temperature.

Meanwhile, preheat an oven to 375°F (190°C).

Pat the chicken dry and sprinkle inside and out with salt and pepper. Stuff the rice mixture into the cavity and sew or skewer closed. Place the chicken on a rack, breast side up, in a roasting pan. In a small bowl stir together the melted butter and salt, pepper and a little honey, cinnamon or allspice (if using) to taste.

Roast the chicken, basting occasionally with the butter mixture, until golden brown and tender and the juices run clear when the chicken is pierced at the thigh joint, about 1½ hours.

Transfer to a warmed platter and let rest for several minutes. Remove the stuffing, carve and serve.

SERVES 4

ANDALUSIA

CORDONICES EN HOJA DE PARRA

Quail in Grapeleaves

These quail, which are very simple to prepare, can be cooked in the oven, braised on top of the stove, or grilled over a charcoal fire. You can, if you like, stuff each quail with a fresh fig in place of the thyme and lemon zest. Traditionally, the quail are served with coarse country-style bread fried in lard.

8 quail, preferably boneless
salt and freshly ground pepper
8 fresh thyme sprigs
8 lemon zest strips
16 bottled grapeleaves, rinsed of brine and stemmed
8 long strips *pancetta* or bacon
½ cup (4 fl oz/125 ml) chicken stock (see glossary), if roasting or braising
½ cup (4 fl oz/125 ml) dry white wine or sherry, if roasting or braising
olive oil, if grilling

Pat the quail dry with paper towels and sprinkle inside and out with salt and pepper. Stuff a thyme sprig and lemon zest strip into each cavity. Wrap each bird in 2 grapeleaves and then wrap in *pancetta* or bacon. (Some recipes reverse the order, wrapping the birds first in the meat and then the leaves.) Tie with string or skewer with toothpicks.

If roasting the birds, preheat an oven to 400°F (200°C). Place the quail in a baking pan and drizzle the stock around them. Roast until they test done when pierced with a knife, about 10 minutes. Remove to a platter and snip the string or remove the toothpicks.

If braising on the stove top, place the quail in a wide sauté pan, pour in the stock, cover and braise over medium heat until quail test done, 15–20 minutes. Remove the quail to a warmed platter and snip the strings or remove the toothpicks.

Add the wine to the baking pan or sauté pan and reduce slightly over high heat. Pour over the quail and serve at once.

If grilling the birds, prepare a fire in a charcoal grill. Brush the wrapped birds with oil, place on the grill rack and grill, turning once, until cooked 4–5 minutes on each side. Transfer to a platter and serve.

SERVES 4

SICILY

CONIGLIO ALL'AGRODOLCE

Sweet-and-Sour Rabbit

Rabbit braised in wine or wine vinegar is enjoyed in Calabria and Sicily. One version, alla cacciatora, *or "hunter's style," adds chopped, pitted green olives and strips of browned celery to the stew. Sage may be added as well. In this Sicilian preparation, pine nuts and raisins are mixed in and, if needed, additional vinegar and some sugar are added to give the dish an* agrodolce, *or "sweet-and-sour," accent. In some versions of the recipe, the rabbit pieces are floured before frying; others add a little tomato purée to the sauce.*

2 rabbits, 2½–3 lb (1.25–1.5 kg) each, cut into serving pieces
1 large onion, sliced
2 celery stalks, chopped
2 carrots, chopped
2 bay leaves
⅓ cup (3 fl oz/80 ml) olive oil
1 cup (8 fl oz/250 ml) red wine vinegar, plus red wine vinegar to taste
1 cup (8 fl oz/250 ml) dry red wine, or as needed
salt and freshly ground pepper
¼ cup (2 oz/60 g) lard or ¼ lb (125 g) *pancetta,* diced
2 onions, sliced
2–3 anchovy fillets in oil, drained and minced
3 or 4 fresh sage leaves (optional)
12 green olives, pitted
3 tablespoons capers, rinsed
½ cup (2½ oz/75 g) pine nuts
½ cup (3 oz/90 g) raisins, plumped in hot water to cover and drained
sugar

Pat the rabbit pieces dry with paper towels. Place in a nonreactive container. Add the onion, celery, carrots, bay leaves, a few tablespoons of the oil, the 1 cup (8 fl oz/250 ml) wine vinegar and enough wine to cover. Cover and refrigerate overnight. Bring to room temperature at least 2 hours before cooking.

Remove the rabbit from the marinade, reserving the marinade, and pat dry with paper towels. Sprinkle with salt and pepper. Strain the marinade and reserve. Working in batches, in a sauté pan over high heat, warm the remaining oil and fry the rabbit pieces, turning, until golden brown on all sides, about 10 minutes. Remove to a platter.

Melt the lard or render the *pancetta* in the same pan over medium heat. Add the onions and sauté until tender and translucent, about 10 minutes. Add the anchovies and sage (if using) and sauté for a few minutes.

Return the rabbit to the pan. Add enough of the marinade almost to cover the rabbit and simmer until tender, about 30 minutes. Add the olives, capers, pine nuts and raisins and simmer for a few minutes. If the sauce is too thin, remove the rabbit to a platter and keep warm. Reduce the sauce over high heat until thickened. Add salt and pepper to taste. Adjust the sweet-and-sour ratio by adding sugar or vinegar, as needed for balance.

Transfer to a warmed serving dish. Serve immediately.

SERVES 6

PROVENCE

POULET À LA NIÇOISE

Sautéed Chicken with Tomatoes, Olives and Wine

A basic braise that can be made with chicken or rabbit. It can be prepared ahead of time and reheated. Greek cooks make a similar dish, called koto kapama, *but they omit the salt pork and olives and season the tomato sauce with ground cinnamon and cloves. For* pollo alla cacciatora, *add strips of sweet red or green pepper (capsicum) to the stew during the last 30 minutes. Serve with mashed potatoes,* gnocchi *or rice.*

1 chicken, 3–4 lb (1.5–2 kg), cut into serving pieces
1 lemon, halved
salt and freshly ground pepper
5–8 tablespoons (3–4 fl oz/80–125 ml) olive oil
½ cup (3 oz/90 g) chopped lean salt pork (green bacon) or *pancetta*
4 onions, cut into eighths
2–4 cloves garlic, minced
2 teaspoons chopped fresh thyme
1 teaspoon chopped fresh sage
½ cup (4 fl oz/125 ml) dry white wine
6 large ripe tomatoes, peeled, seeded and chopped
½ cup (2½ oz/75 g) sharply flavored black olives, pitted
½ cup (¾ oz/20 g) chopped fresh flat-leaf (Italian) parsley or basil, or a mixture

Clockwise from top left: Quail in Grapeleaves, Sweet-and-Sour Rabbit, Quail with Pomegranate

Rub the chicken pieces with the cut sides of the lemon. Sprinkle with salt and pepper. In a large sauté pan over high heat, warm 5 tablespoons of the oil. Add the chicken pieces and salt pork or *pancetta* and fry quickly, turning, until golden on all sides, about 10 minutes. Using a slotted spoon remove to a platter and set aside.

Add the onions to the oil in the pan and sauté over medium heat until well browned, about 15 minutes. You may need to add a bit more oil if they begin to stick. Then add the garlic, thyme, sage, wine and tomatoes and bring to a boil. Reduce the heat and simmer, uncovered, for 10 minutes. Return the chicken and salt pork or *pancetta* to the pan, cover and cook over low heat until the chicken is cooked through, about 30 minutes longer.

During the last 5 minutes of cooking, uncover, add the olives and simmer to reduce the sauce. Taste and adjust the seasonings.

Transfer to a warmed dish. Sprinkle with the parsley or basil, or a combination, and serve at once.

SERVES 4 *Photograph pages 154–155*

SICILY

QUAGLIE ALLA MELAGRANA

Quail with Pomegranate

In this very old Sicilian recipe, Arabic influence is apparent in the use of pomegranate, which adds a tartness that is balanced by the sweetness of the orange zest and juice. (In Greece, this dish would be called Byzantine, referring to the cooking style of Constantinople.) Chopped mint and Marsala add another level of sweetness, making this a complex dish. Unsalted butter or a combination of butter and olive oil can be used for browning the quail in place of the olive oil. A Catalan version of this dish omits the mint and orange juice and zest, adds onion and tomato to the chicken stock and simmers the pomegranate seeds in the sauce rather than stuffing them in the quail cavities. Serve the quail with saffron rice with almonds.

1½ cups (12 oz/375 g) pomegranate seeds (see glossary)
½ cup (4 fl oz/125 ml) pomegranate juice (see glossary)
½ cup (4 fl oz/125 ml) fresh orange juice, plus orange juice as needed for pan juices
½ cup (4 fl oz/125 ml) Marsala, plus Marsala as needed for pan juices
4 tablespoons chopped fresh mint
2 tablespoons grated orange zest
12 quail, preferably boneless
salt and freshly ground pepper
12 slices *pancetta*
¼ cup (2 fl oz/60 ml) olive oil
1 cup (8 fl oz/250 ml) chicken stock (see glossary)
orange segments from 2 oranges

In a small bowl combine the pomegranate seeds, pomegranate juice, ½ cup (4 fl oz/125 ml) of the orange juice, the ½ cup (4 fl oz/125 ml) Marsala, mint and orange zest. Marinate the quail for 2–3 hours at room temperature. Drain, reserving the liquid and seeds separately.

Preheat an oven to 400°F (200°C).

Stuff most of the pomegranate seeds into the quail, reserving some seeds for garnish. Sprinkle the quail with salt and pepper, then wrap each one in a *pancetta* slice. In a large sauté pan over high heat, warm the oil. Add the quail and turn to brown well on all sides, about 8 minutes. Using a slotted spatula, transfer to a baking dish in which they will fit in a single layer. Pour the chicken stock and reserved marinade into the sauté pan and deglaze over high heat, scraping up any browned-on bits and reducing by half. Pour over the quail. Roast until they test done when pierced with a knife, about 10 minutes.

Remove the quail to a warmed platter or individual plates and keep warm. Taste the pan juices and add more orange juice or Marsala. Add the orange segments to the pan and sauté over medium heat for a few minutes in the pan juices.

Using a slotted spoon remove the orange segments. Pour the pan juices over the quail. Garnish with the orange segments and the reserved pomegranate seeds. Serve at once.

SERVES 6

MOROCCO

MROUZIA

Lamb Tagine with Honey, Almonds and Raisins

This tagine is quite sweet, so a little goes a long way. It is usually served alongside two lighter tagines, *such as chicken with lemon and olives (recipe on page 177) and lentils and pumpkin (recipe on page 205), as part of a meal. Shoulder or neck of lamb is best for stewing, not the lean leg. For an Algerian version, substitute 2–3 cups (12–18 oz/375–560 g) pitted prunes for the raisins and sugar for the honey, or beef may be combined with the prunes and sugar and strips of lemon zest can be added. Rabbit can be used in place of the lamb as well, in which case the dish is called* arnab mrouzia.

3 lb (1.5 kg) lamb shoulder or neck, trimmed and cut into 2½-in (6-cm) cubes
1 teaspoon ground ginger
1 teaspoon freshly ground black pepper
1 tablespoon *ras el hanout* (see glossary)
¼ teaspoon saffron threads
½ cup (4 fl oz/125 ml) water
½ cup (4 oz/125 g) unsalted butter
2 onions, finely chopped
2 garlic cloves, finely minced
2 cinnamon sticks, each about 2 in (5 cm) long
1½–2 cups (9–12 oz/280–375 g) raisins
1½ cups (8 oz/250 g) blanched almonds
¾ cup (9 oz/280 g) dark honey
1–2 teaspoons ground cinnamon

Place the meat in a nonreactive container. In a small bowl combine the ginger, pepper, *ras el hanout,* saffron and water and mix well. Rub half of this paste on the meat, coating evenly. Cover the meat and the remaining paste and refrigerate overnight.

Transfer the meat to a dutch oven or other heavy pot and add the butter, onions, garlic and cinnamon sticks. Add enough water just to cover the meat, bring to a boil and skim off any scum. Reduce the heat to low, cover and simmer until tender, about 1½ hours. Stir from time to time and add more water if the pot becomes too dry.

While the lamb is cooking, place the raisins in a small bowl with hot water to cover and stir in the remaining spice paste. Let sit for 1 hour.

Add the raisins and their soaking liquid, almonds, honey and ground cinnamon to the lamb and simmer covered, stirring often to prevent scorching, until very soft and almost falling apart, 30 minutes longer. (If it is too soupy, simmer uncovered to reduce sauce to a syrupy glaze.)

Transfer to a warmed serving dish and serve immediately.

SERVES 6

MOROCCO

MOUKH M'CHARMEL

Brains with Tomato Sauce

Brains must be very fresh and cooked the day they are purchased. This dish is good hot or at room temperature. Decorate if you like with black olives and strips of preserved lemon peel (see glossary).

3 calves' brains, 6–8 oz (185–250 g) each
juice of 1 lemon, plus 1–2 tablespoons lemon juice
3 tablespoons olive oil
5 cloves garlic, minced
1 lb (500 g) tomatoes, peeled, seeded and chopped
1 tablespoon paprika
¼ teaspoon cayenne pepper
½ teaspoon ground cumin
salt
1 small bunch fresh cilantro (fresh coriander), chopped

Place the brains in a bowl and add the juice of 1 lemon and water to cover. Soak for about 1 hour, then drain, remove the membranes and rinse under cold water. Quarter the brains.

In a large sauté pan over medium heat, warm the oil. Add the garlic and sauté for a few minutes but do not allow it to color. Add the tomatoes, paprika, cayenne, cumin and salt to taste and stir well. Bring to a boil and then reduce the heat to low. Add the brains and simmer gently for 15 minutes, turning them occasionally in the sauce. Add the 1–2 tablespoons lemon juice and the cilantro and simmer until the brains are firm, about 5 minutes longer.

Transfer to a serving dish and serve hot or at room temperature.

SERVES 6

MOROCCO

TAGINE BIL SFARDJEL

Lamb and Quince Tagine

Quinces are rather difficult to find, but this tagine, *called* ayva yahnisi *in Turkey, is so fine you'll want to try it with apples or pears. You can cook the quince separately in water to cover with the cinnamon stick and honey, then add them to the completed stew and simmer together for about 20 minutes to combine the flavors. Pitted dates can be used in place of the quinces as well; garnish with fried whole blanched almonds and sesame seeds. Or use 1½–2 cups (8–12 oz/250–375 g) diced apricots and ⅔ cup (4 oz/125 g) raisins for the quinces. You may also make this with 6 lamb shanks in place of the shoulder. Some versions of this recipe brown the meat first and then combine it with onions, spices and water. In Turkey they add 1 cup (8 fl oz/250 ml) pomegranate juice (see glossary) to the cooking liquids. In Greece, pork is substituted for the lamb and the dish, called* hirino me kythonia, *is less sweet.*

3 lb (1.5 kg) lamb shoulder, cut into 2-in (5-cm) pieces
2 onions, finely chopped
2 tablespoons chopped fresh flat-leaf (Italian) parsley
3–4 tablespoons unsalted butter
1 teaspoon ground ginger
1 cinnamon stick
⅛ teaspoon saffron threads
1½ lb (750 g) quinces, quartered and cored
3–4 tablespoons honey
1 teaspoon ground cinnamon

Place the lamb, onions, parsley, butter, ginger, cinnamon stick and saffron in a dutch oven or other heavy pot. Add enough water just to cover the meat, bring to a boil and skim off any scum. Reduce the heat to low, cover and simmer until the meat is just tender, about 1 hour.

Using a slotted spoon remove the meat to a bowl and set aside. Add the quinces, honey and ground cinnamon to the pan juices. Add enough water to half-cover the quinces and stir well. Cover and simmer over low until the quinces are tender. (Some quince varieties take a very long time to soften, so don't be alarmed if this step takes longer than 1 hour; the quinces will have turned red when they are ready.)

Return the meat to the pan, cover and simmer for 15–20 minutes to blend the flavors. Taste and adjust the seasonings, then serve.

SERVES 6

Clockwise from top: Lamb Tagine with Honey, Almonds and Raisins; Lamb and Quince Tagine; Brains with Tomato Sauce

CATALONIA

PINCHO MORUNO

Pork Brochettes

You will find these spicy pork morsels at tapas bars all over Spain. The name of the dish, which literally means Moorish or Arabic mouthfuls, gives away its origin. Obviously, pork was not served in Arab countries and lamb was the meat used for such kebabs (this recipe is reminiscent of the Moroccan qodban *on page 172.) But in Spain pork has become the meat of choice. If you wish to serve these brochettes as tapas, cut the meat into 1-inch (2.5-cm) cubes; this amount will serve eight. The marinade can also be rubbed on a boneless pork loin, which can be roasted or grilled.*

2 lb (1 kg) pork, cut into 1½-in (4-cm) cubes
½ cup (4 fl oz/125 ml) olive oil
1 tablespoon paprika
2 tablespoons ground cumin
1 teaspoon chopped fresh thyme
2 teaspoons cayenne pepper
1 teaspoon oregano
2 teaspoons minced garlic

Place the meat in a nonreactive container.

In a small frying pan over low heat, warm together the oil and all the remaining ingredients. Let cool and rub the spice mixture on the meat to coat evenly. Cover and refrigerate overnight.

Bring the meat to room temperature. Prepare a fire in a charcoal grill, or preheat a broiler (griller).

Thread the meat onto skewers and place on the grill rack or on a broiler tray in the broiler. Grill or broil, turning once, until done to taste, about 4 minutes per side for medium-rare.

Transfer to a warmed platter and serve.

SERVES 4

CATALONIA

HABAS ALLA CATALANA

Bean and Sausage Stew with Mint

If you can find them, fresh favas may be used instead of dried beans for this savory ragout; reduce the cooking time to about 10 minutes. Flavorful sausages add richness to the beans, and chopped mint is the accent that completes the dish. The Sardinians, who were, of course, once under Spanish rule, prepare a similar stew, favata, *but they add cabbage and fennel tops and accompany the dish with fried bread and grated cheese. Although the combination can sound strange, cooked clams may be used instead of sausages. Steam them with chopped onion, tomatoes, garlic and wine and reserve the juices to add when reheating the beans. A pinch of red pepper flakes is a nice accent, as well as a little grated lemon zest. The salt pork in this case is optional.*

2 cups (14 oz/440 g) dried white beans or fava (broad) beans
2 onions, chopped
2 cloves garlic
1 bay leaf
salt and freshly ground pepper
1 lb (500 g) chorizo or *butifarra* sausages (see glossary)
olive oil, as needed
¼ lb (4 oz/125 g) salt pork (green bacon) or bacon, finely diced
3 cloves garlic, minced
1 teaspoon paprika (optional)
2 or 3 tomatoes, peeled, seeded and chopped
½ cup (4 fl oz/125 ml) water or stock (see glossary)

½ cup (4 fl oz/125 ml) dry white wine
2–3 tablespoons chopped fresh mint

Place the beans in a bowl with water to cover generously. Refrigerate overnight.

Drain the beans and transfer to a large saucepan. Add 1 of the onions, the garlic cloves, bay leaf and water to cover. Bring to a boil, cover partially, reduce the heat to low and simmer until the beans are tender, about 1 hour. Drain, discard the bay leaf and season to taste with salt and pepper; set aside.

Top to bottom: Bean and Sausage Stew with Mint, Pork Brochettes

Meanwhile, place the sausages in a frying pan and prick with a fork in a few places. Add a little water to the pan, cover and steam gently until cooked through, about 8–10 minutes. Remove from the heat and, when cool enough to handle, cut into chunks. (You can leave them whole if they are small.) Set aside.

In a large saucepan over medium heat, pour in enough oil to form a film on the pan bottom. Add the salt pork or bacon and fry until crispy, 5–8 minutes. Using a slotted spoon remove to a bowl and set aside.

To the fat remaining in the pan, add the remaining onion and sauté over medium heat until tender and translucent, about 10 minutes. Add the garlic, paprika (if using) and tomatoes and cook, stirring, for 3 minutes longer. Add the water or stock, wine, the reserved sausages and salt pork or bacon, and the mint and simmer, uncovered, for 10 minutes. Add the cooked beans, cover and simmer over low heat for 10 minutes to heat through and blend the flavors. Taste and adjust the seasoning.

Transfer to a warmed serving dish and serve hot.

SERVES 4

EGYPT

BAMIA

Meat and Okra Stew

Okra must be cooked so that its slimy texture is eliminated. The Greeks have the best technique for achieving this: Trim the conical tops with a sharp knife, then soak the okra in red wine vinegar for 30 minutes, allowing ½ cup (4 fl oz/125 ml) vinegar per pound. Drain, rinse and dry the okra and proceed with the recipe. This dish is popular throughout the Middle East and can be prepared with lamb or beef. Serve with rice (recipe on page 200).

6 tablespoons (3 oz/90 g) unsalted butter or (3 fl oz/90 ml) olive oil
2 lb (1 kg) stewing lamb or beef, cut into 1-in (2.5-cm) cubes
2 onions, finely chopped
2 cloves garlic, finely minced
1 teaspoon ground cumin
1 teaspoon ground coriander
1 cup (6 oz/185 g) peeled, seeded and chopped tomatoes
3 tablespoons tomato paste
1 cup (8 fl oz/250 ml) stock (see glossary) or water, or as needed
2 tablespoons chopped fresh mint (optional)

salt and freshly ground pepper
1–1½ lb (500–750 g) okra
juice of 1 lemon

Preheat an oven to 325°F (165°C).

In a large frying pan over medium-high heat, warm 4 tablespoons of the butter or oil. Working in batches, add the meat and fry, turning, until browned on all sides, about 10 minutes. Using a slotted spoon transfer to a baking dish or stew pot.

Add the onions to the fat remaining in the frying pan and sauté over medium heat until tender and translucent, 8–10 minutes. Add the garlic, cumin, coriander, tomatoes, tomato paste, the 1 cup (8 fl oz/250 ml) stock and mint (if using). Stir well. Pour over the meat and season to taste with salt and pepper.

Cover and bake until all the liquid is absorbed, about 1½ hours. Taste and adjust the seasonings.

Meanwhile, prepare the okra as directed in the note. In a sauté pan over medium heat, warm the remaining 2 tablespoons butter or oil. Add the okra and sauté for 3 minutes, stirring gently.

Remove the stew from the oven and arrange the okra on top in a spoke pattern. Sprinkle the lemon juice evenly over the surface. Re-cover the dish and return it to the oven. Bake for 35 minutes longer. Add stock or water if the mixture seems too dry.

Serve the stew piping hot.

SERVES 4

MOROCCO

COUSCOUS À SEPT LEGUMES

Couscous with Lamb and Seven Vegetables

Here is a basic couscous. It can also be made with cubed lamb shanks. This version is a cross between a Tangier couscous and one from Fès.

1 cup (7 oz/220 ml) dried chick-peas (garbanzo beans)
2 lb (500 g) boneless lamb shoulder or neck, cut into 2-in (5-cm) cubes
2 large onions, chopped
2 teaspoons salt
2 teaspoons freshly ground pepper
2 teaspoons ground ginger
⅛ teaspoon saffron threads, crushed
6 tablespoons (3 oz/90 g) unsalted butter
water or lamb stock to cover
1 lb (500 g) carrots, peeled and cut into 2-in (5-cm) chunks
1 lb (500 g) turnips, peeled and quartered
1 piece pumpkin squash, about 1 lb (500 g), peeled and cut into 2-in (5-cm) chunks
1 lb (500 g) zucchini (courgettes), cut into 2-in (5-cm) lengths
3 tomatoes, peeled, seeded and chopped
½ cup (6 oz/185 g) raisins
couscous made with water or part stock and seasoned with ginger and a little olive oil or butter (recipe on page 204)
1–2 tablespoons *harissa* (see glossary)

Place the chick-peas in a bowl and add water to cover generously. Refrigerate overnight. Drain well.

Transfer the beans to a saucepan and add water to cover by about 2 in (5 cm). Bring to a boil, reduce the heat to low, cover and simmer until tender, 1 hour or longer. Drain and let cool.

In a large, heavy pot, combine the lamb, onions, salt, pepper, ginger, saffron, and butter. Turn the ingredients in the butter. Then add water or stock to cover by 1–2 in (2.5–5 cm). Bring to a boil, reduce the heat to low, cover and simmer for 1 hour. Add the cooked chick-peas and all the vegetables except the zucchini, re-cover and cook for 20–30 minutes longer. Finally, add the zucchini and raisins and cook until all the vegetables and meat are tender, about 20 minutes longer.

Pile the couscous on a warmed platter. Using a slotted spoon, lift the meat and vegetables from the pan juices and arrange them around the couscous. Alternatively, make a well in the center of the couscous and spoon the vegetables and meats into it. Adjust the seasoning of the pan juices and spoon some of the juices over the meat and vegetables. In a small bowl whisk together the *harissa* and 1 cup (8 fl oz/250 ml) of the pan juices. Serve on the side.

SERVES 6

MEDITERRANEAN

ASSORTED LAMB KEBABS

Everyone loves meat grilled on a skewer over a wood fire or charcoal grill. Sometimes meat is placed on skewers along with onion slices, cubed peppers, mushrooms or cherry tomatoes. Ideally they all will cook at the same time, leaving the vegetables juicy and the meat perfectly done. Peppers and onions are fairly sturdy and don't fall apart or fall off the skewer. Little tomatoes, however, can explode or fall off the skewer and into the fire or your lap, so if you want grilled tomatoes, thread them onto a separate skewer and baste them with the meat marinade.

What follows are Greek, Turkish and Tunisian marinades for lamb kebabs. For a Moroccan version, see the recipe for mechoui *on page 172. Remember to bring the meat to room temperature before grilling.*

1 boned leg of lamb, 3–4 lb (1.5–2 kg), trimmed and cut into 1½-in (4-cm) cubes

FOR GREEK MARINADE:

½ cup (4 fl oz/125 ml) olive oil
¼ cup (2 fl oz/60 ml) dry white wine
juice of 2 lemons
1 tablespoon dried oregano
4 or 5 cloves garlic, minced
3 bay leaves, broken up (optional)
freshly ground black pepper

Clockwise from left: Meat and Okra Stew, Assorted Lamb Kebabs, Couscous with Lamb and Seven Vegetables

FOR TURKISH MARINADE I:

½ cup (4 fl oz/125 ml) olive oil
1 onion, grated
1 tablespoon minced garlic
1 teaspoon ground cinnamon
2 teaspoons ground cumin
1 tablespoon thyme
pinch of cayenne pepper
salt and freshly ground black pepper to taste
½ cup (¾ oz/20 g) chopped fresh mint or flat-leaf (Italian) parsley, or a mixture (optional)

FOR TURKISH MARINADE II:

1 cup (8 oz/250 g) yogurt
1 onion, grated
salt and freshly ground black pepper, to taste
2 cloves garlic, minced
pinch of ground allspice
pinch of ground cinnamon

FOR TUNISIAN MARINADE:

¼ cup (2 fl oz/60 ml) olive oil
¼ cup (2 fl oz/60 ml) fresh lemon juice
1 tablespoon *harissa* (see glossary) mixed with ½ cup (4 fl oz/125 ml) water
2 teaspoons caraway seeds, toasted and ground
1 teaspoon ground coriander
salt and freshly ground black pepper

❀ Place the meat in a nonreactive container. Select one of the marinades and combine the ingredients for it in a small bowl. Whisk together to combine well, then pour over the lamb. Turn the lamb to coat evenly, then cover and refrigerate for 24 hours.
❀ Bring the meat to room temperature. Prepare a fire in a charcoal grill, or preheat a broiler (griller).
❀ Thread the meat onto skewers and place on the grill rack or a broiler tray in the broiler. Grill or broil, turning once, until done to taste, about 4 minutes on each side for medium-rare. Serve hot.

SERVES 6–8

Clockwise from left: Stuffed Meat Roll; Lamb Ragout with Mushrooms and Sweet Peppers; Veal Rolls, Messina Style

SICILY

FARSU MAGRU

Stuffed Meat Roll

Unlike the small veal rolls that are skewered and broiled, this is a large meat roll, which is known as braciolone *in Italian and called* farsu magru *("false lean") in Sicilian dialect. It is stuffed with slices of* mortadella *and/or* prosciutto, *ground seasoned beef, cheese strips and hard-cooked eggs, rolled and then tied. The roll is then browned and finally it is braised in red wine and tomato sauce. The sauce that results in the braising is also superb spooned over pasta. Veal can be used in place of the round steak.*

2½ lb (1.25 kg) round steak, in one piece
½ lb (250 g) ground (minced) beef
2 slices bread, soaked in water to cover, drained and squeezed dry

1 egg
3 tablespoons chopped fresh flat-leaf (Italian) parsley
salt and freshly ground pepper
4 slices *mortadella* or prosciutto, or a mixture
4 hard-cooked eggs
¼ lb (125 g) *caciocavallo* or provolone cheese, cut into long strips
olive oil, as needed
3 cups (15 oz/465 g) diced onion
4 cups (32 fl oz/1 l) tomato sauce
2 cups (16 fl oz/500 ml) dry red wine

❀ Butterfly the round steak and open it flat like an opened book. Place between sheets of plastic wrap and pound until about ½ in (12 mm) thick. Set aside.

❀ In a bowl combine the ground beef, bread, egg, parsley and salt and pepper to taste. Mix well.

❀ Place the *mortadella* slices atop the pounded beef, covering as much of the beef as possible. Top with the prosciutto, if using. Spread the ground-meat mixture in an even layer on top. Place the hard-cooked eggs in a row lengthwise down the center of the meat and then lay the cheese strips alongside the eggs. Starting from a long side, roll up the beef and tie with kitchen string in 3 or 4 places.

❀ In a large, heavy-bottomed pot, warm a little oil over medium-high heat. Add the beef roll and cook, turning, until browned on all sides, about 10 minutes. Remove from the pot and set aside.

❀ Pour more oil as needed into the same pot and place over medium heat. Add the onion and sauté until tender and translucent, 8–10 minutes. Add the tomato sauce and wine and bring to a boil. Return the meat roll to the pot, reduce the heat to low, cover and braise until tender, about 2 hours.

❀ Transfer the roll to a warmed platter. Snip the strings. Cut the meat into slices ½ in (12 mm) thick. Spoon the sauce into a bowl and pass at the table.

SERVES 6

SICILY

AGNELLO AL FORNO ALLA MADONITA

Lamb Ragout with Mushrooms and Sweet Peppers

The combination of mushrooms and sweet peppers with lamb is an unusual one for Sicily. The flavors seems rather Spanish, but the perfume is pure Mediterranean. A similar Spanish dish, cordero al chílíndrón, *omits the mushrooms and adds dried tomatoes to the sweet peppers.* Capretto, *or "kid," can be used in place of the lamb in the Sicilian dish. This version is from the region of Madonie; for a Palermo-style ragout, add 1 cup (8 fl oz/250 ml) of dry red wine to the marinade.*

3 lb (1.5 kg) lamb shoulder, trimmed and cut into 2-in (5-cm) cubes
3 onions, thickly sliced
4 cloves garlic, crushed, plus 2 cloves garlic, minced
2 tablespoons fresh rosemary
¼ cup (2 fl oz/60 ml) fresh lemon juice, plus lemon juice to taste
½ cup (4 fl oz/125 ml) olive oil, plus olive oil for sautéing
½ cup (4 fl oz/125 ml) dry white wine
3 red or yellow sweet peppers (capsicums), seeded, deribbed and cut lengthwise into wide strips
1 lb (500 g) fresh large brown cultivated mushrooms or porcini, tough stems trimmed and quartered
salt and freshly ground pepper

❀ Place the lamb in a nonreactive container. Add the onions, crushed garlic, rosemary, the ¼ cup (2 fl oz/60 ml) lemon juice and the ½ cup (4 fl oz/125 ml) oil, cover and marinate for a few hours at room temperature or overnight in the refrigerator.

❀ Preheat an oven to 400°F (200°C).

❀ Drain the lamb, reserving the onions, garlic and rosemary from the marinade. Place the lamb in a baking dish. In a large sauté pan over medium heat, warm a few tablespoons oil. Add the onions from the marinade and sauté briefly; scatter them over the lamb. Add the rosemary and crushed garlic from the marinade to the lamb, along with the white wine. Cover tightly and bake for 30 minutes.

❀ While the lamb is baking, heat 2 tablespoons oil in the same sauté pan over medium heat. Add the pepper strips and sauté until soft, about 5–8 minutes. Using a slotted spoon remove to a bowl. Set aside. To the oil in the pan add a few more tablespoons oil. Add the mushrooms and minced garlic cloves and sauté until soft, about 5 minutes.

❀ When the lamb has cooked 30 minutes, reduce the oven temperature to 325°F (165°C). Add the pepper strips and mushroom mixture to the lamb and cook until the meat is tender, about 1 hour longer. Taste and adjust the seasoning with salt, pepper and lemon juice. Transfer to a serving dish and serve at once.

SERVES 6

SICILY

INVOLTINI DI VITELLO ALLA MESSINESE

Veal Rolls, Messina Style

Messina is sometimes called the gateway to Sicily as it is only two miles from the mainland and the most common point of entry by car ferry. It was settled first by the Greeks and their influence is seen here in the use of pine nuts and currants in the filling. These veal rolls are stuffed and threaded onto skewers alternately with sliced onions and bay leaves. Cazzilli *(recipe on page 57) or mashed potatoes are a good accompaniment.*

1½ lb (750 g) veal tenderloin, cut into 18 slices each ½ in (12 mm) thick
¼ cup (2 fl oz/60 ml) olive oil, plus olive oil for brushing
1 onion, chopped
1½ cups (3 oz/90 g) fresh bread crumbs
½ cup (2 oz/60 g) grated *caciocavallo* cheese
½ cup (2½ oz/75 g) pine nuts, toasted
½ cup (3 oz/90 g) dried currants or raisins, plumped in hot water and drained
salt and freshly ground pepper
2 red (Spanish) onions, thickly sliced
bay leaves

❀ Place the veal slices between sheets of plastic wrap and pound until they are ¼ in (6 mm) thick. Set aside.

❀ In a sauté pan over medium heat, warm the ¼ cup (2 fl oz/60 ml) oil. Add the onion and sauté until tender and translucent, 8–10 minutes. Add the bread crumbs and cook for a few minutes longer. Remove from the heat. Add the cheese, pine nuts, currants or raisins, and salt and pepper to taste and mix well. Let cool.

❀ Prepare a fire in a charcoal grill, or preheat a broiler (griller).

❀ Place a heaping spoonful of stuffing on each veal slice and roll up. Thread onto skewers alternately with onion slices and bay leaves. Brush lightly with oil and sprinkle with salt and pepper.

❀ Place the skewers on a grill rack or a broiler pan and grill or broil, turning once, until golden, 3–4 minutes on each side.

❀ Transfer to a warmed platter and serve.

SERVES 6

GREECE

Kokkoretsi

Grilled Innards

This skewer of intestine-wrapped innards is a traditional part of the Greek Easter meal. The diced innards are marinated in herbs, spices, garlic and lemon, then wrapped or stuffed into sheep casings and grilled over a hot fire. In Sardinia, a similar dish is called cordula.

liver, heart, kidneys and sweetbreads of 1 lamb
2–3 tablespoons red wine vinegar
½ cup (4 fl oz/125 ml) olive oil
¼ cup (2 fl oz/60 ml) fresh lemon juice
1 tablespoon dried oregano
1 teaspoon dried thyme
3 cloves garlic, minced
salt and freshly ground pepper
½ lb (250 g) sausage casings, preferably sheep casings

Trim all fat, sinews, valves and membranes from organ meats and cut them into ½-in (12-mm) cubes. Combine all of the remaining ingredients except the intestines in a bowl. Add the cubed lamb innards and toss to coat evenly. Cover and refrigerate for 1 hour.

Rinse the sausage casings by running cold water through them for a few minutes. Using a slotted spoon remove the meats from the marinade; reserve the marinade. Using the sausage stuffing attachment on a grinder, a pastry bag fitted with the large plain tip or a funnel with a 1-in (2.5-mm) or larger opening, stuff the meats into the casings. Tie off the ends, and then form into a coil, if you like.

Prepare a fire in a charcoal grill, or preheat a broiler (griller). Place the sausages on the grill rack or on a broiler pan and grill or broil, turning them once and basting with the marinade, until crisp and cooked through, about 10 minutes.

Cut into thick slices, arrange on a platter and serve hot.

SERVES 8

SICILY

Capretto e Carciofi all'Uovo e Limone

Kid and Artichokes with Egg and Lemon

While the addition of egg and lemon to the pan juices is reminiscent of the Greek avgolemono, *such sauces appear throughout Italian cuisine and are probably of Sephardic origin. This recipe is from Calabria, but* agnello brodettato *or* capretto alla guidea, *the Passover recipes of Lazio and Tuscany, are nearly identical. Instead of all olive oil, lard or prosciutto fat may be used in those recipes not of Jewish origin. The artichokes can be cooked separately and added during the last 10 minutes. Peas may also be added, as well as favas and asparagus. You can make this stew with lamb, chicken or rabbit. In the Greek kitchen, fresh dill is added in place of the marjoram or mint and fennel bulbs or quartered lettuce heads can be added.*

½ cup (4 fl oz/125 ml) olive oil, or as needed
3½ lb (1.75 kg) kid or lamb, cut into 2-in (5-cm) pieces
1 large onion, chopped
4 tablespoons chopped fresh flat-leaf (Italian) parsley
salt and freshly ground pepper
2 tablespoons all-purpose (plain) flour (optional)
1 cup (8 fl oz/250 ml) dry white wine
6 small artichokes
1 cup (5 oz/155 g) cooked shelled peas or fava (broad) beans (optional)

juice of 3 large lemons
3 egg yolks
1 tablespoon chopped fresh marjoram or mint

In a large saucepan or wide sauté pan over medium-high heat, warm the oil. Add the lamb, onion and 3 tablespoons of the parsley and sauté until the lamb is golden. Sprinkle with salt, pepper and flour (if using) and mix well. Add the wine and bring to a boil. Cook over high heat for about 5 minutes, then cover and reduce the heat to low. Simmer for about 40 minutes.

Meanwhile, remove and discard the tough outer leaves from the artichokes. Trim off the stems and prickly points of the leaves. Cut into quarters lengthwise and scoop out and remove the prickly choke. As each artichoke is cut, drop it into a large bowl of water to which has been added the juice of 1 lemon.

Drain the artichokes, pat dry and add to the lamb. Re-cover and simmer until the lamb and artichokes are tender, about 25 minutes longer. Add the cooked peas or favas and warm through. Taste and adjust the seasonings.

In a bowl whisk together the egg yolks, the remaining lemon juice, the remaining parsley and the marjoram or mint until foamy. Remove the stew from the heat and whisk in the egg-lemon mixture, stirring constantly. Re-cover the pan and allow the eggs to thicken the sauce, just a few minutes.

Transfer to a warmed bowl and serve at once.

SERVES 6

GREECE

Moussaka

Eggplant and Lamb Casserole

A classic casserole found in both Greek and Turkish cuisines, moussaka *combines two of the most popular ingredients in Mediterranean cooking, lamb and eggplant. Many recipes for* moussaka *use a thicker, more floury cream sauce. Here the ricotta acts as a stabilizer, so the top custard does not need to be so rich. You can use olive oil in place of butter for sautéing the ingredients for the meat sauce. Some Turkish versions add potato slices to the dish, frying the potatoes when the eggplant is fried. The* moussaka *can be assembled a day ahead and refrigerated and then baked just before serving.*

2 or 3 eggplants (aubergines), about 2 lb (1 kg) total weight
salt and freshly ground pepper
olive oil

FOR THE MEAT SAUCE:

¼ cup (2 oz/60 g) unsalted butter
2 onions, chopped
4 cloves garlic, finely minced
2 teaspoons ground cinnamon
1–2 teaspoons dried oregano
1 lb (500 g) ground (minced) lamb
1 cup (8 fl oz/250 ml) tomato purée or 2 or 3 fresh large tomatoes, peeled, seeded and diced
2 tablespoons tomato paste
½ cup (4 fl oz/125 ml) dry red wine
4 tablespoons chopped fresh flat-leaf (Italian) parsley
salt and freshly ground pepper

FOR THE CREAM SAUCE:

2 cups (16 fl oz/500 ml) milk
¼ cup (2 oz/60 g) unsalted butter
¼ cup (1½ oz/40 g) all-purpose (plain) flour
½ teaspoon freshly grated nutmeg
salt and freshly ground pepper
4 eggs, lightly beaten
1 cup (8 oz/250 g) ricotta cheese

Clockwise from left: Kid and Artichokes with Egg and Lemon, Eggplant and Lamb Casserole, Grilled Innards

⅓ cup (1⅓ oz/45 g) grated *kasseri* (see glossary) or Parmesan cheese
⅓ cup (1⅓ oz/45 g) fine dried bread crumbs

Peel the eggplants completely, or peel them lengthwise in a striped pattern. Cut into slices ⅓ in (9 mm) thick. Sprinkle with salt and set aside in a large colander for 1 or 2 hours. Pat the slices dry with paper towels and squeeze out any excess moisture as you do.

Working in batches, in a large sauté pan over medium heat, pour in oil to a depth of ½ in (12 mm). Add the eggplant slices and fry, turning once, until lightly browned on both sides. Using a slotted spoon remove to paper towels to drain. Alternatively, brush the eggplants with oil, sprinkle with pepper and bake in a 400°F (200°C) oven until golden, 10–15 minutes.

To make the meat sauce, in a large sauté pan over medium heat, melt the butter. Add the onions and garlic and sauté until tender and translucent, about 10 minutes. Add the lamb, breaking it up, and sauté until the meat loses its red color, about 10 minutes. Add the cinnamon, oregano, tomato purée or tomatoes, tomato paste and wine; simmer until most of the liquid is absorbed, about 15 minutes. Add the parsley and season to taste with salt and pepper.

To make the cream sauce, warm the milk in a small saucepan. In a large saucepan over medium heat, melt the butter. Stir in the flour and cook, stirring constantly, for 2–3 minutes. Slowly stir in the hot milk and continue stirring until the mixture thickens and comes to a boil. Remove from the heat and stir in the nutmeg and salt and pepper to taste. Beat in the eggs and ricotta. Set aside.

Preheat an oven to 375°F (190°C). Combine the grated cheese and bread crumbs in a bowl.

Lightly oil a 4-qt (4-l) ovenproof casserole. Sprinkle the bottom with a little of the crumb-cheese mixture. Arrange one-third of the eggplant slices in a layer on top. Pour on one half of the meat sauce. Sprinkle evenly with the remaining crumbs and top with half of the remaining eggplant. Pour on the remaining meat sauce and then top with the remaining eggplant. Pour the cream sauce evenly over all.

Bake until golden and the top is set but still slightly quivery, 45–60 minutes. If the top is browning too quickly, cover with aluminum foil.

Remove from the oven and let stand for 15 minutes, then cut into squares to serve.

SERVES 8

Left to right: Roast Lamb, Lamb Kebabs with Yogurt and Tomato Sauces

TURKEY

YOĞURTLU KEBAB

Lamb Kebabs with Yogurt and Tomato Sauces

This is one of the most wonderful kebab dishes imaginable. The meat is marinated and grilled, then removed from the skewers and placed atop a bed of warmed pita bread that has been torn into large bite-sized pieces. Two sauces are then drizzled over the meat and bread, a spicy tomato sauce and a yogurt-and-garlic sauce. As if this isn't enough, a little melted butter seasoned with cayenne pepper and paprika and a few strips of hot green chilies crown the dish. The long green peppers Turkish cooks use are not easily found outside of Turkey, so poblano *chilies have been substituted here. You can omit this chili topping, if you like, and the dish will still be irresistible.*

2 lb (1 kg) lamb sirloin or leg, trimmed and cut into 1-in (2.5-cm) cubes
½ cup (4 fl oz/125 ml) plus 2 tablespoons olive oil
¼ cup (1¼ oz/40 g) grated onion
2 cloves garlic, minced, plus 2 teaspoons finely minced garlic
2 tablespoons fresh lemon juice
1 tablespoon chopped fresh thyme
4 or 5 tomatoes
pinch of red pepper flakes, crushed
dash of red wine vinegar
salt
6 tablespoons (3 oz/90 g) unsalted butter
1½ cups (12 oz/375 g) plain yogurt
freshly ground pepper
4 large pita breads (recipe on page 82)
paprika and cayenne pepper for seasoning butter
2 fresh *poblano* chilies, roasted, peeled, seeded and diced or cut into long strips (optional; see glossary)

Place the lamb in a nonreactive container. In a small bowl stir together the ½ cup (4 fl oz/125 ml) oil, onion, the 2 cloves minced garlic, lemon juice and thyme. Pour over the lamb, turn to coat well, cover and marinate in the refrigerator for several hours, or preferably overnight.

Heat a griddle or a cast-iron skillet over medium heat. Add the tomatoes and roast, turning, until blistered on all sides, about 4 minutes. Remove from the heat and, when cool enough to handle, peel, chop and put into a saucepan. Add the 2 tablespoons oil and the pepper flakes and cook over medium heat for about 5 minutes. Add the vinegar and salt to taste. Set aside and keep warm.

In a small sauté pan over medium heat, melt 2 tablespoons of the butter. Add the finely minced garlic and sauté for 1–2 minutes. Remove from the heat and let cool, then combine it with the yogurt in a small bowl. Add salt to taste and stir well. Cover and refrigerate, but bring to room temperature before serving.

Bring the lamb to room temperature. Preheat a broiler (griller), or prepare a fire in a charcoal grill.

Remove the lamb cubes from the marinade and thread onto skewers. Sprinkle with salt and pepper. Place on a broiler pan or grill rack and broil or grill, turning once, until done to taste, about 4 minutes on each side for medium-rare.

Meanwhile, warm the pita bread by wrapping it in aluminum foil and placing in a 350°F (180°C) oven for 7 minutes, or by placing it on the grill rack for a few minutes. Tear it into pieces and arrange on 4 individual plates. Melt the remaining 4 tablespoons (2 oz/60 g) butter and add paprika and cayenne to taste.

Reheat the tomato sauce. Top the bread with some of the warm tomato sauce and the yogurt sauce. Divide the lamb evenly among the plates. Top with the remaining tomato and yogurt sauces. Drizzle with the seasoned melted butter and the chilies (if using). Serve at once.

SERVES 4

MOROCCO

MECHOUI

Roast Lamb

Technically mechoui *is a whole lamb roasted on a spit over charcoal. It is unlikely that many of us will be cooking a whole lamb very often. But the flavors of the* mechoui *marinade, or* chermoula, *are so wonderful, there is no reason not to use it on leg of lamb, chops or even on kebabs, which are called* qodban. *(To be truly authentic when preparing the kebabs, skewer them alternately with cubes of lamb fat.)*

Moroccans prefer their lamb well done. You can, however, cook it to the degree of doneness you prefer. An instant-read thermometer will indicate 125°F (52°C) for rare, 135°F (57°C) for medium, 145°F (63°C) for well done. Either butter or oil can be used for the chermoula. *If you are roasting the lamb in the oven, baste it as it roasts with the pan drippings. If you are cooking on a charcoal grill or in a broiler, try to reserve a little of the* chermoula *for basting or make a little extra. Cubed liver or sweetbreads can be marinated in this same* chermoula, *then skewered and grilled.*

1 leg of lamb, about 5 lb (2.5 kg), boned and butterflied; 12 lamb chops; or 2½ lb (1.25 kg) boneless leg of lamb meat, trimmed and cut into 1½-in (4-cm) cubes

FOR THE MARINADE:

1 cup (8 oz/250 g) unsalted butter, at room temperature, or 1 cup (8 fl oz/250 ml) olive oil

1 large onion, grated
4 garlic cloves, finely minced
1 teaspoon salt
2 teaspoons ground cumin
1 teaspoon paprika
½ teaspoon cayenne pepper
½ teaspoon ground cinnamon
½ teaspoon ground ginger
1 teaspoon freshly ground black pepper
¼ cup (2 fl oz/60 ml) lemon juice
4 tablespoons chopped fresh flat-leaf (Italian) parsley
4 tablespoons chopped fresh cilantro (fresh coriander)

melted butter or olive oil seasoned with a little marinade

Trim all excess fat and sinew from the lamb. Place in a nonreactive container. In a bowl combine all the marinade ingredients, stirring to form a paste. Rub the paste on the meat to coat completely. For boneless lamb leg to be roasted in the oven, rub the inside with half of the marinade, roll the leg and tie in several places with kitchen string, then rub the rest of the marinade over the surface. Cover and marinate the meat overnight in the refrigerator.

Bring the meat to room temperature. Prepare a fire in a charcoal grill, or preheat a broiler (griller). If roasting in the oven, preheat to 350°F (180°C).

Remove the meat from the marinade. For grilled or broiled boneless lamb leg, place on the grill rack or broiler pan and grill or broil until done to taste, 10–15 minutes per side for medium-rare; baste with a little butter or oil seasoned with the marinade as it cooks. For roasted boneless lamb leg, place in a roasting pan and roast, basting with the pan drippings, until done to taste (see introduction). For chops, grill or broil, turning once, until done to taste, about 4–6 minutes per side, depending upon thickness of chops, for medium-rare. For kebabs, thread the cubes onto skewers and grill or broil, turning once, until done to taste, about 4 minutes per side for medium-rare.

Transfer to a warmed platter, carve, if necessary, and serve.

SERVES 6

MEDITERRANEAN

Grilled Chicken

Grilled chicken is always welcome at the table. Whether you use whole butterflied poussins, game hens, broiler halves, chicken parts or boneless chicken cubes on skewers, you will find the following marinades intensely flavorful. The Egyptian marinade is especially good on whole butterflied squab (pigeon). Marinate the meat overnight in the refrigerator and bring to room temperature before cooking. If you like, thread blanched vegetables such as sweet pepper (capsicum) and onion chunks onto skewers and cook alongside the chicken (or thread them onto the same skewers). Serve the grilled chicken with pita bread (recipe on page 82) and lemon wedges.

2 lb (1 kg) boneless chicken breasts or part boneless thighs and part breasts or 6 small birds or broiler halves, about 1 lb (500 g) each (see note)

FOR A LEBANESE MARINADE:

4–6 cloves garlic, finely minced
½ cup (4 fl oz/125 ml) fresh lemon juice
2 teaspoons chopped fresh thyme
1 teaspoon paprika
¼–½ teaspoon cayenne pepper (optional)
1 teaspoon salt
½ teaspoon freshly ground black pepper
½ cup (4 fl oz/125 ml) olive oil

FOR A TURKISH MARINADE:

1 cup (8 oz/250 g) plain yogurt
1 tablespoon paprika
1 teaspoon ground cinnamon or 1 tablespoon ground cumin
¼ teaspoon cayenne pepper, or to taste
4 cloves garlic, minced
juice of 1 lemon
6 tablespoons (3 fl oz/90 ml) olive oil
½ teaspoon freshly ground black pepper
½ cup grated onion

FOR A MOROCCAN MARINADE:

1 tablespoon paprika
2 teaspoons ground cumin
½ teaspoon cayenne pepper
1 teaspoon ground ginger
½ cup (4 fl oz/125 ml) melted unsalted butter or olive oil
juice of 1 large lemon
salt and freshly ground black pepper, to taste

FOR AN EGYPTIAN MARINADE:

½ cup (4 fl oz/125 ml) olive oil
2 tablespoons ground cumin
1 tablespoon ground coriander
1 onion, grated
3 cloves garlic, finely minced
1 teaspoon cayenne pepper

salt and freshly ground pepper to taste

If using boneless chicken pieces, cut into 1-in (2.5-cm) cubes and place in a shallow nonreactive container. If using whole birds, butterfly them; if using broiler halves, leave whole. Select one of the marinades, then combine the ingredients for it in a bowl and pour over the chicken. Cover and marinate in the refrigerator for 6 hours or overnight.

Bring the meat to room temperature. Meanwhile, prepare a fire in a charcoal grill or preheat a broiler (griller).

Remove the meat from the marinade, reserving the marinade. If using chicken cubes, thread onto skewers. Place the skewers or butterflied or halved birds on the grill rack or a broiler pan and grill or broil until cooked through, basting with reserved marinade while cooking. Cooking time will depend upon size of poultry pieces; do not let the meat become dry.

SERVES 6

Grilled Chicken

TURKEY

TAVSAN KEBABI

Grilled Rabbit

In the Mediterranean, rabbit is usually cut up and braised or sautéed quickly. It can also be left whole and slowly grilled on a spit over a wood fire. Since few of us have spits or are able to build a fire pit, in all likelihood we will be broiling the rabbit or cooking it on a charcoal grill. In both cases it is easier if you cut the rabbit in half, which will reduce the cooking time. The loin yields most of the meat, so you will need two rabbits to serve four persons. Here is a Turkish recipe for grilled rabbit adapted from spit-roasting.

2 rabbits, about 2 lb (1 kg) each, livers reserved
6 cloves garlic, cut into slivers, plus 3 cloves garlic, finely minced
12 whole cloves
1 cup (8 fl oz/250 ml) olive oil
3 tablespoons chopped fresh mint
3 tablespoons chopped fresh tarragon
6 tablespoons (½ oz/15 g) chopped fresh flat-leaf (Italian) parsley
salt and freshly ground pepper
3 tablespoons unsalted butter
1 cup (8 fl oz/250 ml) dry red wine
juice and zest of 1 lemon
1 teaspoon ground allspice

Pat the rabbit dry with paper towels. Make shallow slits all over the rabbits and insert the garlic slivers and cloves together into the slits. Place the rabbits in a nonreactive container. In a bowl combine the oil, mint, tarragon, parsley and salt and pepper to taste. Rub the mixture over the rabbits, cover and refrigerate overnight.

Prepare a fire in a charcoal grill or preheat a broiler (griller). Remove the rabbits from the marinade, reserving the marinade. If you have a spit, secure the 2 rabbits to it and position it about 2 feet (60 cm) from the heat source. Cook slowly until cooked through when pierced with a knife, about 1 hour. For grilling or broiling the rabbits, split them in half lengthwise. Place on an oiled grill rack or broiler pan and grill or broil, turning once, until tender, about 8 minutes on each side. In each case baste the rabbits as they cook with the reserved marinade.

While the rabbits are cooking, cut the livers into small pieces. In a small sauté pan over medium heat, melt the butter. Add the livers and the minced garlic and sauté for about 4 minutes. Add the wine, lemon juice and zest and allspice and sauté until the livers are done but still pink, 1–2 minutes longer.

Remove the rabbits to a warmed platter. Spoon the sauce over the rabbits and serve.

SERVES 4

MOROCCO

DJEJ MATISHA MESLA

Chicken with Sweet Tomato Sauce

In this especially delicious dish, the tomatoes cook down to a slightly caramelized thick purée and their sweetness is heightened by the addition of honey and cinnamon. Two noted cooks and food writers, Latifa Bennani Smires and Paula Wolfert, simmer the chicken with the tomatoes, remove the chicken, thicken the sauce over high heat, and then reheat the chicken in the sauce. Another respected authority, Fattouma Benkirane, cooks the chicken and tomatoes separately, then pours the thickened sweet tomato purée over the chicken almost as if it is a condiment. For maximum richness of flavor, reheat the chicken in the sauce, whether you've cooked them together or separately. If you like, add 1 cup (5½ oz/170 g) toasted almonds to the sesame seeds before sprinkling them over the top. Also, you may omit the marinating step and simply combine all the ingredients for the marinade with the onions and water and proceed as directed.

1 teaspoon freshly ground pepper
¼ teaspoon saffron threads, crushed
½ teaspoon ground ginger
2 cloves garlic, finely minced
¼ cup (2 fl oz/60 ml) olive oil
2 chickens, about 3 lb (1.5 kg) each, quartered
2 onions, grated
2 cups (16 fl oz/500 ml) water
5–6 lb (2.5–3 kg) ripe tomatoes, peeled, seeded and diced
1 tablespoon ground cinnamon
salt
6 tablespoons (5 oz/155 g) dark honey
¼ cup (1 oz/30 g) sesame seeds, toasted

In a small bowl stir together the pepper, saffron, ginger, garlic and oil. Place the chicken quarters in a nonreactive container and rub the mixture on them to coat evenly. Cover and refrigerate overnight.

In a large, wide pan, combine the chicken and marinade, onions and the water. Bring to a boil, reduce the heat and simmer for 20 minutes. Add the tomatoes, ½ tablespoon of the cinnamon and a little salt. Simmer the chicken, turning it often in the sauce, until tender, about 30 minutes. When the chicken is cooked, remove it from the pan and set aside.

Reduce the sauce over high heat, stirring often to prevent scorching. When the sauce is thick and the oil starts to rise to the top, add the honey and remaining ½ tablespoon cinnamon and cook for a few minutes longer. Return the chicken to the sauce and reheat.

Transfer to a warmed serving dish. Sprinkle with sesame seeds and serve at once.

SERVES 8

TURKEY

KADIN BUDU

Lady's Thigh

Every country's standard of beauty is different. No thin fashion models here. These round kefta *are said to resemble a woman's thighs. Beauty may be in the eye of the beholder, but we can all agree that these taste wonderful.*

2 tablespoons unsalted butter
1 large onion, finely chopped
⅓ cup (2½ oz/75 g) long-grain white rice
1 cup (8 fl oz/250 ml) water
1½ teaspoons salt
1½ lb (750 g) lamb, ground twice
3 eggs
1 teaspoon freshly ground pepper
1 teaspoon ground cinnamon, plus 1 teaspoon cinnamon for garnish (optional)
1 teaspoon ground cumin
⅓ cup (1½ oz/45 g) fresh *kasseri* cheese (see glossary)
½ cup (¾ oz/20 g) chopped fresh dill (optional)
1 cup (5 oz/155 g) all-purpose (plain) flour
vegetable oil for frying

In a saucepan over medium heat, melt the butter. Add the onion and sauté until soft, 10–15 minutes. Add the rice, the water and ½ teaspoon of the salt. Bring to a boil, cover, reduce the heat to low and cook until the water is absorbed and rice

Clockwise from left: Grilled Rabbit, Chicken with Sweet Tomato Sauce, Lady's Thigh

is cooked, 15–20 minutes. Remove from the heat and let cool. In a dry sauté pan over medium heat, sauté half of the meat, stirring often, until the meat absorbs its juices, about 10 minutes. Remove from the heat and let cool.

❀ In a bowl combine the cooled rice and meat, the raw meat, 1 of the eggs, pepper, 1 teaspoon cinnamon, cumin, the remaining 1 teaspoon salt, cheese and the dill (if using). Knead the mixture well. Dip your hands into cold water and form the meat mixture into 18 large or 24 smaller flattened ovals. Place on baking sheets lined with parchment paper until ready to fry.

❀ To fry, spread out the flour on a plate. In a small bowl whisk the remaining 2 eggs lightly with a fork. In a large sauté pan over medium-high heat, pour in oil to a depth of ¼ in (6 mm).

❀ When the oil is ready, dip each oval into the flour and then into the egg. Working in batches, fry, turning once, until golden, 3–5 minutes on each side. Using a slotted spatula remove to paper towels to drain, and repeat with the remaining balls.

❀ Arrange on a platter and sprinkle with the remaining 1 teaspoon cinnamon, if you like. Serve warm or at room temperature.

SERVES 8

MEDITERRANEAN THE BEAUTIFUL COOKBOOK

MEDITERRANEAN THE BEAUTIFUL COOKBOOK

THE MIDDLE EAST

THE MIDDLE EAST

Syria, Lebanon, Israel, Egypt

The artificiality of many of the frontiers in the contemporary Middle East is betrayed, among other things, by cuisine. The lands now divided among Syria, Lebanon and Israel (including the occupied territories) were known traditionally as *Bilad al-Sham,* "the Lands of (Greater) Syria," and they formed a single cultural unit with a shared culinary tradition that varied only slightly by region. This tradition overlapped, moreover, with the cuisine of Iraq, Egypt and the Arabian Peninsula, and it is therefore more or less coterminous with the cuisine of the entire Arab East. In its heyday, lasting roughly from the eighth to the fourteenth centuries, this was one of the most brilliant and influential cuisines of the Mediterranean world.

The diet of the Arabs before their emergence from the peninsula in the seventh century was a frugal and straightforward affair, consisting for the most part of dates, bread and mutton, supplemented on festive occasions by the meat and the milk of the camel; even today, this remains the essential menu of the Bedouin throughout the Arab world. Pre-Islamic Arabia was by no means exclusively nomadic, and the cities of western Arabia where Islam came into being were important centers of international commerce. Their citizens were, however, interested in the spices from Asia that passed through their hands en route to the eastern Mediterranean only as commodities

Previous pages: The pyramids of Giza, built circa 2550–2400 B.C., are the only survivors among the Seven Wonders of the World.
Left: Colorful Egyptian tents, often hand appliquéd, are used for festivals, funerals and entertaining dignitaries.

in which to trade, not as a source of enrichment for their own food. This sparseness of diet was reinforced by the ascetic spirit of early Islam. Although the Prophet Muhammad is recorded to have had his favorite dishes, such as a mixture of dates, butter and milk, he would eat only one type of food at each meal and recommended his followers leave their stomachs one-third empty. The gastronomic future of Islam was, however, guaranteed in a sense by the verses in the Koran *(Qur'an)* that draw attention to the fruits of the earth as God's gift; encourage the pursuit of agriculture; and command the believers to eat *al-tayyibat,* "pure and wholesome food."

The lands to the north of the peninsula that the Muslims conquered with amazing speed soon after the death of the Prophet are often referred to as the Fertile Crescent, an arc of territory extending from Syria to Iraq in which climatic conditions are infinitely more favorable to agriculture than the parched wastes of Arabia. The origins of many things are attributed to this area, and agriculture is one of them. Such a categorical assertion is difficult if not impossible to prove, but it is safe to assume that the ancient civilizations of the Middle East—Assyrians, Babylonians, Phoenicians and the rest—developed their own culinary traditions, even if we know little of them today.

The date palm flourished in some regions of the Mediterranean as far back as 50,000 B.C.

Before the Muslim conquest, Syria had been under Byzantine control, and Iraq under Persian, although the frontiers of each empire fluctuated with great frequency. The first center of the caliphate outside the peninsula was Damascus, and it is to be presumed that the Umayyad caliphs who made their home there came under the influence not only of Byzantine administrative systems but also of Byzantine cuisine. The Persian influence was, however, infinitely greater in the formation of classical Arab cuisine. This was in part a function of chronology. The transfer of the caliphate to Baghdad, near the old centers of Persian imperial splendor, came at a time when the early territorial expansion had been completed and the stage was set for the elaboration of a civilization impressive in both its intellectual and material aspects. Foodstuffs from the entire Middle East and lands as far distant as France, Russia and China flowed into the markets of Baghdad, almost demanding the elaboration of a sophisticated cuisine. Perhaps most important, the Abbasid caliphs of Baghdad abandoned the frugal ways of early Islam, to which the Umayyads had still in some measure subscribed, and, ably assisted by a horde of Persian cooks, began to indulge freely in the pleasures of the table.

The importance of the Persian contribution can be gauged by glancing at the contents of a thirteenth-century manual of gastronomy written in Baghdad. Many of the dishes listed here, particularly the more intricate ones such as *bazmaward* (roast meat prepared with a multitude of spices, nuts and rose water), bear Persian names, easily distinguishable by their phonetic form. The delight commonly taken in combining nuts, fruits and vegetables with meats, often yielding a melange of sweet-and-sour tastes, is also verifiably Persian in origin.

It can in general be said that classical Arab cuisine built on Persian traditions of ingenuity and complexity to evolve a new style. One hallmark of this was the intensive but subtle use of spices, some of them now cultivated for the first time in the Middle East and others imported along a farflung network of trading routes in greater quantity than ever before. Herbs, seeds and even flowers, gathered and analyzed with scientific precision, were also put to good use. Rice had been known in the Middle East before the rise of Islam, but it was more extensively planted than before by the Arabs (who also, as we have seen, introduced it to Europe by way of Spain and Sicily); this enhanced availability of rice made it possible to begin its full incorporation into cuisine, a process completed by the Turks. Techniques for the preparation of food became more sophisticated and elaborate. The Arabs were masters of preservation by means of salt and vinegar, or lemon juice and honey; the crystallization of fruit; and numerous methods of frying, baking and grilling.

This classical cuisine of the Arab East was, in its full richness, naturally beyond the means of many people, whose sustenance was primarily dependent upon lentils and beans. But even those humble preparations were enlivened with a few vegetables and a handful of spices and herbs. The splendors of the Abbasid caliphate were, in any

The Western Wall (or Wailing Wall), remnants of the Temple Mount in Jerusalem, is considered a holy place by Jews.

event, utterly destroyed by the Mongols in the thirteenth century. The invaders also took care to destroy the intricate irrigation systems of Iraq, a blow from which the area's agriculture—and hence cuisine—never fully recovered.

As has been pointed out, the Ottoman Turks were heirs to the entire civilization of classical Islam, and this included its culinary traditions. In a sense, then, Arab cuisine continued in a new setting and guise. But the imprint and style of Ottoman cuisine were new and distinct, reflecting the great stretch of the empire and the products to which it had access. It enjoyed also the prestige of great political and military success, and soon became the favored cuisine of the affluent throughout the Arab East. The assimilation of Ottoman cuisine was particularly marked in Syria, closest of the Arab provinces in both geography and culture to the Turkish heartland of the empire. This is not to say that Turkish cuisine extinguished all traces of regional style. *Kibbee* in its numerous varieties, still popular in Syria and Lebanon, is an exoticum in Turkey, and the various religious minorities packed into Lebanon have always retained their culinary specialties, in true Mediterranean style. By and large, however, the food of Syria and Lebanon has been down to recent times a variation on that of Turkey. The principal gastronomic centers of the area have been Damascus, which surrounded by the vast leafy oasis of the Ghutah has always been well supplied with fresh produce; Aleppo, renowned for its pastries; and Beirut, which with its cosmopolitan population and devotion to pleasures of various kinds boasted the best restaurants in the Middle East before the storms of war ravaged it to near destruction. It must be admitted that the general disarray of the Arab Middle East today is mirrored in its gastronomic impoverishment. Other than a few staples like *hummus, falafel* and a handful of dishes from the Turkish kitchen, little remains of a once brilliant culinary heritage.

The various traditions of Sephardic Jews from North Africa and Turkey, Ashkenazi Jews from Eastern Europe, and other immigrants from places as diverse as Yemen

Fellucas *are a common sight along the Nile, the world's longest river and the main artery linking southern Egypt to the Mediterranean.*

The golden dome of the Mosque of Omar, built in the seventh century, is a prominent feature on the Jerusalem skyline.

and the United States, have not yet amalgamated into a distinctively Israeli cuisine, something with its own genius and amounting to more than the sum of the parts. This mirrors not only the recent origins of the state but also the continued ethnic segmentation of Israeli society. Indeed, while some cookbook writers have called *falafel,* a kind of vegetarian hamburger made from chick-peas (garbanzos), "the Israeli national dish," it is perhaps more accurately described as a perennial favorite of the eastern Arab world, particularly beloved of the Palestinians.

A description of Egypt and its cuisine as Mediterranean might appear to the uninitiated inoffensively true. Egypt has, after all, a lengthy Mediterranean coastline that includes Alexandria, the country's second largest city. In the 1940s, however, controversy raged in Egypt as to whether it was primarily a Mediterranean country, enjoying its most important affinities with, for example, France and Italy, or an Arab and Muslim country, intermediate between North Africa and the Arab East (not to mention its African identity). Like most such disputes, this one was misconceived, because Egypt has been and is all these things, although in unequal measure: both Mediterranean and Arab, both northward looking and eastward looking. These varying orientations have inevitably reflected themselves in the food, creating not so much local variations on a national cuisine as entirely separate styles and traditions. Economics have also played a great role, the affluent showing great receptivity to foreign cuisines and the poor depending upon the immemorial staples of the indigenous diet. The varied and truly Mediterranean cuisine of pre-1952 Alexandria, where Greeks, Italians, Armenians and Jews lived in great numbers, was entirely unknown to the peasant masses toiling in the narrow strip of arable land that lines the Nile Valley. Polyglot Alexandria is now but a memory, but a similar social and culinary fission currently exists between the fashionably attired students at the American University in Cairo who patronize Pizza Hut in the intervals between classes and the great majority of Cairenes who can barely afford bread.

We are fairly well informed about the cuisine of ancient Egypt. Like their Greek counterparts, the Egyptian gods seem to have taken an interest in food; Isis is said to have first taught people the use and cultivation of the olive. Poultry farming was widespread, a particular fondness being shown for geese and ducks; the latter were often force-fed to make them fatter and more delicious, a kind of ancient rehearsal for making *pâté de foie d'oie gras.* Fish were also popular, although shellfish were shunned, possibly as a result of influence by the Israelites during their Egyptian exile. The ancient Egyptians may well have been the first people to bake leavened bread, and it is certain that bread was established very early as a staple of the diet. Bread came in many forms, dates sometimes being mixed in with the dough, and the loaves might be artfully shaped like animals, a homely display of the ancient Egyptian genius for plastic representation of the animal realm. A fairly narrow range of vegetables—okra, leeks and onions—was cultivated, but they were so well appreciated that every prosperous home had a vegetable garden attached to it. Mushrooms were reserved for the pharaohs because of the magical properties they were believed to possess. Spices imported from India and points farther east were a luxury item, reserved for the privileged, as indeed they were throughout the ancient and classical Mediterranean world.

The coming of Islam in the seventh century marked a definite break with the Pharaonic past (as well as with its Coptic continuation, over which we pass in culinarily justifiable silence). It is highly remarkable, therefore, that several of the dishes most common in Egypt even today go back to ancient origins. Pride of place among these dishes goes to *ful mudammas,* the ubiquitous concoction of slowly cooked fava beans that for centuries has been the indispensable staple of the masses. The word *mudammas,* used exclusively to describe this dish, appears to mean "buried in ashes," since the pot of beans was traditionally left in the hot ashes of an oven or bathhouse to cook overnight, although now other methods are used. Beans have been a part not only of Egyptian cuisine, but also of the Egyptian psyche itself for millennia: The ancient Egyptians called the realm in which the dead await resurrection a "bean field." (Does a common devotion to beans tend to corroborate the theories of those who take one look at the pyramids of Giza and Teotihuacan and proclaim Mexico and Egypt to have been in ancient communication?)

Of comparable antiquity are *melokhia,* a kind of peasant soup made with the glutinous leaves of the plant of the same name and sometimes adding rabbit, not a meat generally favored by Muslims; and *batarekh,* the salted and dried roe of the gray mullet, a delicacy for special occasions.

Apart from these Pharaonic relics, Egypt does not seem to have made any noteworthy contribution to classical Arab cuisine. This is curious, given the high demand in which Egyptian cooks once stood throughout the eastern Arab world. Until the coming of the Ottomans in the sixteenth century, rulers and the well-to-do appear to have eaten much the same fare as their counterparts in Syria and Iraq; then it was the sophisticated cuisine of the Ottomans that took their fancy.

E. W. Lane, the great Arabic lexicographer who was also a careful observer of Egyptian life in the early nineteenth century, describes a typical Cairene meal as consisting of a *yakhni,* a meat stew containing okra or other vegetables; stuffed vine, lettuce or cabbage leaves; stuffed squash and other vegetables; kebab; and *pilav.* All this is clearly Turkish, and it argues, too, for a higher degree of prosperity than that now available. But in Lane's day there were those who could not afford such ample fare and would make a meal of bread and *dukkah,* a mixture of salt, pepper, mint or cumin seeds, and other seasonings.

Like Syria and Lebanon, Egypt is subject to multiple stresses and transformations; social, economic, cultural and political. The future of its cuisine, together with that of the Middle East as a whole, is correspondingly unpredictable.

The camel, introduced to Egypt by the Persians in the 6th century B.C., was a crucial link between the trans-Saharan trade route and the Mediterranean.

VEGETABLES, PASTA AND GRAINS

Pasta is found in varying forms in most Mediterranean cuisines.

VEGETABLES, PASTA AND GRAINS

The traditional cuisines of the Mediterranean are plant-based. They revolve around vegetables, legumes, pastas and grains, with fish and shellfish, poultry and meat served in small portions and not every day. This healthful diet is being corrupted. As people leave the village for the city, they want to dine on larger portions of meat as often as possible, as a sign of personal success. The Greeks euphemistically call this the "northern diet." As well-known fast-food emporia take over the spaces that used to be cafes, tavernas and trattorias, and as the leisurely two-hour lunch shrinks to twenty minutes of hovering at a counter, we not only regret the loss of a less stressful life-style, but also the deterioration of a healthful diet and the gradual disappearance of traditional foods. Sadly, a treasury of great recipes is threatened with being replaced by french fries, a burger and a shake.

While we can't stop "progress," we can keep in mind that healthful Mediterranean foods can be the basis of a satisfying and varied diet. At a 1992 conference at Harvard University, scientists, doctors and nutritionists discussed the relative health advantages of the traditional diet of the Mediterranean, a region recognized for its low incidence of heart disease and cancer. Their conclusion was that the ideal diet for good health should be based on recipes like those in this chapter, accompanied with fruits, small amounts of dairy products such as yogurt and cheese, some olive oil, and only occasional bites of fish and animal protein.

In the Mediterranean, vegetables are not looked upon only as an accompaniment to meat or fish. Indeed, they are often the centerpiece of the meal. An assortment of vegetable *dolmas,* a casserole of baked vegetables with tomatoes and cheese, a ragout of vegetables braised in olive oil and herbs, a pilaf studded with eggplant, or a pasta with vegetables makes a delectable meal.

The variety of Mediterranean vegetables is bountiful. At the apex is the eggplant (aubergine). It is frequently combined with the other three most popular Mediterranean vegetables, peppers, zucchini and tomatoes. (Although peppers and tomatoes were gifts from the New World, they have been firmly established in the Mediterranean repertoire for two centuries.) There are also many recipes for artichokes, pumpkins and other squashes, beets, broccoli, cauliflower, carrots, turnips, potatoes, onions, leeks, garlic, cucumbers, mushrooms, fennel, okra, green beans, fava (broad) beans, asparagus, peas and greens such as spinach, Swiss chard (silverbeet), cabbage, dandelion, radicchio, chicory (curly endive) and kale. Each time a vegetable comes into season it is eaten daily until it is no longer at its best, and it is likely to be served as a course by itself. A harvest of the first new peas or wild asparagus is cause for celebration. A platter of grilled wild mushrooms basted with garlic and olive oil, a rice-filled tomato, or *imam bayildi* (garlic-and-tomato-stuffed eggplant) is a glorious meal.

Previous pages: left to right; Fish flavored Rice (recipe page 215), Rice from Valencia (recipe page 208)

Vegetables are not viewed as merely accompaniments to meat, but are often the centerpiece of the Mediterranean meal.

Pasta is not only an Italian phenomenon, although it is clearly a driving passion and has attained its highest art form there. Flat noodles called *laganum* were part of the early Roman diet and pasta tools have been found in Etruscan tombs. Vermicelli were referred to in a twelfth-century Arab text, where they were known as *itriya,* which became shortened to *tria* in Sicilian dialect. Noodles served in ancient Persia were termed *lakhsha,* which evolved into the Arabic *rishta;* today they are still called *lakshen* in Yiddish. Ravioli appear in Sardinia as *culingiones,* and in Turkey under the name *mantı,* after the Chinese *mantou.* Dried pastas are a staple of the southern Italian diet and the number of sauce and noodle combinations are countless. Volumes on the subject of pasta will continue to be written because the body of recipes is so vast and the noodle, fresh or dried, is so highly versatile.

The ubiquitous tomato, originally a gift from the New World, has been firmly established in Mediterranean cooking for over two centuries.

Couscous, coarse semolina pellets that are a kind of mini pasta, is the premiere North African grain dish. Pre-Islamic and pre-Arabic, it is to Morocco, Tunisia and Algeria what pastas are to Italy. It has even become part of the Italian diet, having migrated to Sicily. A similar pellet, called *fregula,* appears in Sardinian cooking.

Rice of both long-grain and short-grain varieties is a staple of many Mediterranean cuisines, forming the basis for pilafs, paellas and risottos. Short-grain rice, which tends to be stickier and gives off a sort of starch that thickens sauces, is used for Spanish rice dishes and is a specialty of Valencia. The Italian Arborio rice used in risotto and in the Sicilian deep-fried rice balls called *arancini,* is its close relative. Long-grain rice is the staple grain in Greece, Turkey and most of the Middle East, and the most fragrant variety is basmati. In these cultures rice is used for a main course, a pilaf and as a filling for grapeleaves, cabbage leaves, tomatoes, peppers, eggplants (aubergines), artichokes and zucchini as well as for baked chicken and fish.

Bulgur, or cracked wheat, is the other staple grain in the Arab diet. It imparts a nutty flavor and is served hot as a pilaf or cold, as in the familiar *tabbouleh* salad. Combined with meat, fish and vegetables as in baked *kibbee,* bulgur is the signature grain of Syria and Lebanon, although rice and noodles are also found in their diets.

Clockwise from top left: "Angry" Pasta, Raviolis Filled with Cheese and Greens, "Little Ear" Pasta with Broccoli Rabe

CALABRIA

Penne all'Arrabbiata

"Angry" Pasta

Arrabbiare means "to get angry," a simple but effective title for pasta with a fiery tomato sauce. The sauce can be prepared a little ahead of time and rewarmed before tossing it with the noodles. You can also mate this sauce with spaghetti or rigatoni.

4 tablespoons olive oil or 2 tablespoons each olive oil and lard
2 or 3 cloves garlic, minced
2 onions, sliced
2 small dried chili peppers, cut into pieces
6 large tomatoes, peeled, seeded and chopped
salt and freshly ground black pepper
1 lb (500 g) *penne* or other dried pasta
grated pecorino cheese

❀ In a large sauté pan over medium heat, warm the oil or the oil and lard. Add the garlic, onions and peppers and sauté until the onions are translucent and tender, 8–10 minutes. Add the tomatoes and cook, stirring occasionally, until thickened, about 8 minutes. Season to taste with salt and black pepper and keep warm until the pasta is ready.

❀ Bring a large pot three-fourths full of water to a boil. Add the pasta and cook until al dente, about 10 minutes (it will take about 10 minutes to cook; check the package directions). Drain.

❀ Place the pasta on a warmed platter. Spoon the sauce over the top and toss well. Sprinkle with cheese and serve immediately.

SERVES 6

SARDINIA

CULINGIONES

Raviolis Filled with Cheese and Greens

Here, cheese raviolis from Sardinia are flavored with a pinch of saffron and lightened by the addition of greens. Pecorino is available in two forms: as a fresh, soft, mildly tangy cheese and as a dry aged cheese for grating.

1½ lb (750 g) Swiss chard (silverbeet), green part only
salt
2½ cups (1¼ lb/625 g) ricotta or fresh pecorino cheese
2 eggs
pinch of saffron threads, crushed and steeped in 2 tablespoons hot water
3–4 tablespoons all-purpose (plain) flour (optional)
salt and freshly ground pepper
dough for *manti* (recipe on page 198)
tomato sauce or meat-flavored tomato sauce (see glossary), heated
grated aged pecorino cheese

Bring a large pot three-fourths full of water to a boil. Add the Swiss chard and salt to taste and cook until tender, about 5 minutes. Drain well, squeeze dry and chop finely. Place in a bowl and let cool completely.

Add to the chard the ricotta or fresh pecorino, eggs, saffron and steeping liquid, and enough flour to bind the filling (if using). Season to taste with salt and pepper. Place the filling in a sieve set over a bowl and let drain in the refrigerator for a few hours or as long as overnight.

Prepare the dough as directed and let it rest for 1 hour.

Roll out the dough into long strips about 4 in (10 cm) wide and fill and cut into 2-in (5-cm) squares as directed for the *manti*. Bring 1 large pot or 2 small ones three-fourths full of water to a boil, add salt to taste and the raviolis and cook until tender, 8–10 minutes. Drain well.

Layer the raviolis in a warmed wide serving dish with the hot sauce and grated cheese. Serve immediately.

SERVES 6

APULIA

ORECCHIETTE CON BROCCOLI DI RAPA

"Little Ear" Pasta with Broccoli Rabe

These small pasta rounds resemble little ears, thus their name. The depression in the middle traps the sauce. Cooked white beans or chick-peas (garbanzo beans) may be added to the sauce. Broccoli rabe is a slightly bitter green popularly served in southern Italy. It has 6–8-inch (15–20-cm) stalks topped by small florets.

1½ lb (750 g) broccoli rabe or other bitter greens or a combination of broccoli, cauliflower and bitter greens (about 5 cups)
salt
1 lb (500 g) *orecchiette*
olive oil
1 tablespoon finely minced anchovy fillet, or to taste
3 cloves garlic, minced
freshly ground black pepper or red pepper flakes
grated pecorino cheese

Wash the greens well and trim away any tough stalks. Cut into 2-in (5-cm) lengths for the greens and into florets for the broccoli or cauliflower. Bring a large pot three-fourths full of water to a boil. Add the prepared vegetable and salt to taste and boil until tender, 5–10 minutes; timing will depend upon what vegetable you are using. Using a slotted spoon remove to a bowl and set aside.

Return the water to a boil and drop in the *orecchiette*.

While the pasta cooks, warm the oil in a wide sauté pan over medium heat. Add the anchovy and garlic and warm through. Add the cooked vegetable and heat through. Season to taste with black pepper or pepper flakes.

When the pasta is al dente (it will take about 10 minutes to cook; check the package directions), drain and place on a warmed platter. Pour the vegetables and oil over the top and toss. Sprinkle with cheese and serve immediately.

SERVES 6

CALABRIA

MELANZANE ALLA PARMIGIANA

Eggplant Parmesan

Despite the name this dish has nothing to do with either the city of Parma or Parmesan cheese. The eggplant is fried and layered with tomato sauce and sometimes with slices of mozzarella or caciocavallo *cheese and sometimes with onions or hard-cooked eggs. It is then topped with bread crumbs and grated pecorino cheese. This version is from Calabria. Greeks make a similar dish with feta cheese and tomato sauce.*

3 eggplants (aubergines), about 2½ lb (1.25 kg) total weight
salt
olive oil
1 onion, thinly sliced
2 cloves garlic, minced (optional)
2 cups (12 oz/375 g) peeled, seeded and diced tomatoes
freshly ground pepper
1 lb (500 g) mozzarella, sliced ⅛ in (3 mm) thick
2 or 3 hard-cooked eggs, sliced
½ cup (2 oz/60 g) freshly grated pecorino cheese
½ cup (2 oz/60 g) fine dried bread crumbs

Peel the eggplants and slice crosswise about ½ in (12 mm) thick. Sprinkle the slices with salt and drain in a colander for 30 minutes. Rinse and pat dry with paper towels.

Preheat an oven to 400°F (200°C).

In a large sauté pan over medium heat, pour in oil to a depth of ¼ in (6 mm). Working in batches, add the eggplant and sauté, turning once, until lightly browned, about 5 minutes. Using a slotted utensil transfer to paper towels to drain. Add oil to the pan only as needed, or the eggplant will absorb too much of it.

To the oil remaining in the pan, add the onion and garlic (if using) and sauté over medium heat for about 5 minutes. Then add the tomatoes and cook, stirring, until a saucelike consistency forms, about 10 minutes. Season to taste with salt and pepper.

Spoon about one-third of the tomato sauce into a large baking dish. Top with half of the eggplant, the mozzarella cheese (if using), then half of the remaining sauce, half of the sliced eggs, and all of the remaining eggplant. Top with the remaining eggs and then the remaining sauce. In a small bowl stir together the pecorino cheese and crumble and then sprinkle them over the top.

Bake until golden, about 20 minutes. Remove from the oven and let rest 15 minutes before serving. Cut into squares to serve.

SERVES 6 *Photograph page 203*

GREECE

PILAFI ME MELITZANES

Eggplant Pilaf

A fine accompaniment for chicken or meat dishes.

2 globe eggplants (aubergines), about 1½ lb (750 g) total weight
6 tablespoons (3 oz/90 g) unsalted butter or (3 fl oz/90 ml) olive oil
1 onion, chopped
3 large tomatoes, peeled, seeded and diced
2 oz (60 g) vermicelli, broken into 1-in (2.5-cm) lengths (about ½ cup)
1½ teaspoons salt
½ teaspoon freshly ground pepper
½ teaspoon ground cinnamon (optional)
1¼ cups (9 oz/280 g) long-grain white rice, washed and drained
3 cups (24 fl oz/750 ml) chicken or vegetable stock (see glossary), heated
⅓ cup (2 oz/60 g) currants, plumped in hot water and drained (optional)
chopped fresh mint or flat-leaf (Italian) parsley (optional)

Peel the eggplants and cut into ¾-in (2-cm) cubes. Place in a colander, sprinkle with salt and set aside for about 20 minutes to drain off the bitter juices. Dry the eggplant with paper towels.

In a large sauté pan over high heat, melt 4 tablespoons of the butter or warm 4 tablespoons of the oil. Add the eggplant and sauté, stirring often, until golden, about 10 minutes. Remove from the heat and set aside, keep warm.

In a large saucepan over medium heat, melt the remaining 2 tablespoons butter or warm the remaining 2 tablespoons oil. Add the onion and sauté until softened, 5–7 minutes. Add the tomatoes, vermicelli, salt, pepper, and cinnamon (if using). Cook, stirring often, for about 4 minutes. Add the rice and sauté, stirring often until the rice is translucent and coated with fat, about 3 minutes. Add the heated stock, bring to a boil, reduce the heat to low, cover and cook until the liquid has been absorbed and the rice is tender, about 20 minutes.

Fold into the rice the cooked eggplant and the mint or parsley and the plumped currants, if using. Turn off the heat and let the rice rest, covered, for 10 minutes. Taste and adjust the seasoning. Fluff once with a fork and transfer to a warmed platter. Serve at once.

SERVES 6

TURKEY/LEBANON

BULGUR PILAV

Bulgur Pilaf

A staple in Turkey and the Middle East, bulgur (cracked wheat) comes in a variety of grinds, from very fine for tabbouleh (recipe on page 44) and kibbee *(recipe on page 182) to coarse. Medium grind is what is found in most stores. A coarse grind will do for pilaf, however, if that is all you can find. Most bulgur recipes call for too much liquid and the resulting pilaf is often soggy. To maintain a crunchy texture, with each grain separate, a ratio of 1½ cups (12 fl oz/375 ml) liquid to 1 cup (6 oz/185 g) grain is best. If the pilaf still seems too wet, place it on a baking sheet and dry it out in a 350°F (180°C) oven for 10–15 minutes. If it seems too dry, add a bit more liquid.*

2¼–2½ cups (18–20 fl oz/560–625 ml) water or chicken stock (see glossary)
2 teaspoons salt
¼ cup (2 oz/60 g) unsalted butter
1 onion, chopped
1½ cups (9 oz/280 g) bulgur (cracked wheat)

In a saucepan combine the water or stock and salt and bring to a boil. Reduce the heat to low and keep warm. In a large sauté pan over medium heat, melt the butter. Add the onion and sauté until tender and translucent, about 10 minutes. Add the bulgur and continue to cook, stirring, for a few minutes.

Add the hot water or stock. Stir once, and reduce the heat to low, cover and cook for about 15 minutes. Turn off heat and let stand until the bulgur absorbs all the liquid, about 15 minutes longer.

Transfer to a warmed dish and serve immediately.

SERVES 6

TURKEY

MANTI

Lamb Dumplings with Yogurt Sauce

Manti *are similar to dumplings found in Cyprus, Iran and Afghanistan. Such dumplings are generally filled with lamb or cheese and the sauce is often yogurt with garlic and mint, or a combination of yogurt and tomato sauces. Some recipes place the* manti *in a low oven for about 25 minutes to color them, then ladle the hot stock over the dumplings, cover the dish and bake until the stock is absorbed and the dumplings are tender, about 25 minutes longer. The yogurt sauce and the garnish are then spooned on top. In Cyprus, melted butter forms the sauce and mint is included in the filling. Beef can replace the lamb in this recipe.*

FOR THE DOUGH:
3 cups (15 oz/470 g) all-purpose (plain) flour
1 teaspoon salt
3 eggs
3–4 tablespoons cold water

FOR THE FILLING:
¾ lb (375 g) finely ground (minced) lean lamb
¾ cup (4 oz/125 g) finely minced onion
4 tablespoons finely minced fresh flat-leaf (Italian) parsley
1 teaspoon salt
½ teaspoon freshly ground black pepper

FOR THE SAUCE:
3 cups (1½ lb/750 g) plain yogurt, drained in a sieve lined with cheesecloth (muslin) for 3 hours
6 cloves garlic, finely minced
salt and freshly ground pepper

2–2½ qt (2–2½ l) light stock (see glossary), part stock and part water, or water

FOR GARNISH:
¼ cup (2 oz/60 g) unsalted butter
1 tablespoon finely crushed dried mint
good pinch of cayenne pepper

To make the dough, sift together the flour and salt into a bowl. Make a well in the center and add the eggs and most of the water to the well. Gradually stir the dry ingredients into the wet ingredients, mixing until all the liquid is absorbed and a stiff dough forms. Add more water as needed if the dough is too dry. Turn the dough out onto a floured board and knead for 10 minutes until smooth. Cover with a towel and let rest for 1 hour.

Top to bottom: Eggplant Pilaf, Bulgur Pilaf, Lamb Dumplings with Yogurt Sauce

Alternatively, make the dough in a food processor fitted with the metal blade. Sift the flour and salt into the processor container and then, with the motor running, add the eggs and water through the feed tube and process until a stiff, workable dough forms. Knead by hand on a floured board for a few minutes until smooth, then cover and let rest for 1 hour.

To make the filling, in a bowl combine the lamb, onion, parsley, salt and pepper. Knead to mix well. Alternatively, combine in a food processor fitted with the metal blade and process to mix.

Divide the dough into 4 equal portions. Roll out each portion on a pasta machine, gradually adjusting the machine until the dough passes through the rollers adjusted to their narrowest setting. Alternatively, on a floured board roll out each portion as thinly as possible. Cut the dough into 1-in (2.5-cm) squares or into rounds 1 in (2.5 cm) in diameter. Put a scant teaspoon of the filling on the dough, moisten edges lightly with water and fold into a half-moon, if working with rounds, or bring together the points to form a triangle, if working with squares.

Alternatively, roll out the dough into long strips 2 in (5 cm) wide. Place spoonfuls of filling at regular intervals along one side of each strip, moisten the edges, fold over the uncovered side, press edges together and cut into squares with a pastry wheel. You will have 60–80 tiny dumplings.

Just before cooking the dumplings, make the sauce. In a bowl stir together the yogurt and garlic. Season to taste with salt and pepper. (If you prepare the yogurt sauce ahead of time, bring it to room temperature just before serving.)

To cook the dumplings, divide the stock and/or water between 2 pots. Bring to a boil, add the dumplings and simmer, uncovered, until tender, 10–15 minutes.

While the dumplings are cooking, make the garnish. Melt the butter in a sauté pan and add the mint, sage and cayenne pepper. Simmer for 1 minute. Using a slotted spoon, remove the dumplings from the stock and distribute evenly among 6–8 warmed plates. Spoon the yogurt-garlic sauce on top, then drizzle with the mint-cayenne mixture. Serve at once.

SERVES 6–8

GREECE

DOMATES YEMISTES ME RIZI

Tomatoes Stuffed with Rice

Vegetable dolmas, *or stuffed vegetables, are an important part of Mediterranean cuisine. They can be filled with an aromatic rice or a rice-and-meat mixture. The filling for stuffed grapeleaves (recipe on page 61) can be placed in hollowed-out cooked vegetables and served garnished with yogurt, or simply dressed with lemon juice and olive oil. The stuffed tomato is the epitome of the Greek vegetable* dolma *and appears on every table during the summer. To make stuffed bell peppers (capsicums),* piperies yemistes, *cut off the tops, remove the ribs and seeds and parboil the shells 4–5 minutes before stuffing. To make stuffed small eggplants (aubergines),* melitzanes yemistes, *cut in half lengthwise, scoop out some of the pulp to make a shell, chop the pulp and sauté with the onion and rice for the filling, and then sauté the eggplant cases in olive oil for 5 minutes to soften before stuffing. To make stuffed zucchini (courgettes),* kolokythakia yemistes, *cut in half lengthwise, scoop out some of the pulp to make a shell, chop the pulp and sauté with the onion for the filling and parboil the shells for 3 minutes before stuffing. Turkish cooks would use 2 large onions, chopped fresh dill in place of the parsley and ½ teaspoon ground allspice in the filling. Toasted bread crumbs can be used to top the vegetables in place of their own caps. If you decide to do an assortment of vegetables, select those that are about the same size. This recipe makes enough filling for about 4 pounds (2 kg) of vegetables.*

12 ripe tomatoes
salt
sugar
½ cup (4 fl oz/125 ml) olive oil
1 large onion, chopped
2 cloves garlic (optional)
1½ cups (10½ oz/330 g) long-grain white rice
½ cup (3 oz/90 g) currants or raisins
1½ cups (12 fl oz/375 ml) plus ⅓ cup (3 fl oz/80 ml) hot water
4 tablespoons chopped fresh flat-leaf (Italian) parsley
3 tablespoons chopped fresh mint
freshly ground pepper
¼ cup (1¼ oz/40 g) pine nuts, toasted (optional)

Cut off the tops from the tomatoes and scoop out the pulp. Reserve the tomato pulp and all juices as well as the tops. Sprinkle the insides of the tomatoes with salt and a little sugar. Set aside. Put the tomato pulp in a blender or in a food processor fitted with the metal blade and purée. Reserve.

In a sauté pan over medium heat, warm ¼ cup (2 fl oz/60 ml) of the oil. Add the onion and sauté until tender and translucent, 8–10 minutes. Add the garlic, rice, currants or raisins, the 1½ cups (12 fl oz/375 ml) hot water, the reserved tomato juices, parsley and mint and bring to a boil. Reduce the heat to low and simmer, uncovered, until all the liquid is absorbed, 10–12 minutes. Taste and adjust the seasonings. Let cool slightly.

Preheat an oven to 350°F (180°C).

Divide the rice mixture evenly among the tomatoes; do not fill too tightly as the rice will continue to expand. Place close together in a baking dish and replace the reserved tops. Pour the ⅓ cup (3 fl oz/80 ml) hot water into the dish. Spoon the remaining ¼ cup (2 fl oz/60 ml) oil evenly over the tomatoes. Bake, basting occasionally with the pan juices, until the tomatoes are tender, about 30 minutes.

Remove to a platter and serve hot or at room temperature.

SERVES 6

Tomatoes Stuffed with Rice

SICILY

PEPERONATA

Stewed Peppers

This dish is typical of southern Italy. Red and yellow peppers are most commonly used, but use green ones if you cannot find the others. Some versions of this dish add tomato; others do not. Some add a splash of vinegar at the end of cooking; others add sugar and vinegar for an agrodolce, *or sweet-and-sour taste. Almonds and raisins can be added as well. Serve warm or at room temperature. These peppers also make a satisfying sauce for pasta.*

3 large red bell peppers (capsicums)
3 large yellow or green bell peppers (capsicums)
½ cup (4 fl oz/125 ml) olive oil
1 or 2 onions, sliced ¼ in (6 mm) thick
2 cloves garlic, finely minced
3 ripe tomatoes, peeled, seeded and diced
1 fresh chili pepper, minced (optional)
¼ cup (2 fl oz/60 ml) red wine vinegar (optional)
2 tablespoons sugar (optional)
¼ cup (1 oz/30 g) sliced almonds, toasted (optional)
¼ cup (1½ oz/45 g) raisins, plumped in hot water and drained (optional)
salt and freshly ground pepper

Cut the peppers in half lengthwise. Remove the seeds and thick ribs and then slice lengthwise into strips about ½ in (12 mm) wide. In a sauté pan over medium heat, warm the oil. Add the onions and sauté until softened, 5–8 minutes. Add the bell peppers and garlic, cover and cook over low heat until the peppers are tender, about 20 minutes.

Add the tomatoes and any of the optional ingredients and season to taste with salt and pepper. Simmer for a few minutes for the flavors to mellow.

Transfer to a dish and serve warm or at room temperature.

SERVES 6

Clockwise from top left: Eggplant Parmesan (recipe page 197); Stewed Peppers; Eggplant, Taranto Style

APULIA

Melanzane alla Tarantina

Eggplant, Taranto Style

This recipe can be prepared with large or small eggplants; only the cooking time will vary. The technique described is called scoring and it is used all over the Mediterranean. This recipe is from Apulia, but it could easily be mistaken for a Provençal or Greek dish. In fact, given the influence of Greek cuisine on this region of Italy, it may well be a Greek recipe. If you like, add 3 cloves garlic, minced and sautéed in oil for 1 minute, to the paste. The eggplants can also be cooked in a broiler (griller) rather than an oven.

3 globe eggplants (aubergines) or 12 slender (Asian) eggplants
½ cup (2½ oz/75 g) sharply flavored black olives, pitted and chopped
¼ cup (1½ oz/45 g) capers, rinsed and chopped
4 tablespoons chopped fresh basil
4 tablespoons chopped fresh mint
½ cup (2 oz/60 g) grated pecorino cheese
salt and freshly ground pepper
olive oil for drizzling

❀ Cut the eggplants in half lengthwise and salt the cut sides. Place in a colander to drain for 30 minutes.

❀ Preheat an oven to 375°F (190°C).

❀ Rinse the eggplants and pat dry with paper towels. Using a sharp knife score the top of the eggplant, making the cuts about ¼ in (6 mm) deep and forming a pattern of tiny squares; be careful not to cut all the way through. In a bowl stir together the olives, capers, basil, mint, cheese, and salt and pepper to taste. Rub this paste into the scored eggplant. Place the eggplants in a baking dish, cut sides up. Drizzle oil over them. Bake until the eggplants are tender when pierced with a knife, about 30 minutes for the globe eggplants and 10–15 minutes for the small ones.

❀ Transfer to a platter and serve hot or warm.

SERVES 6

Clockwise from top: Steamed Semolina Grain, Chick-peas in Spicy Sauce, Potatoes in Spicy Olive Oil, Lentils and Pumpkin

MOROCCO/TUNISIA

Couscous

Steamed Semolina Grain

The signature grain of North Africa, couscous is a very fine pellet made from semolina. The classic method of preparation calls for steaming the grain in a couscousière *over hot liquids. First the couscous is spread on a baking sheet and sprinkled with a little warm salted water. Then it is steamed over hot water or a stew for 20–30 minutes. The slightly swelled grains are poured back onto a baking sheet and then are raked with fingertips to break up any lumps. There is more sprinkling with warm water, steaming again for 12–15 minutes, fluffing again with a fork, steaming and so on, until the grain has puffed to the maximum and is light. If you do not have a* couscousière, *you can improvise one by placing a sieve over a pot.*

With the advent of instant couscous (available at most stores today), the method of preparation has been simplified. The hot water may be added all at once, the grain covered and left to rest, and then fluffed and held over hot water or in a warm place until serving time. It is important for the couscous to puff up completely or it will continue to puff in the stomach, causing some discomfort to the diner.

2 cups (12 oz/375 g) instant medium-grind *(moyen)* couscous
3 cups (24 fl oz/750 ml) water or stock (see glossary)
1 teaspoon salt
2 tablespoons unsalted butter or olive oil (optional)
pinch of ground cinnamon, ginger, cumin or freshly ground pepper (optional)

Place the couscous in a small baking pan that will hold 6 cups (48 fl oz/1.5 l), plus allow a little room for fluffing. In a saucepan combine the water or stock, salt and the butter or oil and spice, if using. Bring to a boil and pour over the couscous. Stir well once and cover the pan with aluminum foil. Let rest for 10 minutes.

Fluff the couscous with a fork. Re-cover and place over hot water or set in a warm place such as a turned-off gas oven until needed. Serve in a warmed dish.

SERVES 6

ALGERIA

Hmissa bil Dersa

Chick-peas in Spicy Sauce

Dersa *is a spicy Algerian sauce. The heat is provided by* harissa *(see glossary) or cayenne and garlic, and tomato. The spices can vary: Cumin and paprika are standard, but the addition of cinnamon, coriander and caraway is the choice of the cook. Lentils, white beans and cauliflower may be prepared this same way.*

2¼ cups (1 lb/500 g) dried chick-peas (garbanzo beans)
½ cup (4 fl oz/125 ml) olive oil
2 cloves garlic, finely minced
1 teaspoon cayenne pepper
½ teaspoon freshly ground black pepper
1 teaspoon paprika
1 teaspoon ground cumin
2–3 tablespoons tomato purée
4–5 cups (32–40 fl oz/1–1.25 l) water
1½–2 teaspoons salt
chopped fresh basil, thyme or cilantro (fresh coriander), optional

In a bowl combine the chick-peas and water to cover generously. Refrigerate overnight. Drain and set aside.

In a large saucepan over medium heat, warm the oil. Add the garlic, cayenne and black peppers, paprika and cumin and sauté for a few seconds. Add the tomato purée and the water and bring to a boil. Add the drained chick-peas, reduce the heat to low, cover and simmer until the chick-peas are tender, 45–60 minutes. Add the salt and simmer, uncovered, until most of the liquid has been absorbed or has evaporated, about 15–20 minutes. Transfer to a serving bowl and sprinkle with basil, thyme or cilantro (if using).

SERVES 6

MOROCCO

Ads be Qar wa Khli

Lentils and Pumpkin

A tagine *is a North African ceramic cooking utensil that gives its name to a variety of stews. For this* tagine *you can use pumpkin, butternut or acorn squash. Dried white beans can replace the lentils, but they will need to be soaked over night. Occasionally, ¼ pound (125 g)* khlii *(dried seasoned beef) is added to impart a meat flavor. It should be added to the pan in one piece with the onions and then removed just before the greens are added, cut into thick strips and returned to the pan. Look for* khlii *in shops specializing in North African foods.* Smen *is the Moroccan term for clarified butter (see glossary). Serve with couscous (recipe on preceding page) for a complete dinner.*

2 tablespoons *smen,* unsalted butter or olive oil
2 onions, diced
2 fresh chili peppers, thinly sliced
1 tablespoon paprika
½ teaspoon cayenne pepper
1 teaspoon ground cumin
1 cup (7 oz/220 g) dried lentils
4 tomatoes, peeled, seeded and chopped
¼ cup (2 fl oz/60 ml) tomato purée
1 piece pumpkin squash, 2 lb (1 kg), peeled and cut into 1-in (2.5-cm) cubes
1 lb (500 g) greens such as Swiss chard (silverbeet), dandelion, kale, blanched 3–5 minutes, drained well and coarsely chopped (optional)

In a saucepan over medium heat, warm the *smen*, butter or oil. Add the onions and chilies and cook until the onions begin to soften, about 10 minutes. Add the paprika, cayenne and cumin and continue to sauté until the onions are tender, a few minutes longer.

Add the lentils, tomatoes and tomato purée and water just to cover. Simmer for about 20 minutes. Add the squash and simmer until tender, about 20 minutes. Add the greens, if using, during the last 5 minutes of cooking.

Transfer to a warmed serving dish and serve immediately.

SERVES 6

MOROCCO

Batata bil Zait

Potatoes in Spicy Olive Oil

Here is a spicy potato stew, not unlike Sicilian patate al diavolicchio, *or "devilishly hot potatoes." In Italy they use hot-pepper oil and in North Africa* harissa *adds the fire. In Algeria parsley rather than mint is used, and in Tunisia caraway rather than cumin is added. Instead of cooking the potatoes fully in a sauté pan, they can be parboiled first and then sautéed in the spiced oil and garnished with the parsley or mint.*

⅓ cup (3 fl oz/80 ml) olive oil
3 cloves garlic, thinly sliced
2 tablespoons tomato purée
½–1 teaspoon *harissa* (see glossary)
1 teaspoon ground cumin (optional)
½ teaspoon salt, or to taste
2 cups (16 fl oz/500 ml) water
2 lb (1 kg) potatoes, peeled and sliced ½ in (12 mm) thick
4 tablespoons chopped fresh flat-leaf (Italian) parsley or mint

In a large sauté pan over medium heat, warm the oil. Add the garlic, tomato purée, *harissa* , cumin (if using) and salt and stir well. Add the water and the potato slices and mix well. Bring to a boil, reduce the heat to low and simmer until the potatoes are nearly cooked, 10–15 minutes. Add the parsley or mint and simmer until the potatoes are tender, about 5 minutes longer.

Transfer to a serving dish. Serve hot or at room temperature.

SERVES 6

APULIA

Zucca alla Ricotta Forte

Winter Squash with Sharp Ricotta

A specialty of Brindisi, this dish can also be made with pumpkin squash. If you cannot find ricotta salata, *a salted, hard ricotta, use a sharp or salty cheese such as pecorino or* ragusana.

5 tablespoons (3 fl oz/80 ml) olive oil
2–3 anchovy fillets in olive oil, drained and minced
1 or 2 cloves garlic, minced
1 large celery stalk, chopped
1 onion, chopped
1 butternut squash, about 1½ lb (750 g), peeled, seeded and diced
2–3 tablespoons capers, rinsed and chopped
¼ cup (1½ oz/45 g) sharply flavored black olives, pitted
2–3 tablespoons freshly grated sharp cheese
salt and freshly ground pepper
toasted bread

In a large sauté pan over medium heat, warm 2½ tablespoons of the oil. Add the anchovies, garlic, celery and onion and sauté until the vegetables begin to soften, about 5 minutes. Transfer to a bowl and set aside.

Heat the remaining 2½ tablespoons oil in the same pan over medium heat. Add the squash and brown quickly, turning to color evenly, just a few minutes. Return the onion mixture to the pan and add the capers and olives. Stir well, cover and cook until the squash is tender, about 15 minutes. Add the cheese and salt and pepper to taste and toss to mix.

Transfer to a warmed dish and serve with toasted bread.

SERVES 6 *Photograph page 4*

Left to right: Stuffed Mushrooms; Spinach with Raisins and Pine Nuts; Roasted Eggplants, Peppers and Onions

ANDALUSIA

Paella Valenciana

Rice from Valencia

Paella takes its name from a two-handled shallow pan called a paellera. *Traditionally, Valencian paella is made with short-grain rice, rabbit or chicken, tomatoes, beans and often snails. In Spain, rosemary and snails rarely appear in the same recipes, since the snails feed on wild rosemary and have taken on the flavor of the herb. Here, the canned snails lack that extra flavor, so the rosemary is added. Less traditional versions include shellfish and occasionally sausage, ham or meatballs. If you want to add shrimp (prawns) to this paella, omit the snails and sauté 1 pound (500 g) shrimp in the tomato-onion mixture, remove them from the pan and then return them during the last five minutes of cooking. You can also add 36 mussels and/or clams, well scrubbed (mussels debearded), in place of the snails; tuck them into the rice once it has been stirred in, placing them with the edge that will open facing up. Chorizo (see glossary) or meatballs can be browned after the chicken and rabbit, removed from the pan and then returned to the pan with them.*

Paella is usually cooked outdoors over an open fire, but you can cook this on a stove top with great success. You will probably need two burners to accommodate a large paellera. *The rice is cooked uncovered so that it does not steam, and the cooking is stopped when the rice is still a bit underdone. It finishes cooking off the heat, where it absorbs the last of the juices. You can, if you prefer, cook the paella uncovered in a 350°F (180°C) oven for about 20 minutes once all the ingredients have been combined on the stove top. While this recipe looks like a lot of work, much of the cooking can be done in stages.*

2⅓ cups (8 oz/250 g) dried large white beans
5 tablespoons (3 fl oz/80 ml) olive oil
1½ lb (750 g) chicken parts
1–1½ lb (500–750 g) rabbit parts
salt and freshly ground pepper
1 large onion, chopped
1 clove garlic, minced (optional)
3 or 4 tomatoes, peeled, seeded and chopped
4–5 cups (32–40 fl oz/1–1.25 l) chicken stock (see glossary) or part stock and part water, heated
24 canned snails, drained
½ teaspoon saffron threads, crushed
2 fresh rosemary sprigs, chopped
2 cups (14 oz/440 g) short-grain white rice

½ lb (250 g) green beans, trimmed, cut into 3-in (7.5-cm) lengths, blanched 5 minutes and drained

❀ Place the white beans in a bowl, add water to cover generously and let soak overnight. Drain and place in a saucepan. Add water to cover by 2 in (5 cm), bring to a boil, reduce the heat to low, cover and simmer until tender, 45–60 minutes. Drain and set aside.

❀ In a *paellera* or very large sauté pan over medium-high heat, warm the oil. Season the chicken and rabbit pieces with salt and pepper. Add the chicken and brown on all sides, about 10 minutes. Using a slotted spoon remove from the pan and set aside. Add the rabbit pieces and brown in the same manner; set aside.

❀ To the oil remaining in the pan, add the onion, garlic (if using) and tomatoes and sauté for about 10 minutes. Return the chicken and rabbit pieces to the pan, add the heated stock and simmer for 10 minutes.

❀ Add the snails, white beans, saffron, rosemary and rice, stir well and cook, uncovered, over a medium heat without stirring until the liquid has been absorbed and the rice is cooked but still slightly underdone, about 20 minutes. Add the green beans during the last 5 minutes of cooking. Do not let the rice scorch and lower the heat if the rice is cooking too quickly. Cover and let stand for 5–10 minutes, until the rice is fully cooked, then serve directly from the pan.

SERVES 6–8 *Photograph pages 192–193*

CATALONIA

Champiñones Rellenos

Stuffed Mushrooms

Most baked stuffed mushrooms take a long time to cook and often do not cook evenly. The most foolproof method for preparing them is to sauté the mushroom caps quickly in olive oil or butter to brown and soften them a bit before stuffing; they can then be finished in the oven without additional liquid. In Spain, France and Italy, prosciutto, sausage or ham and onion and garlic are added to the chopped mushroom stems for the filling. The stuffed mushrooms are then topped with bread crumbs or a combination of grated cheese and crumbs. To use sausage, sauté ¼ pound (125 g) chorizo or fennel sausage meat (see glossary) until cooked and use in place of the ham or prosciutto in the recipe. The mushrooms can be assembled several hours in advance and baked just before serving.

12 large fresh mushrooms
3 tablespoons olive oil
3 tablespoons unsalted butter, plus melted butter for basting
6 tablespoons (2 oz/60 g) finely minced onion
2 cloves garlic, minced finely
¼ cup (1½ oz/45 g) minced ham or prosciutto
2 tablespoons chopped fresh flat-leaf (Italian) parsley, thyme or marjoram
¼ cup (1 oz/30 g) fine dried bread crumbs
salt and freshly ground pepper
freshly grated Parmesan cheese (optional)

Preheat an oven to 400°F (200°C).

Wipe the mushrooms clean with a damp towel or a brush. Carefully remove the stems and chop the stems finely. You'll need only 8–10 tablespoons (1½–1¾ oz/45–68 g) chopped stems.

In a large sauté pan over high heat, warm the oil. Add the mushroom caps and brown quickly. Remove from the heat and set aside, hollow side up, on a baking sheet.

In a small sauté pan over medium heat, melt the 3 tablespoons butter. Add the onion and sauté until soft, about 5 minutes. Add the garlic and mushroom stems and sauté until the stems are wilted, about 3 minutes. Add the ham or prosciutto and cook for 2–3 minutes. Stir in the parsley and bread crumbs and season to taste with salt and pepper. (Remember that prosciutto and ham will give off more salt as they heat.) Pile the sautéed mixture into the mushroom caps. Sprinkle with grated cheese (if using).

Bake, basting with a little melted butter if desired, until tender when pierced with a knife, about 15 minutes.

Transfer to a platter and serve hot or warm.

SERVES 6

CATALONIA

Escalivada

Roasted Eggplants, Peppers and Onions

Many restaurants in Spain roast vegetables in the oven, as it is easier and less time-consuming than grilling them. Grilling, however, gives the characteristic smoky taste that is essential to escalivada *(*escalivar *means "to grill"). If you do not feel like lighting a charcoal fire every time you crave this dish, you can broil the vegetables or cook them directly on the stove-top flame or on a stove-top griddle. Tomatoes can also be grilled and added to this mixture, as can garlic, which is then mashed and mixed with the oil before tossing with the vegetables.*

4 small globe eggplants (aubergines) or 8–10 slender (Asian) eggplants
3 or 4 red bell peppers (capsicums)
2 small or medium red (Spanish) onions, unpeeled
virgin olive oil, as needed
2–4 cloves garlic, minced
salt and freshly ground pepper

Prepare a fire in a charcoal grill.

Place the eggplants and peppers on the grill rack and grill, turning often, until charred on all sides and tender; the timing will depend upon the size of the vegetables and the intensity of the fire.

Place the peppers in a paper bag or a covered plastic container to steam for 15 minutes. Then peel the peppers and remove the seeds and ribs. Slice into strips about ½ in (12 mm) wide.

Place the eggplants in a colander and, when cool enough to handle, peel and discard the skin. Allow the pulp to drain in the colander to release its bitter juices, about 15 minutes. Then cut into large strips or large dice.

While the onions can be grilled, it is easiest to prepare them in a 400°F (200°C) oven unless they are very small. Rub the onions with oil and place them in a small baking pan. Bake until tender, about 45 minutes. Remove from the oven and, when cool enough to handle, peel and cut into slices about ½ in (12 mm) thick.

Combine the cooked vegetables in a serving bowl and dress with a little olive oil, minced garlic and salt and pepper to taste. Serve at room temperature.

SERVES 6–8

CATALONIA

Acelgas con Pasas y Piñónes

Spinach with Raisins and Pine Nuts

A popular dish in Spain, but also in Italy, Greece and Turkey. The Arabic influence is evident in the use of raisins and pine nuts. You can toast the pine nuts in a 350°F (180°C) oven for about 8 minutes, or you can fry them until lightly golden in the olive oil used for the dish and then remove them before you sauté the onion in the same oil.

2 lb (1 kg) spinach or Swiss chard (silverbeet)
3 tablespoons olive oil
1 small onion, finely chopped
1 clove garlic, minced
⅓ cup (2 oz/60 g) raisins, plumped in hot water and drained
¼ cup (1¼ oz/40 g) pine nuts, toasted
salt and freshly ground pepper

Chop the greens coarsely if the leaves are very large. Wash in several changes of water and drain.

In a wide sauté pan over medium heat, warm the oil. Add the onion and sauté until golden and sweet, 15–20 minutes. Add the garlic and cook for 1–2 minutes longer.

Add the greens in batches and stir well until wilted; add more as each batch shrinks. You do not need to cover the pan, as the greens will cook down in the moisture clinging to the leaves. When all the leaves are wilted, add the raisins and pine nuts and season to taste with salt and pepper.

Transfer to a serving dish and serve hot or warm.

SERVES 6

Top to bottom: Pasta with Eggplant and Tomatoes, Pasta with Sardines

SICILY

PASTA CON SARDE

Pasta with Sardines

This is one of the most famous and interesting pastas from Sicily. The Arabic influence is seen in the addition of raisins and nuts to what seems like a simple fish sauce. Do not worry if you cannot find wild fennel. Cultivated fennel will do. Use the stalks and fronds as well as the celery-textured bulb.

1½ lb (750 g) wild fennel greens
5 tablespoons (3 fl oz/80 ml) olive oil
2 onions, minced
⅓ cup (2 oz/60 g) raisins or currants, plumped in hot water and drained
⅓ cup (2 oz/60 g) pine nuts, toasted
6 anchovy fillets in oil, drained and coarsely chopped
large pinch of saffron, crushed and steeped in 2 tablespoons hot water
1 lb (500 g) fresh sardines, boned and cut into large pieces
1 lb (500 g) *bucatini, perciatelli* or other dried pasta
1 cup (4 oz/125 g) fine dried bread crumbs, toasted (optional)

Trim the fennel bulbs and remove and discard any dry or discolored leaves. Cut the bulbs in half or into quarters lengthwise. Bring a large pot three-fourths full of water to a boil. Add salt to taste and the fennel. Cook until tender, 8–10 minutes. Using a slotted spoon remove the fennel to a cutting board. Chop and set aside. Reserve the water.

In a large sauté pan over low heat, warm 2 tablespoons of the oil. Add the onions and sauté until they are pale gold, 10–15 minutes. Add the raisins or currants, pine nuts, anchovies, and saffron and steeping liquid. Simmer over low heat for 5 minutes. Remove to a bowl; keep warm.

In the large sauté pan over medium heat, warm the remaining 3 tablespoons oil. Add the sardines and sauté, turning once, until golden, 3–4 minutes on each side. Using a slotted spoon remove to a dish; keep warm. Add the chopped fennel to the sardine-flavored oil and cook over low heat to warm through. Return the sardines and the onion mixture to the pan and keep warm.

Meanwhile, return the fennel water to a boil. Add the pasta and cook until al dente, about 10 minutes (it will take about 10 minutes to cook; check the package directions). Drain.

Place the pasta on a platter. Spoon the sardine sauce over the top and toss well. Sprinkle with the bread crumbs, if using. Serve immediately or at room temperature.

SERVES 6

SICILY

PASTA ALLA NORMA

Pasta with Eggplant and Tomatoes

Vincenzo Bellini was born in Catania, where this pasta was born as well. It is named for one of his best-known operas, Norma. *If vine-ripened tomatoes are not available, canned plum (Roma) tomatoes can be substituted.*

2 globe eggplants (aubergines) or 8 slender (Asian) eggplants, about 1½ lb (750 g) total weight
salt
olive oil
2 lb (1 kg) tomatoes, peeled, seeded and coarsely chopped
2 cloves garlic, minced
12 large fresh basil leaves, chopped
freshly ground pepper
1 lb (500 g) *maccheroni* or spaghetti
grated pecorino cheese

Peel the eggplants lengthwise in a striped pattern. If the eggplants are large, cut them in half lengthwise and then thinly slice them crosswise. If they are long and thin, or if you are using long, slender eggplants, simply thinly slice them crosswise. Sprinkle the slices with salt, place in a colander and let stand for 20–30 minutes to drain off the bitter juices. Pat dry with paper towels.

In a large sauté pan over high heat, pour in oil to a depth of ¼ in (6 mm). When the oil is hot, working in batches, fry the eggplant slices, turning once, until golden brown and tender, just a few minutes. Using a slotted spoon remove to a dish.

In another sauté pan over medium heat, warm 2 tablespoons oil. Add the tomatoes and garlic and cook, stirring occasionally, until the tomatoes take on a saucelike consistency, 10–15 minutes. Add the fried eggplant and basil and warm the eggplant through. Season to taste with salt and pepper. Meanwhile, bring a large pot three-fourths full of water to a boil. Add the pasta and cook until al dente (it will take 7–10 minutes to cook; check the package directions). Drain.

Place the pasta on a warmed platter. Spoon the sauce over the top and toss well. Sprinkle with cheese and serve immediately.

SERVES 6

PROVENCE

TOMATES PROVENÇALE

Baked Tomatoes with Garlic, Parsley and Bread Crumbs

In one sense, this recipe is so simple there seems no reason to write it down. The dish, however, often suffers from flavorless tomatoes with too much liquid. Seek out vine-ripened tomatoes and be sure to rid them of excess liquid, so the tops will acquire a crusty finish.

6 large, firm but ripe tomatoes
salt
4 tablespoons (2 fl oz/60 ml) olive oil
salt and freshly ground pepper
½ cup (2 oz/60 g) fine dried bread crumbs
3 cloves garlic, minced
½ cup (¾ oz/20 g) chopped fresh flat-leaf (Italian) parsley

Preheat an oven to 375°–400°F (190°–200°C). Lightly oil a baking dish. Cut the tomatoes in half crosswise. Sprinkle with salt and drain, cut sides down, in a colander, for about 10 minutes. Dry well with paper towels.

In a large sauté pan over medium-high heat, warm 2 tablespoons of the oil. Add the tomato halves, cut side down and 4–6 at a time, and fry until golden, about 5 minutes.

Place the tomatoes, cut side up, in the prepared baking dish. Sprinkle with salt and pepper. In a small bowl stir together the bread crumbs, garlic and a little of the parsley. Spread atop the tomatoes. Drizzle with remaining 2 tablespoons oil. Bake until the tops are golden, 10–15 minutes.

Transfer to a platter and sprinkle with the remaining parsley. Serve warm or at room temperature.

SERVES 6

PROVENCE

FENOUIL BRAISÉ

Braised Fennel

Although fennel is most often eaten raw with salt and olive oil in France and Italy, it is also tasty when cooked. Precooking the fennel can be done two ways: It can be sautéed in oil or butter and then braised in stock until tender, or it can be cooked in boiling salted water. The fennel is then served as is or dressed with butter and grated Parmesan cheese and bread crumbs. Or it can be placed in a baking dish, sprinkled with cheese and crumbs and glazed under the broiler (griller). Both versions are given here.

6 large bulbs fennel, cut in half lengthwise and cored
¼ cup (2 oz/60 g) butter or (2 fl oz/60 ml) olive oil for sautéing, plus more as needed for drizzling
1 cup (8 fl oz/250 ml) chicken stock (see glossary), if braising
salt and freshly ground pepper
freshly grated nutmeg (optional)
¼ cup (1 oz/30 g) freshly grated Parmesan cheese
¼ cup (1 oz/30 g) fine dried bread crumbs, toasted

2–3 tablespoons heavy (double) cream (optional)

Preheat an oven to 400°F (200°C).

If you are sautéing the fennel, cut the fennel bulbs lengthwise into thick slices. In a large sauté pan over medium heat, warm the butter or oil. Add the fennel and sauté until golden, 8–10 minutes. Add the stock, cover and braise until tender and most of the stock is absorbed, 15–20 minutes. Season to taste with salt, pepper and nutmeg (if using). Transfer the fennel to a gratin dish, arranging it in a single layer. Cover with the cheese, crumbs and a bit of oil or butter. Bake until the top is golden, about 10 minutes. Alternatively, warm briefly in the oven and then brown under a preheated broiler (griller). Serve immediately.

Alternatively, bring a saucepan three-fourths full of water to a boil. Drop in the fennel halves and add salt to taste. Cook, uncovered, until the bulbs are tender, about 25 minutes. Drain in a colander, let cool and squeeze out excess moisture. Cut bulbs lengthwise into thick slices, keeping slices intact as much as possible. Butter or oil a baking dish and place fennel slices in it. Sprinkle with salt, pepper, and nutmeg (if using). Then top with the butter or oil, cream (if using), cheese and crumbs. Bake until the top is golden, about 10 minutes. A few tablespoons of cream may be added.

SERVES 6

Top to bottom: Baked Tomatoes with Garlic, Parsley and Bread Crumbs, Braised Fennel

Clockwise from top left: Rice Pilaf with Currants and Nuts, Pilaf Wrapped in Filo, Saffron Pilaf with Shrimp

TURKEY

YUFKALİ PİLAV

Pilaf Wrapped in Filo

Some versions of this recipe combine chicken and an almond rice pilaf in a shallow baking dish lined with overlapping sheets of filo, fold the filo over the top, bake, and then cut for serving much as one would cut baklava. You can use ½ pound (250 g) lamb in place of the chicken: Cut the lamb into ½-in (12-mm) cubes, brown in ¼ cup (2 oz/60 g) unsalted butter for a few minutes, and then simmer in 1 cup (8 fl oz/250 ml) meat stock until tender; use meat stock in place of the chicken stock for cooking the rice.

FOR THE CHICKEN:

1 small chicken, about 2½ lb (1.25 kg), or about 2 lb (1 kg) chicken pieces
1 onion, halved
1 carrot, halved
salt
6 peppercorns

¾ cup (6 oz/180 g) unsalted butter
½ cup (3 oz/90 g) almonds

1 onion, chopped
1½ cups (10½ oz/330 g) long-grain white rice, washed and drained
½ teaspoon ground cinnamon or allspice
¼ teaspoon ground cardamom
salt and freshly ground pepper
8 *filo* sheets (see glossary)

To prepare the chicken, in a saucepan combine the chicken, onion, carrot, salt to taste, peppercorns and water to cover. Bring to a boil, reduce the heat to low, cover and simmer until the chicken is tender, about 30 minutes for chicken pieces and 50 minutes for whole chicken. Remove the chicken and, when cool enough to handle, remove the bones and skin and cut the chicken meat into bite-sized pieces. Strain the stock and place in a saucepan; bring to a simmer.

In a large saucepan over medium heat, melt ¼ cup (2 oz/60 g) of the butter. Add the almonds and fry, stirring, until golden brown, a few minutes. Using a slotted spoon remove to a dish. Add the onion to the butter remaining in the pan and sauté until tender and translucent, 8–10 minutes. Add the cinnamon or allspice, cardamom and salt and pepper to taste and sauté for a few more minutes. Add the rice and sauté, stirring, until the rice is translucent and coated with fat, about 3 minutes. Add the fried almonds, chicken meat and 3 cups (24 fl oz/750 ml) of the simmering stock and bring to a boil. Reduce the heat to low, cover and cook until the liquid has been absorbed and the rice is cooked, about 20 minutes. Turn off heat and let the rice sit until cool.

Preheat an oven to 450°–500°F (230°–260°C).

In a small pan melt the remaining ½ cup (4 oz/125 g) butter. Brush a deep 2-qt (2-l) baking dish (a soufflé dish works well) generously with some of the butter. Now line the dish with the *filo* sheets, allowing each one to overhang the sides and brushing them with the butter. Make sure there is enough *filo* overhanging the sides of the dish to enclose the pilaf. Spoon the cooled pilaf evenly into the dish and bring the *filo* sheets up over the top to enclose neatly. Brush the top with the remaining butter.

Bake until golden, 15–20 minutes. Remove from the oven and let rest for 2–3 minutes. Invert onto a serving platter. Slice and serve.

SERVES 6–8

TURKEY

IC PİLAV

Rice Pilaf with Currants and Nuts

A good accompaniment to many Turkish dishes. You can expand the dish with the addition of cooked chicken or lamb, sautéed together with the onion. Long-grain rice is essential and basmati is the best, as it holds its firmness and fragrance longer than any other varieties.

¼ cup (2 oz/60 g) unsalted butter or (2 fl oz/60 ml) olive oil
1 onion, chopped
¼ teaspoon ground allspice
½ teaspoon ground cinnamon or coriander
2 cups (14 oz/440 g) long-grain white rice, washed and drained
4 cups (32 fl oz/1 l) chicken stock (see glossary) or water, heated
1 teaspoon salt, plus salt to taste
1 cup (6 oz/185 g) currants, plumped in hot water and drained
½ cup (2½ oz/75 g) pine nuts, toasted, pistachios or almonds, toasted
freshly ground pepper (optional)
4 tablespoons chopped fresh flat-leaf (Italian) parsley or dill (optional)

In a large saucepan over medium heat, melt the butter or warm the oil. Add the onion and sauté until just translucent, about 7 minutes.

Add the allspice and cinnamon or coriander and cook, stirring, for 2 minutes. Add the rice and stir over medium heat until the grains become translucent and coated with the fat, about 3 minutes. Add the heated stock or water and the 1 teaspoon salt. Bring to a boil, reduce the heat to low, cover and simmer until the liquid has been absorbed and the rice is cooked, about 20 minutes. Turn off heat and let the rice rest, covered, for 10 minutes.

Add the currants and nuts to the rice and fluff with a fork. Season to taste with salt and with pepper, if using. Transfer to a warmed platter, sprinkle with the parsley or dill (if using) and serve.

SERVES 6

TURKEY

KARIDESLI PİLAV

Saffron Pilaf with Shrimp

Seafood and rice pilaf are popular in Greece as well as Turkey. While this recipe specifies shrimp, scallops, squid or cooked octopus would also be nice. Mussels are a particular favorite in Turkey. To make the pilaf with mussels, scrub and debeard about 40 mussels and then steam them open in a little white wine or water, discarding any that do not open. Shell the mussels and strain the steaming liquid. Steep the saffron in the strained liquid. Proceed with the recipe, sautéing the mussels in the butter.

¼ cup (2 oz/60 g) unsalted butter
1 lb (500 g) shrimp (prawns), peeled and deveined
1 onion, chopped
2 cloves garlic, minced
2 celery stalks or 1 small bulb fennel, trimmed and chopped (optional)
3 large tomatoes, peeled, seeded and chopped
1½ cups (10½ oz/330 g) long-grain white rice, washed and drained
¼–½ teaspoon saffron threads, crushed and steeped in ¼ cup (2 fl oz/60 ml) hot water
1 teaspoon salt
½ teaspoon freshly ground pepper
3 cups (24 fl oz/750 ml) fish or chicken stock (see glossary) or water, heated
4 tablespoons chopped fresh flat-leaf (Italian) parsley or dill

In a large saucepan over medium-high heat, melt the butter. Add the shrimp and sauté, stirring constantly, until pink, for about 2 minutes. Using a slotted spoon, remove the shrimp to a bowl.

Add the onion and garlic to the butter remaining in the pan and sauté over low heat until beginning to soften, about 7 minutes. Add the celery (if using) and tomatoes and sauté for 3 minutes longer. Add the rice and stir well. Add the saffron and its steeping liquid, salt, pepper and heated stock or water. Bring to a boil, reduce the heat to low, cover and cook until the liquid has been absorbed and the rice is cooked, about 20 minutes.

Return the shrimp to the pan, stir once, and cover the pan. Turn off the heat and let the rice rest, covered, for 10 minutes. Fluff once with a fork, transfer to a warmed platter, sprinkle with the parsley or dill and serve.

SERVES 4

Clockwise from top left: Fried Cauliflower, Green Beans with Tomatoes, Simmered Fava Beans

EGYPT

FUL MUDAMMAS

Simmered Fava Beans

In Egypt these flavorful brown beans are served for breakfast as well as other meals. Simply put, this is the national dish of Egypt. The beans can also be puréed and served as a meze *with the same garnishes as those used for the simmered beans. If fava beans are unavailable, pinto beans can be substituted. Pita bread, of course, is an ideal accompaniment.*

2 cups (14 oz/440 g) dried fava (small broad) beans
5–6 cups (40–48 fl oz/1.25–1.5 l) water, to cover
3 or 4 cloves garlic, minced
1 teaspoon ground cumin (optional)
salt
chopped fresh flat-leaf (Italian) parsley
lemon wedges
olive oil
beid hamine (recipe on page 50)
freshly ground pepper
pita bread (recipe on page 82)

❀ In a bowl combine the fava beans and water to cover generously and let soak in the refrigerator overnight. Drain.
❀ Place the beans in a saucepan and add the water making sure the beans are covered. Bring to a boil, reduce the heat to low, cover and simmer until tender, 2–5 hours. The cooking time will depend on the age and the size of the beans. When the beans are ready, add the garlic, cumin (if using) and salt to taste.
❀ Ladle into bowls. Set out the parsley, lemon wedges, oil, *beid hamine* and pepper for diners to add as they like. Pass the pita.

SERVES 6

LEBANON

KARNABEET MAKLEE

Fried Cauliflower

Not quite a fritter, but very delectable indeed. You can steam the cauliflower rather than boil it; use the same timing. In Turkey, cauliflower florets are dipped in flour, then in a mixture of eggs and grated kasseri *(see glossary) or Parmesan cheese and fried. In Sicily, cauliflower florets are placed in a baking dish; topped with a mixture of minced garlic, chopped parsley, grated* caciocavallo *cheese and fine dried bread crumbs; drizzled with melted butter; and baked in a moderately hot oven until crusty and golden. In Greece, cauliflower is cooked, then layered with tomato sauce and feta cheese and baked.*

1 large head cauliflower, separated into florets
salt to taste, plus 1 teaspoon salt
4 eggs
⅓ cup (3 fl oz/80 ml) water, or as needed
¾ cup (4 oz/125 g) all-purpose (plain) flour
½ cup (3 oz/90 g) finely minced onion or (1½ oz/45 g) green (spring) onions
½ cup (¾ oz/20 g) chopped fresh flat-leaf (Italian) parsley
½ cup (¾ oz/20 g) chopped fresh mint
½ teaspoon ground cinnamon
½ teaspoon ground allspice
½ teaspoon freshly ground pepper
vegetable oil for deep-frying
lemon wedges

❀ Bring a saucepan three-fourths full of water to a boil. Add the cauliflower and salt to taste and simmer until cooked but still firm, about 4 minutes. Drain and immerse in cold water to cool. Drain again and pat dry with paper towels. Let cool completely.
❀ In a bowl combine the eggs, ⅓ cup (3 fl oz/80 ml) water and the flour and whisk until smooth. Add the onion, parsley, mint, cinnamon, allspice, the 1 teaspoon salt and the pepper.

Stir well. Alternatively, mix the ingredients in a blender or in a processor fitted with the metal blade.

In a deep sauté pan, pour in oil to a depth of 3 in (7.5 cm) and heat to 375°F (190°C), or until a bit of batter dropped into the oil begins to color within moments. When the oil is ready, dip the florets into the batter, allowing the excess to drip back into the bowl, and then slip them into the hot oil; do not crowd the pan. Fry, turning once, until golden, 3–5 minutes. Using a slotted spoon transfer to paper towels to drain, and repeat with the remaining florets.

Arrange on a platter and serve with lemon wedges.

SERVES 4–6

LEBANON

Loubia Bzeit

Green Beans with Tomatoes

In the Middle East, green beans are often seasoned with sautéed onion and diced tomatoes or tomato sauce. Sometimes garlic is added; oregano, dill or mint is also sometimes used. In Greece, feta cheese is crumbled atop the cooked beans. In Turkey, ½ teaspoon ground allspice is added with the tomatoes. Okra can be prepared in the same way: Cut off the hard stems and dry the okra well with paper towels. Simmer for about 1 hour and add a squeeze of lemon juice at the end of cooking. In Greece, the okra is trimmed, soaked in 1 cup (8 fl oz/250 ml) red wine vinegar for 30 minutes and then drained and rinsed before cooking. The beans are cooked for a long time until very soft. This style of cooking may seem unappealing to those accustomed to tender, crisp vegetables, but try it.

1 lb (500 g) green beans, trimmed
3 tablespoons olive oil
1 cup (4 oz/125 g) chopped onion
1 or 2 cloves garlic, minced (optional)
4 cups (1½ lb/750 g) chopped tomatoes
pinch of sugar, if needed
½ cup (4 fl oz/125 ml) canned tomato purée (optional)
salt and freshly ground pepper
chopped fresh flat-leaf (Italian) parsley, mint, dill or oregano (optional)

Ideally the green beans are young, small beans. If they are large, however, remove any strings and cut into 2-in (5-cm) lengths. Set aside.

In a large sauté pan over medium heat, warm the oil. Add the onion and sauté until lightly browned and soft, 12–15 minutes. Add the garlic, if using, and cook for 1–2 minutes. Add the green beans and sauté for a few minutes longer. Then add the tomatoes and the purée, if using, and bring to a simmer. Cover and cook over very low heat until the tomatoes form a thick sauce, 45–60 minutes.

Season to taste with salt and pepper and with one of the herbs, if using. Transfer to a serving dish and serve hot, warm or at room temperature.

SERVES 6

CATALONIA

Arroz a Banda

Fish-Flavored Rice

In Spain, Valencia is the home of rice cultivation and cuisine. Spanish rice is a short-grain variety, rather like the Italian Arborio. This is an unusual rice dish in that it is served in two parts. The fish is cooked in stock and set aside for a second course. The stock is strained and reduced, then the rice is browned in oil and cooked in the reduced stock. The rice is served as a course by itself, a banda, *or "apart," accompanied by a very garlicky aioli (garlic sauce). A similar dish,* fideus a banda, *is made with thin dried pasta that is browned and cooked slowly in fish stock.*

FOR THE FISH STOCK:

2 lb (1 kg) fish heads, bones, small bony fish and shellfish shells, if available
2 tablespoons olive oil
1 large onion, coarsely chopped
2 cloves garlic (optional)
1 or 2 dried chili peppers (optional)
1 leek, chopped
2 carrots, chopped
2 bay leaves
1 lemon slice
12 peppercorns
few fresh sprigs of thyme, parsley and marjoram
6–8 cups (48–64 fl oz/1.5–2 l) water
salt

FOR THE FISH COURSE:

2 lb (1 kg) halibut, monkfish (anglerfish), cod or other white fish fillets or 1½ lb (750 g) fish fillets and 1 lb (500 g) shrimp (prawns), peeled and deveined

FOR THE RICE:

6 tablespoons (3 fl oz/90 ml) olive oil
4 cloves garlic, minced
2 tomatoes, peeled, seeded and chopped, or 2 tablespoons tomato paste
2 teaspoons paprika
2 cups (14 oz/440 g) short-grain rice, washed and drained
¼ teaspoon saffron threads, crushed
salt and freshly ground pepper

aioli made with 8 cloves garlic (recipe on page 144)

To make the stock, rinse the fish parts well and set aside. In a stockpot over medium heat, warm the oil. Add the onion, garlic and chili peppers (if using) and sauté for a few minutes. Add the fish parts and sauté, stirring often, for 1–2 minutes. Add all the remaining ingredients except the salt, adding the water as needed to cover.

Bring to a boil, skimming off any scum that forms on the surface. Reduce the heat to a simmer and cook for 25 minutes, skimming often. Strain the stock and reduce further over high heat to intensify the flavor. It will be used for cooking the fish and rice; you will need a little more than 4 cups (32 fl oz/1 l). Season to taste with salt.

To prepare the fish, bring the fish stock to a simmer in a wide, shallow saucepan. Add the fish and poach gently until it is cooked through but not falling apart; timing will depend upon thickness of fillets. Using a slotted spatula remove from the stock and set aside in a dish. Cover with just a little of the stock to keep it moist. If using shrimp add them to the stock separately and poach them until they turn pink, just a few minutes. Set aside with the fish.

In a paella pan or wide sauté pan over medium heat, warm the oil. Add the garlic and when it starts to turn pale gold, add the tomatoes or tomato paste. Cook, stirring, for about 5 minutes, then add the paprika and cook for 2 minutes longer. Add the rice and cook, stirring often, until colored a bit, about 3 minutes. Stir in the saffron and salt and pepper to taste.

Add 4 cups (32 fl oz/1 l) fish stock and cook for 5 minutes over high heat. Reduce the heat to low and simmer, uncovered, until the liquid has been absorbed and the rice is tender, about 15 minutes. Alternatively, cook the rice over high heat, uncovered, for 5 minutes, then place in a 350°F (180°C) oven for 15 minutes. Turn off the heat (or remove from the oven) and let the rice rest, covered, for 10 minutes.

Taste and adjust the seasoning.

Transfer the rice to a warmed platter and serve with the aioli. Serve the poached fish as a second course.

SERVES 6 *Photograph pages 192–193*

NORTH AFRICA

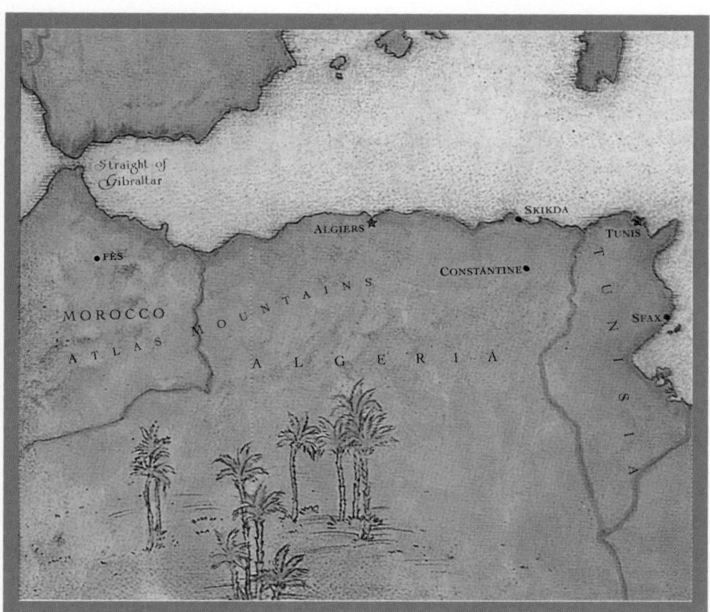

NORTH AFRICA

Morocco, Algeria, Tunisia

We complete our circuit of the Mediterranean by advancing in the footsteps of the Muslim armies of the seventh century, from Egypt along the coast of North Africa until we face Spain, our point of departure, from across the Strait of Gibraltar. The three modern states through which we pass, Morocco, Algeria and Tunisia, form a coherent geographical whole, consisting of a fairly narrow coastal plain separated from a vast desert hinterland by the Atlas and Aurès mountains. The western and eastern extremities of the region—northern Morocco and eastern Tunisia—are almost within shouting distance of Europe. North Africa thus served both as the base from which the Arab conquests of Spain and Sicily were launched, and as a refuge for Andalusians fleeing before the Reconquista. And as we noted earlier in connection with Marseilles, traffic between the North African and northern shores of the Mediterranean still continues unabated.

North Africa also possesses a distinct identity within the Arab world, being known as *al-Maghrib,* "the West," as opposed to *al-Mashriq,* "the East," consisting of historic Syria, Iraq and the Arabian peninsula. The dialects of Arabic spoken in North Africa are barely comprehensible to the easterner, and the specificity of the region is further underlined by the presence of the Berbers, its indigenous inhabitants since time immemorial. North Africa pos-

Previous pages: Although 85 percent of Algeria lies in the vast Sahara Desert, it has fertile oases that produce the most delicately flavored dates in the world. Left: Romans were perfecting the art of pottery in Nabeul, Tunisia, as early as 2000 years ago.

sesses accordingly its own rich and distinctive cuisine, one not only different, in large part, from the cuisine of the Arab East, but also infinitely better preserved. (Not surprisingly, this is true of traditional culture in general; no country in the Arab East, with the possible exception of Yemen, can boast of a perfectly preserved medieval city like Fès.)

If we except Ulysses's visit to the lotus eaters of Djerba, an island off the Tunisian coast (who may in any event have been eating ground jujube), North Africa is largely absent from the gastronomic lore of the ancient Mediterranean world. Essential elements of the Mediterranean diet were nonetheless available there quite early; the Carthaginians planted fruit trees, olive trees and cereal crops in the fifth century B.C. They were, however, essentially traders, and it was left to the Romans to develop North African agriculture on the grand scale. They treated the whole area as they did Spain and Sicily, as a granary to supply Rome, and to this end they built the canals and barrages, of which traces still remain, and organized the fertile lands of Numidia—eastern Algeria, in terms of contemporary geography—into latifundia, vast monocultural estates for the growing of wheat. It is doubtful that the Romans had any effect on the eating habits of the Berbers; the similarity between couscous, the grain, and polenta, that Etruscan remnant in the Roman diet, is slight and probably fortuitous.

Roman rule was brought to an end in the early fifth century A.D. by the Vandals, who after their expulsion from Spain were eager to pounce on the wheat fields of Numidia. As might be expected of a people whose achievements are immortalized in the word *vandalism,* the Vandals made no contribution, culinary or otherwise, to North Africa during their century of dominion. A degree of prosperity returned with the Byzantines, who repaired irrigation systems and reorganized the latifundia in keeping with their overall ambition of restoring the traditions of Roman rule throughout the Mediterranean. Unlike the Romans, however, the Byzantines believed in the need to impose direct rule, as well as their own mores, on the Berbers; this led to constant uprisings that combined with internecine strife among the Byzantines to devastate North African agriculture anew.

Sousse, a Tunisian port town that has recently found its niche as a tourist resort, caters to visitors searching for rugs and carpets.

The Arab-Muslim conquest of North Africa in the seventh century fixed the character and destiny of the region permanently as a distinct and culturally important zone of the Islamic world, linked not only to the Arab East but also to Spain (until the end of the fifteenth century) and to the Muslim lands of West Africa. All these connections were reflected in its cuisine, a circumstance that was in part the consequence of the unified rule established over Spain, Morocco, western Algeria and parts of Senegal by the Almoravide dynasty in the twelfth century. As in the Fertile Crescent, Spain and Sicily, the coming of Islam to North Africa ushered in a great flourishing of agriculture. The Roman irrigation systems were put in order once more, and in both Tunisia and Morocco subterranean canals were dug on the Iranian model to prevent the water from evaporating. The invasion of North Africa by the Bani Hilal nomads in the eleventh century damaged many of these installations, but they remain operative down to the present. The skill of the Arabs in extracting, conserving and channeling water contributed to the gastronomic well-being of North Africa in two interconnected ways. First, it increased the land available for cultivation of the new crops that arrived from the East: all manner of citrus fruits, a wider range of vegetables than those previously available, rice and sugar. Second, as the great reservoir outside the now-deserted city of Qayruwan makes clear, it made possible the foundation of great cities that, with their abundantly stocked markets and affluent courts, developed, almost automatically, regional styles of cuisine. It is no accident that what the Moroccan tourist brochures call the Royal Cities—Fès, Marrakech, Meknes and Rabat—are even today the principal centers of traditional Moroccan cuisine.

The two chief strands in North African cuisine are the Arab and the Berber. Most of its best-known dishes contain elements that can be assigned to the one or the other, but by and large it can be said that the Berber contribution is the original conception, and that of the Arab, the use of new ingredients and more sophisticated techniques of preparation. The word *couscous,* designating both the granules of semolina that are the foundation of the dish and the complete, bipartite preparation, including both the semolina and the stew poured over it, is an etymological mystery, being neither Berber nor Arab. The names *seksu* in Morocco and *ta'am* in Algeria (the latter having, significantly enough, the literal meaning of "food") are, in any event, more common. But the dish itself began no doubt as a simple Berber preparation of grain flavored only with butter. Then, as agriculture and abundance increased after the arrival of the Arabs, first chick-peas (garbanzos), pumpkins and gourds were added for extra flavor and substance, and then the dish was perfected with vegetable and meat stews. Couscous is justifiably the most celebrated food of North Africa, coming in a wide range of styles that reflect both different degrees of prosperity and regional preferences. The brightest star in the couscous constellation is perhaps that of Fès, prepared with chicken and lamb, seven vegetables, and seven spices that are offset by the sweetness of raisins. Tunisia likes its couscous unambiguously spicy, and often substitutes fish for chicken and lamb. Most lavish of all couscous dishes and furthest removed from Berber origins are those ceremonial preparations in which stuffed pigeons are embedded in the grain. Couscous is also the most widely traveled of all North African dishes; it is found in Sicily, Senegal and even Brazil.

The standard accompaniment for couscous is *harissa,* a hot sauce of red chilies. Chili peppers being an import from the New World, *harissa* cannot be ascribed to the original repertoire brought to North Africa by the Arabs. The suggestion that its name is derived from Orissa, a chili-growing district in India, is quite baseless, but there is a remarkable similarity between *harissa* and the *sambal oelek* of Malay-Indonesian cuisine, although the latter is made of only chilies and salt while spices go into *harissa.*

Tagine, the rich and varied stew of North Africa, belongs by contrast quite clearly to the classical Arab cuisine that was so heavily influenced by Iran. The mixture of sweet-and-sour tastes and the combination of a wide range of fruits as well as vegetables with a variety of meats were after all hallmarks of that cuisine, although it is now almost exclusively in North Africa that they are honored. Noticeable, too, is the frequent use of pigeons in *tagines,* as well as in some other dishes. Elsewhere in the Arab world, with the exception of Egypt, pigeons are these days generally spared from the cooking pot, their only role being to flutter peacefully in the courtyards of mosques. Among *tagines* particularly challenging to the palate we can mention lamb *tagine* with artichokes, lemons, and olives, and pigeon *tagine* with prunes and onions.

The jewel in the crown of North African cuisine is *b'stilla,* the intricate, flaky pie of pigeon or chicken prepared in differing ways in Fès, Rabat, Tetuan, Meknes and Marrakech. Its origins are sometimes thought to be Andalusian, since the word sounds vaguely Spanish and the rich combination of tastes proffered by *b'stilla* seems somehow to mirror all the restrained opulence of Hispano-Arab culture. As Paula Wolfert points out, however, *bestila* is a Berber word meaning "chicken cooked in butter and saffron," which is the very foundation of *b'stilla;* we may therefore conclude that the creation of this magnificent dish was a joint Berber and Arab enterprise. Here, the Arab contribution appears to have been the Persian-derived concept of enclosing meat with spices and nuts in pastry; the technique of making *ouarka,* thin layers of pastry akin to the *filo* used in making Turkish and Balkan *börek* but differing from it in some important respects; and the use of cinnamon and other seasonings.

Despite its tempestuous political history, North Africa has remained largely impregnable to external culinary influences after the Arab-Muslim conquest. It is to be noted, however, that the Andalusian refugees and migrants who came to North Africa in continuous waves, from the twelfth until the seventeenth century, brought with them something of their own culinary traditions. One of them, Ibn Zarin al-Tujibi, compiled a book of recipes with the express purpose of preserving Andalusian traditions; it is useful also for the comparisons it makes with the culinary styles of the Arab East. Andalusian cuisine, marked among other things by a complete eschewal of the butter beloved of the Berbers in favor of olive oil, is still cultivated in Tetuan and some districts of Fès.

Decorative mosaic art was an Eastern technique perfected in Andalusia and imported to Morocco by the Muslims of Spain.

North Africa underlined its separate identity by resisting full absorption into the Ottoman Empire, unlike the Arab East. Morocco never came under Ottoman dominion, and Ottoman rule was generally nominal in Algeria and Tunisia. There are, nonetheless, some traces of Ottoman culinary influence, faint in Morocco and somewhat stronger in Algeria and Tunisia. They consist of *kefte,* grilled mincemeat, the Turkish *köfte;* the *briks* of Tunisia, reminiscent, perhaps, of Moroccan *b'stilla,* but more clearly indebted in both substance and name to the Turkish *börek;* and *shurba,* the rich, pungent soup of Algeria and Tunisia, which mirrors in its name the Turkish fondness for soups, while using a hotter combination of spices than most Turks would countenance.

It is curious to note that it was the English merchants of Tangier who introduced the Moroccans to tea, although the tea they now drink—poured over mint leaves—is quite different; fortunately, there is no other trace of English influence on the food of North Africa. As for the French who colonized Algeria for 130 years and established shorter-lived protectorates in Morocco and Tunisia, their influence on the North African diet appears to have been minimal; not even the Francophone ruling elite that they trained saw any reason to trade in its cuisine for that of the conquerors.

Desserts, Preserves and Beverages

While the most common dessert is fruit, Mediterranean cuisines excel in rich and sugary pastries.

DESSERTS, PRESERVES AND BEVERAGES

In the Mediterranean, the most common dessert is a piece of fruit, and sweets and pastries are reserved for special occasions or for accompanying afternoon coffee or tea. When fruits are in season they are served at both lunch and dinner, on plates or in big bowls; during the hot-weather months, they are set in vessels filled with ice water. While these fruits can be eaten out of hand, they are often pared and sliced deftly with a knife and fork.

When fruits are in great abundance and cannot be eaten instantly, they are turned into compotes, baked, dried, candied or put up into jewellike jams and preserves. The assortment of Mediterranean fruits is rich with diversity: peaches, apricots, plums, strawberries, raspberries, tart and sweet cherries, green and black figs, dates, all kinds of melons, loquats, quince, apples, pears, pomegranates, persimmons, grapes and a variety of citrus fruits. Bananas and avocados are grown in Israel, and even pineapple and mangoes appear at the market.

While many fruit preserves in the Mediterranean are eaten with bread, in the eastern countries they are more often served with rich black coffee or eaten from a spoon with a glass of ice cold water for sipping afterward. Sometimes the preserves are served with a bit of thickened cream. Rose-petal preserves are especially nice spooned on top of vanilla ice cream and add an exotic closing note to dinner. Candied fruit peels are served with little pastries as part of coffee service.

Ice creams, sherbets and *granite* are seldom made at home; they are served in cafes and special ice cream shops or sold from carts by street vendors. The variety of flavors—apricot, chocolate, coffee, vanilla, lemon, hazelnut, strawberry, pistachio—is amazing and one is tempted to sample as many as possible, followed by a cool glass of water and a long walk. In the eastern Mediterranean, ice cream is made with *sahleb* (ground dried orchid) and mastic, which give it a chewy texture that may seem out of place to those familiar only with creamy custard-based ice creams.

Along with ice creams, puddings made with dried fruit, rice, bread, semolina and milk are much enjoyed. Both honey and sugar are used for sweetening desserts and pastries. Nuts appear in profusion: walnuts, almonds, hazelnuts, pine nuts and pistachios. Dried fruits—apricots, figs, dates—and nuts are cooked in compotes flavored with rose water or orange-blossom water, or are tucked into cookies, *filo* and *konafa* pastries, and tarts. Fresh soft-curd cheese is used as a filling for tarts and small pastries. Because coffee and tea are so central to Mediterranean culture, there is a whole range of cookies, small pastries and candies that are associated with these drinks. Some are baked and others are fried.

The popularity of French and Italian bakeries and restaurants throughout the world has given many people the opportunity to experience fine examples of pastries and sweets of southern France and Italy. Most of us are more poorly informed about the pastries of the eastern Mediterranean, which, when discovered in shops outside

Previous pages: Rose Petal Preserves (recipe page 228)

the region, are too often leaden, overly sweet and soggy with syrup. The pastries presented here will assure that these same sweets can be as light and delicate as any French creation. They are usually prepared with *konafa* or *filo* dough. The former looks like wiry strands of wheat and is sometimes sold under the name *kadayifi filo.* It is made by passing a batter of flour and water through a brass sieve onto hot metal sheets. The dough sets up in moments and then the strands are pushed to the side to clear the way for making more. *Filo* leaves are the well-known thin pastry sheets of Greece. *Ouarka,* their Moroccan and Tunisian cousins, like *filo,* require considerable skill to make and thus are usually purchased from shops that specialize in turning out the fragile dough.

While wine is served with meals throughout France, Italy, Spain and Greece, in the Muslim countries alcoholic beverages are replaced by teas, yogurt drinks, and syrups and fruit juices mixed with ice, soda or water and called *sharbat,* from the Arabic *shariba,* "to drink." In France, Italy, Spain and Greece flavored liqueurs are savored after dessert and coffee. Some of these are made at home according to recipes that have been in families for years, such as the Provençal orange brandy called *ratafia.* Liqueurs are made from nuts or fruits or are scented with spices and herbs and even flower petals.

Coffee is an important part of daily life in Italy, France and the Middle East. The Arabs, Turks and Greeks prepare coffee in a special single-handled pot with very finely ground coffee powder and sweeten it according to personal taste, which is sometimes too sweet for the outside visitor. Cardamom seeds, rose water or orange-blossom water may be added. After the coffee is drunk, the cups are turned upside down and left for about ten minutes. They are then righted and the sediment is "read" by a fortune-teller.

Coffee houses emerged in Mediterranean cities in the sixteenth century.

The ritual of serving coffee and sweets is the essence of Mediterranean hospitality. Today, with so many women active in the workplace, home baking is gradually becoming only a memory. Most pastries are now purchased from shops bursting with a tempting variety of traditional sweets. (In Athens I once tasted nine versions of baklava at a single coffee-filled sitting, to discover how they differed and to find my favorite.) For special holidays, however, the old recipes are prepared at home by those who still remember. Some of these recipes appear here, culled from books and family recipe collections.

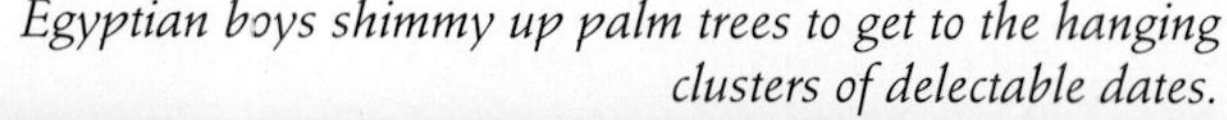

Egyptian boys shimmy up palm trees to get to the hanging clusters of delectable dates.

Left to right: Cherry Pancake, Pears in Red Wine

PROVENCE

Clafouti aux Cerises

Cherry Pancake

Some cooks make this dessert with eggs and milk, and serve it as a warm custard. Others pour the custard into a rich pie shell and serve it as a cherry custard pie. The most popular version, however, adds flour to the custard and turns it into a savory pancake. In France, they seldom pit the cherries, so diners are always on the alert for the pits. You will worry less about your guests if you pit the cherries first.

3 cups (1 lb/500 g) pitted Bing cherries
1½ cups (12 fl oz/375 ml) milk
4 eggs
½ cup (2½ oz/75 g) all-purpose (plain) flour
¼ cup (2 oz/60 g) granulated sugar
2 teaspoons vanilla extract (essence)
1 tablespoon kirsch
confectioners' (icing) sugar

❀ Preheat an oven to 350°F (180°C). Butter a 1½-qt (1.5-l) shallow baking dish or wide gratin dish or a 10-in (25-cm) pie plate.

❀ Pat the cherries dry with paper towels. Spread the cherries on the bottom of the prepared pan.

❀ To make the batter, in a blender or in a food processor fitted with the metal blade, combine the milk, eggs, flour, granulated sugar, vanilla and kirsch. Process until mixed. Stop the machine and scrape down the sides of the container, then process again. Alternatively, in a bowl with an electric mixer set on medium speed, beat together the eggs and granulated sugar. Slowly add the milk, vanilla and kirsch, continuing to beat until fully incorporated. The batter should be lump-free. If it is not, strain it through a fine-mesh sieve.

❀ Pour the batter evenly over the cherries. Bake on the middle shelf of the oven until the top is golden brown and a knife inserted in the center comes out clean, 45–60 minutes. Sprinkle with confectioners' sugar and serve while still very warm.

SERVES 6

FRANCE

Poires au Vin Rouge

Pears in Red Wine

Spain, France, Greece and Italy all claim this dessert with minor variations. While cinnamon, cloves and strips of orange or lemon zest are traditionally added to the poaching liquid, a few black peppercorns or bay leaves will also contribute a wonderful perfume to the pears. The pears become crimson in the syrup and intensify in color the longer they macerate, so you may want to make this dessert a few days ahead.

3 cups (24 fl oz/750 ml) dry red wine
1 cup (8 oz/250 g) sugar
2 cinnamon sticks, each about 2 in (5 cm) long
4 whole cloves
1 orange or lemon zest strip, about 3 in (7.5 cm) long, or both
1 teaspoon fennel seeds or aniseeds (optional)
a few peppercorns (optional)
2 small bay leaves (optional)
6 large firm pears, peeled, and cored from the bottom leaving the stem intact

❀ In a saucepan combine the wine, sugar, cinnamon sticks, cloves, citrus zest and the fennel seeds, aniseeds, peppercorns or bay leaves, if using. Bring to a boil, stirring until the sugar dissolves. Simmer for 5 minutes, then slip the pears into the syrup, cover and simmer until the pears are tender, about 25 minutes.

❀ Using a slotted spoon remove the pears from the syrup and place in a serving bowl. Cover and refrigerate. Remove and discard the citrus zest, cinnamon stick, cloves, peppers and seeds from the poaching syrup. If the syrup is thin, reduce it over high heat until thickened enough to coat a spoon, then remove from the heat and let cool.

❀ When the syrup is cold, pour it over the pears. Re-cover and chill for a few hours before serving.

SERVES 6

PROVENCE

TARTE AU CITRON

Lemon Tart

The perfect balance of sweet and tart, encased in a rich pie shell. You may garnish the tart with whipped cream or berries, if you like.

FOR THE PASTRY:

1¼ cups (6½ oz/200 g) all-purpose (plain) flour
pinch of salt
2 tablespoons sugar
½ cup (¼ lb/125 g) unsalted butter, chilled and cut into ¼-in (6-mm) pieces
1 egg yolk
2 teaspoons fresh lemon juice
1 tablespoon grated lemon zest
1 tablespoon ice water, or as needed

FOR THE FILLING:

4 eggs, separated
¾ cup (6 oz/185 g) sugar
juice of 2 large lemons (about ½ cup/4 fl oz/125 ml)
grated zest of 2 large lemons (about 2 tablespoons)
1 teaspoon cornstarch (cornflour) dissolved in 2 tablespoons water
pinch of salt

❀ To make the pastry, in a food processor fitted with the metal blade, combine the flour, salt and sugar. Add the butter and, using on-off pulses, process until the mixture resembles cornmeal. Add the egg yolk, lemon juice and zest, and the 1 tablespoon ice water and process just until the dough holds together. Add a few drops more ice water if dough is too dry. Gather into a ball, enclose in plastic wrap and refrigerate for about 1 hour. Alternatively, to make by hand, in a bowl stir together the flour, salt and sugar. Add the butter and, using a pastry blender or 2 knives, cut in until the mixture resembles cornmeal. Using a fork, mix in the egg, lemon juice and zest, and ice water. Once the dough forms a rough mass, gather it into a ball and wrap and refrigerate as directed.

❀ Preheat an oven to 400°F (200°C).

❀ On a lightly floured surface, roll out the dough into a round large enough to fit a 9-in (23-cm) tart pan with removable bottom. Transfer the dough round to the pan and ease it into the pan. Trim off the excess dough. Prick with a fork and then line with aluminum foil and weight with pie weights, beans or rice. Bake for about 10 minutes, then remove the weights and foil. Reduce the heat to 350°F (180°C) and continue to bake the crust until set, about 10 minutes longer. Remove from the oven and let cool.

❀ To make the filling, in a bowl with an electric mixer set on high speed, beat together the yolks and half the sugar until pale and thick. Beat in the lemon juice and zest and the cornstarch mixture. Transfer to a saucepan and place over very low heat. Cook, stirring often, until the mixture thickens to the consistency of mayonnaise, about 5 minutes. Remove from the heat and rest in a bowl of ice to cool completely.

❀ Meanwhile, again preheat the oven to 400°F (200°C). In a bowl place the egg whites and the salt. Beat, gradually adding the remaining sugar, until stiff peaks form. Stir about one-fourth of the whites into the yolk mixture to lighten it, then gently fold in the remaining whites.

❀ Spoon the lemon mixture into the pastry shell. Bake until the crust is lightly browned and the filling is set, about 15 minutes.

❀ Remove from the oven to a wire rack to cool, then cut into wedges to serve.

SERVES 8

Lemon Tart

GREECE

Syka Sto Fournou

Baked Figs

Although this dessert has a Greek name, it turns up in Turkey, France, Spain and Italy as well. It doesn't matter if the figs are the green Adriatic or the black Mission variety. They just need to be ripe and heavy in the hand. You can make this dish with lemon zest and add a little lemon juice to the mixture if the orange juice is very sweet. Spanish cooks would use anisette instead of brandy. If you like, omit the almonds and top with a dollop of sweetened thickened yogurt (see glossary).

24 small or 12 large ripe figs
¼ cup (3 oz/90 g) fragrant honey
½ cup (4 fl oz/125 ml) orange juice
¼ cup (2 fl oz/60 ml) brandy
4–6 small bay leaves
a few thin orange zest strips
½ cup (2½ oz/75 g) almonds, toasted (optional)

Preheat an oven to 350°F (180°C).

Prick the figs in a few places with the tines of a fork so that they can absorb the cooking juices. Place upright in a baking dish. In a small bowl stir together the honey, orange juice and brandy and pour over the figs. Add a little water, if necessary, so that the liquid covers the bottom of the dish to a depth of about ¼ in (6 mm). Tuck in the bay leaves and the strips of zest.

Cover and bake, basting occasionally with the pan juices, until the figs are soft, 25–35 minutes. Transfer to individual dishes and sprinkle with the almonds. Serve warm or at room temperature.

SERVES 6

GREECE

Karithopitta

Walnut Cake

This walnut cake is traditionally soaked in syrup, making it quite rich. Without the syrup, however, it is very light and can be served with a fruit compote or a little sweetened yogurt (see glossary) or whipped cream.

FOR THE SYRUP:

¾ cup (6 oz/185 g) sugar
1 cup (8 fl oz/250 ml) water
½ cup (6 oz/185 g) honey
4 whole cloves
1 tablespoon fresh lemon juice
1 lemon zest strip (optional)

½ cup (4 oz/125g) unsalted butter, at room temperature
⅓ cup (3 oz/90 g) sugar
6–8 eggs, separated
¼ cup (1½ oz/45 g) all-purpose (plain) flour
2 teaspoons baking powder
2 teaspoons ground cinnamon
¼ teaspoon ground cloves
pinch of salt
2½ cups (10 oz/315 g) ground walnuts
½ cup (1½ oz/45 g) zweiback crumbs (optional)
1 tablespoon grated orange zest (optional)

To make the syrup, in a saucepan combine the sugar, the water and honey. Bring to a boil over medium heat, stirring to dissolve the sugar. Add the whole cloves and lemon juice and zest (if using), reduce the heat to low and simmer until thickened, about 10 minutes. Remove from the heat and remove and discard the cloves and zest, if used. Let cool completely.

Preheat an oven to 350°F (180°C). Lightly butter and flour a 9-by-12-by-3 in (23-by-30-by-7.5-cm) cake pan.

In a bowl with an electric mixer set on high speed, cream together the butter and sugar until fluffy. Add the egg yolks, one at a time, beating well after each addition. Beat until fully incorporated.

In another bowl sift together the flour, baking powder, cinnamon, ground cloves and salt. Fold this into the egg mixture. Fold in the nuts, the zweiback crumbs and orange zest (if using).

In yet another bowl beat the whites until stiff peaks form. Stir one-third of the whites into the batter to lighten it, then gently fold in the remaining whites. Pour into the prepared pan.

Bake until the cake is dark golden brown and springs back when touched with a finger, about 40 minutes. Remove from the oven and immediately pour the cooled syrup over the cake. Let cool completely in the pan.

To serve, cut into 12–16 squares or lozenges.

MAKES 12–16 PIECES

TURKEY

Gül Reçeli

Rose Petal Preserves

Fragrant and exotic, this preserve is nice over vanilla ice cream or just eaten with a spoon.

½ lb (250 g) pesticide-free fresh red rose petals with a strong fragrance
juice of 2 lemons
1 cup (8 fl oz/250 ml) water
2 cups (1 lb/500 g) sugar
2 tablespoons rosewater

Wash the petals without bruising them and place in a bowl. Squeeze the juice of 1 lemon over them. Let sit for 10 minutes. Transfer to a food processor fitted with the metal blade. Pulse until finely chopped. Or finely chop by hand.

Transfer the petals to a large nonreactive saucepan with any lemon juice remaining in the bottom of the bowl. Add the water and bring to a boil. Reduce the heat to low and simmer until the petals are tender. This can take as little as 10 minutes or as long as 30 minutes, depending upon the roses. Add the sugar and the juice of the second lemon and simmer until the syrup thickens to a jam consistency, about 30 minutes longer. It should register about 220°F (104°C) on a candy thermometer when ready or until a large spoonful dropped onto a saucer chilled in the freezer sets within 2 minutes.

Remove from the heat and stir in the rosewater. Let cool, then skim. Ladle into hot, sterilized jars and seal according to manufacturer's instructions. Store in a cool, dark place.

MAKES 2–3 HALF-PINTS (16–24 FL OZ/500–750 ML)

Photograph pages 222–223

Left to right: Walnut Cake, Baked Figs

TURKEY

KADAYİF

Konafa Pastry

The pastry used to make this sweet resembles shredded wheat or vermicelli, is called konafa *in Arabic and is sold in 1-pound (500-g) packages. It dries out very quickly so keep it covered until you brush it with butter. This pastry can be filled with nuts, semolina cream or sweetened cheese. All three fillings are included here; select the one that appeals to you. The pastry can be prepared in large pans in the same manner as baklava, or it can be cut into 5-inch (13-cm) lengths, some filling placed at one end and rolled. It is usually covered with a cold syrup while it is still hot.*

FOR THE SYRUP:

3 cups (1½ lb/750 g) sugar
2 cups (16 fl oz/500 ml) water
1 tablespoon fresh lemon juice
1 orange zest strip (optional)

FOR THE ALMOND FILLING:

1½ cups (6 oz/185 g) ground almonds
1 cup (8 oz/250 g) sugar
1 tablespoon ground cinnamon
½ cup (4 fl oz/125 ml) fresh orange juice

FOR THE CHEESE FILLING:

1½ cups (12 oz/375 g) ricotta cheese
1 tablespoon rosewater or orange-flower water
½ cup (4 oz/125 g) sugar

FOR THE CREAM FILLING:

2 cups (16 fl oz/500 ml) milk
3 tablespoons sugar
¼ cup (1½ oz/45 g) fine semolina
1 tablespoon rosewater

½–1 cup (4–8 oz/125–250 g) unsalted butter, melted
1 package (1 lb/500 g) *konafa* pastry

To make the syrup, in a saucepan combine the sugar, the water, lemon juice and orange zest (if using). Bring to a boil over medium heat, stirring to dissolve the sugar. Reduce the heat to low and simmer until thickened, about 10 minutes. Remove from the heat and remove and discard the zest, if used. Cool the syrup completely.

Make one of the fillings: To make the almond filling, in a bowl stir together the almonds, sugar, cinnamon and orange juice, mixing well. To make the cheese filling, in a bowl stir together the ricotta, flower water and sugar, mixing well. To make the cream filling, in a small saucepan over medium heat, combine the milk and sugar and bring to a boil, stirring to dissolve the sugar. Place the semolina in a small bowl and stir a little of the warm milk into it to make a smooth paste. Stir this paste into the pan of milk and then cook over low heat, stirring, until the mixture thickens, about 5 minutes. Remove from the heat, stir in the rosewater and let cool.

Preheat an oven to 350°F (180°C). Using a wide pastry brush, spread melted butter on the bottom and sides of a 9-by-12-by-3-in (23-by-30-by-7.5-cm) baking dish. Open the pastry packet and pull apart the strands. In a bowl toss half the pastry with about half of the melted butter, or as needed to coat. Place in the prepared baking dish. Spread with the almond, cheese or cream filling. Toss the remaining pastry strands with as much melted butter as needed to coat. Distribute the pastry evenly atop the filling. Tuck in any loose strands.

Bake until the top is golden, 45–60 minutes. Remove from the oven and immediately pour the cooled syrup over the hot pastry. Let cool completely.

To serve, cut into 16–20 squares.

MAKES 16–20 SQUARES

GREECE

BAKLAVA

Filo Pastry with Nuts

The most famous of Middle Eastern pastries. The word baklava *is Turkish for "lozenge." The dessert, however, is found in Greek, Turkish and Arab sweets shops and the variations on the theme are countless. Not only can it be filled with nuts, but also with semolina-thickened cream, fruit, and in Athens once I even ate chocolate baklava! The most common baklava is made with walnuts or a combination of walnuts and almonds. Some syrups are made with clove and cinnamon; others include lemon juice or a fragrant flower water. Although most people have come to associate baklava with a rich, sticky honey syrup, most Greek (and Turkish) recipes do not include honey. While this is not a light dessert, it is infinitely lighter minus the honey. Some recipes call for layering half the pastry sheets on the bottom, topping with the nuts and then layering with the remaining pastry; this recipe, however, layers only 6–8 pastry sheets at a time. The story goes that, in any case, there must be 40 layers of pastry, to represent the 40 days of Lent. But who's counting?*

FOR THE SYRUP:

1¼ cups (10 oz/315 g) sugar
½ cup (4 fl oz/125 ml) water
1 tablespoon fresh lemon juice
1 lemon zest strip (optional)
1 cinnamon stick, about 2 in (5 cm) long, and 2 whole cloves (optional)
1 tablespoon orange-flower water or rosewater (optional)

½ lb (250 g) walnuts or half walnuts and half almonds, coarsely ground
3 tablespoons sugar
1 teaspoon ground cinnamon (optional)
1 cup (8 oz/250 g) unsalted butter, melted and clarified or skimmed of froth (see glossary)
28–32 *filo* sheets (see glossary)

To make the syrup, in a saucepan combine the sugar, the water, lemon juice and the lemon zest and cinnamon stick or cloves, if using. Bring to a boil, stirring to dissolve the sugar. Reduce the heat to low and simmer until thickened, about 10 minutes. Remove from the heat and, if necessary, discard the zest, cinnamon stick, and cloves. Stir in the flower water, if using, and set aside to cool and allow the flavors to mellow.

In a bowl stir together the ground nuts, sugar and ground cinnamon (if using).

Preheat an oven to 350°F (180°C). Using a wide pastry brush, spread melted butter on the bottom and sides of a 12-by-15-by-3-in (30-by-37.5-by-7.5-cm) pan or dish (or a pan that is the exact size of the *filo* sheets, if you can find one). One by one and brushing each sheet with butter, layer about 8 *filo* sheets in the pan. Top with about one-third of the nuts. Layer 6–8 more *filo* sheets, buttering each sheet, then half of the remaining nuts. Top with another 6–8 buttered *filo* sheets, then the remaining nuts. End with 8 buttered *filo* sheets on top. Butter the top layer generously. (If possible, cover and refrigerate the baklava for about 30 minutes, so the butter can set up. It will make cutting the pastry easier before baking.) Using a sharp knife, cut the baklava into 25–30 diamond shapes.

Bake for 30 minutes, then reduce the heat to 300°F (150°C) and bake until the top is golden, 15–20 minutes longer.

Remove from the oven and immediately pour the cooled syrup over the hot baklava. Let cool completely. To serve, recut the pastry with a sharp knife.

MAKES 25–30 PIECES

Left to right: Konafa Pastry, Filo Pastry with Nuts, Coffee

TURKEY

KAHVE

Coffee

Turkish coffee, sometimes labeled Arab coffee, is available at stores specializing in foods of the Middle East. It is drunk throughout the region. The coffee comes finely ground and is prepared in a small brass or metal pot variously called a cezve *in Turkey and a* jazoua, ibrik, rakwi *or* tanaka, *depending upon which other country in the region you are in. This pot has a long handle and a narrow neck. In some countries there is a belief that the coffee must boil up 3–5 times for luck; the difference in number of times depends upon tradition. Some people add cardamom seeds, a pinch of cinnamon or some rosewater or orange-flower water. After the coffee boils and is poured, the grounds must not be disturbed. One can ask for his or her coffee to be brewed to a specific sweetness:* helou *or* sekerli *(sweet),* mezbout *or* orta *(medium) and* murra *or* sade *(unsweetened), but the coffee is usually sweet regardless of pronouncements.*

Some people boil the water and sugar first, then stir in the coffee, but it is easier to combine all three and then bring the mixture to a boil. If you are using the seeds, add them while the coffee is boiling. Add the flower water after the coffee has boiled.

FOR EACH SERVING:

1 heaping teaspoon sugar
1 heaping teaspoon finely ground Turkish coffee
½ cup (4 fl oz/125 ml) water
a few cardamom seeds (optional)
a few drops of rosewater (optional)

❀ In a small, narrow pan combine the sugar, coffee, water and cardamom seeds (if using) multiplying the amounts according to the number of people you are serving. Stir well to combine and then bring to a boil and let the mixture foam up to the top of the pan. Remove from the heat for 1 minute. Return the coffee to the heat and bring to a frothy boil. Pour into small cups and serve at once. Be sure that everyone gets some foam, by wiggling the pot while you pour.

SERVES 1

TURKEY

KABAGI TATLISI

Pumpkin with Walnuts

In Turkey, there is a story that Prophet Mohammed ate pumpkin before ascending to heaven, so this dish is usually made on Mirac, his ascension day. In Sicily and Spain, the pumpkin is cooked first in water until tender for 10–15 minutes, drained and then cooked in sugar syrup for about 35 minutes until it forms a jam. It is used as a cake filling. In Sicily the pumpkin might be cooked with jasmine flowers or with a little cinnamon, orange-flower water or rosewater. In Spain this same basic mixture is known as cabello d'angel.

1 small pumpkin or piece of pumpkin, 2 lb (1 kg), peeled, seeded and cut into 1-in (2.5-cm) cubes
⅔–1 cup (5–8 oz/155–250 g) sugar
½ cup (4 fl oz/125 ml) water, or as needed
lemon zest, cinnamon stick or whole cloves (optional)
⅔ cup (2½ oz/75 g) chopped toasted walnuts or almonds
kaymak or clotted cream for serving (see glossary)

❀ Layer the pumpkin pieces in a shallow saucepan, sprinkling the sugar between the layers. Add the water and the lemon zest, cloves or cinnamon stick, if using. Bring to a simmer, cover and cook over low heat until the pumpkin has absorbed almost all the water and is tender, about 30 minutes. Remove from the heat and let cool.

❀ Transfer to a serving dish or individual dishes. Sprinkle with the nuts and serve with *kaymak* (cut into slices) or clotted cream on the side.

SERVES 8

Top to bottom: Quince Compote, Oranges in Fragrant Syrup, Pumpkin with Walnuts

TURKEY

AYVA KOMPOSTOSU

Quince Compote

The seeds of the quinces contribute to the wonderful rosy color of the cooked fruits. So even though you remove the seeds from the fruit for cooking, always add them to the cooking liquids, if you want the quince to turn red. Long simmering is also required for the color to change. If you want to speed up the coloring process, add pomegranate juice to the cooking liquids.

6 quinces, about 2 lb (1 kg) total weight
12 whole cloves
1½ cups (12 oz/375 g) sugar
3 cups (24 fl oz/750 ml) water or part pomegranate juice (see glossary)

❀ Peel the quinces, cut them in half lengthwise and remove the cores and seeds. Tie the peels and seeds in a small piece of cheesecloth (muslin).

❀ Arrange the quince halves hollow side up, in a wide saucepan. Insert a clove in the middle of each quince. Tuck the seed packet among the quinces, then sprinkle with sugar and add the water, or water and pomegranate juice. Bring to a boil, reduce the heat to very low, cover and simmer until the quinces are soft, about 1 hour.

❀ To serve, transfer to individual plates and spoon the syrup over the top. Serve warm or at room temperature.

SERVES 6

TURKEY

PORTOKAL KOMPOSTOSU

Oranges in Fragrant Syrup

A version of this dessert is at home in Turkey, Greece, North Africa and Provence. The oranges are covered in a syrup perfumed with orange-flower water and cinnamon. Serve garnished with just the orange zest in the syrup, or top with toasted almonds or chopped fresh mint.

6 large oranges
1½ cups (12 oz/375 g) sugar
½ cup (4 fl oz/125 ml) water
1 cinnamon stick, about 2 in (5 cm) long
¼ cup (3 oz/90 g) honey
3 tablespoons orange-flower water

❀ Using a vegetable peeler remove the zest from the oranges. Cut away all traces of the bitter white pith. Cut the orange zest into thin, narrow strips. Separate the oranges into segments by carefully cutting between the membranes with a sharp knife. Put the segments into a bowl, cover and refrigerate.

❀ Bring a saucepan three-fourths full of water to a boil. Add the orange zest and boil for 3–5 minutes. Drain and refresh in cold water. Drain again and set aside.

❀ In a saucepan combine the sugar, the water, cinnamon stick and honey and bring to a boil over high heat. Cook briskly until a very thick syrup forms, about 230°F (110°C) on a candy thermometer. Remove from the heat.

❀ Remove and discard the cinnamon stick. Stir in the reserved orange zest and the orange-flower water. Pour the syrup over the orange segments, re-cover and chill for about 4 hours.

❀ To serve, transfer to individual plates. Spoon the syrup with the zest over the top.

SERVES 6

SICILY

Cassata alla Siciliana

Layered Ricotta Cake

The best Italian desserts are arguably found in Sicily. The classic pan di spagna *("Spanish bread"), or sponge cake, is layered with ricotta laced with candied fruits and sometimes shaved chocolate. The assembled* cassata *can be frosted with egg-white icing, a layer of marzipan or chocolate. This* cassata *is not to be confused with* cassata gelata, *a frozen dessert, or* cassata al forno, *a tart filled with the same ricotta mixture. The word* cassata *comes from the Arab* quasat, *which means "round pan" or "bowl." You may find it easier to assemble and serve the* cassata *in a loaf shape, however.*

FOR THE SPONGE CAKE:

6 large eggs
1 cup (8 oz/250 g) sugar
pinch of salt
1 cup (4 oz/125 g) cake flour
pinch of ground cinnamon
1 teaspoon grated orange zest
2 teaspoons vanilla extract (essence)

FOR THE RICOTTA FILLING:

2 cups (1 lb/500 g) ricotta cheese
¼ cup (2 fl oz/60 ml) heavy (double) cream
½ cup (4 oz/125 g) sugar
½ teaspoon ground cinnamon
½ cup (3 oz/75 g) semisweet chocolate bits or chopped chocolate
¼ cup (1 oz/30 g) diced candied fruits such as citron and orange zest

½ cup (4 fl oz/125 ml) sweet Marsala, dark rum, Cointreau or crème de cacao

FOR THE ICING:

¾ lb (375 g) semisweet chocolate, chopped
¾ cup (6 fl oz/180 ml) double-strength brewed coffee
½ cup (¼ lb/125 g) unsalted butter
¼ cup (2 fl oz/60 ml) dark rum or crème de cacao

Preheat an oven to 350°F (180°C). Butter a 10½-by-15½-in (26.5-by-39-cm) jelly roll pan, then line with parchment paper.

To make the cake, in a mixing bowl placed over (not touching) warm water, whisk together the eggs, sugar and salt. Whisk until the sugar is dissolved and the mixture feels warm. Using an electric mixer set on high speed, beat until the mixture is thick and pale and holds a 3-second ribbon when the beater is lifted. Sift together the flour and cinnamon over the batter, then add the orange zest and vanilla and fold until blended.

Pour the batter into the prepared pan. Bake until the cake shrinks away from the sides of the pan and a tester inserted in the center comes out clean, 10–15 minutes. Remove from the oven and cool in the pan.

To make the filling, by hand or with an electric mixer, beat together the ricotta, cream, sugar and cinnamon until light and fluffy. Fold in the chocolate and candied fruits.

To assemble the cassata, line the bottom and sides of a 5-by-9-by-3-in (13-by-23-by-7.5-cm) loaf pan with parchment paper.

Turn the cake out of the pan onto a work surface and peel off the parchment. Cut the cake crosswise into thirds to fit the insides of the loaf pan precisely. Place 1 strip on the bottom of the loaf pan and brush with some of the wine or liqueur. Spread half of the ricotta filling on the cake. Place another strip of cake over the filling, brush with more wine or liqueur and then spread the remaining filling on top. Cover with the third cake strip and brush with the remaining liqueur. Cover with plastic wrap and refrigerate for at least 2 hours, preferably, or for up to 1 day.

Left to right: Layered Ricotta Cake, Lemon Ice

To make the icing, combine the chocolate and coffee in the top pan of a double boiler and heat over simmering water, stirring occasionally, until melted. Remove from the heat and stir in the butter and then the rum or liqueur. Let cool completely, stirring occasionally.

Carefully invert the loaf pan onto a serving platter and lift it off of the cake. Whip the icing until it is fluffy and spread it over the top and sides of the cake. Serve immediately or cover and refrigerate for up to 1 hour, then bring to room temperature before serving.

To serve, bring the cake to room temperature and cut into slices 1 in (2.5 cm) thick.

SERVES 8

SICILY

Granita di Limone

Lemon Ice

Orange or grapefruit juice and zest can be used in place of the lemon. Adjust the sweetness to taste. Berries make a nice garnish.

1 cup (8 fl oz/250 ml) water
1 cup (8 oz/250 g) sugar
pinch of salt
2 cups (16 fl oz/500 ml) strained fresh lemon juice
2 tablespoons grated lemon zest (optional)

In a small saucepan combine the water, sugar and salt. Bring to a simmer over medium heat, stirring until the sugar dissolves. Pour into a shallow metal pan. Cover and place in the freezer until ice crystals begin to form, 2–3 hours, depending upon the freezer.

Break up the crystals with a fork, re-cover and freeze again. Repeat this process every 30 minutes until the mixture is slushy, 2–3 hours.

Spoon the *granita* into dessert bowls and eat promptly before it melts.

SERVES 4–6

TURKEY

EKMEK KADAYİF

Bread and Honey Pudding with Kaymak

If you don't have time to make kaymak *as a garnish for this pudding, use whipped or clotted cream or crème fraîche. This dessert of honey-coated bread is very sweet and rich, but delicious. It needs the cream for relief.*

1 small round loaf white French or Italian bread, unsliced
½ cup (4 fl oz/125 ml) milk
1½ cups (18 oz/560 g) fragrant honey
juice of 2 large lemons (about ½ cup/4 fl oz/125 ml)
kaymak made with 2 cups (16 fl oz/500 ml) heavy (double) cream, sliced (see glossary)

Preheat an oven to 350°F (180°C).

Cut the bread in half horizontally. Remove and discard the crusts. Cut each half into a slice 1½ in (4 cm) thick. Place the 2 bread slices on a baking sheet.

Bake until toasted, golden and almost crisp, 15–20 minutes. Remove from the oven, sprinkle the slices with the milk and then wrap them in a cloth towel until the milk is absorbed, about 5 minutes. Reduce the oven temperature to 300°F (150°C).

In a saucepan combine the honey and lemon juice and bring to a boil. Meanwhile, unwrap the bread slices and place them in a shallow baking dish just large enough to hold them. If you like, cut the bread into 2–3-in (5–7.5-cm) square pieces.

Pour the hot honey mixture evenly over the bread. Bake until the honey is absorbed and the bread is golden, about 30 minutes. Remove from the oven and let rest until warm.

Transfer the warm pudding to individual plates and garnish with the slices of *kaymak* cream. (If the kaymak is not firm enough to slice, it will still be wonderful as thickened cream atop the dessert.) Serve at once.

SERVES 6–8

LEBANON

MUHALLABIA AMARDINE

Amardine Cream

Sheets of dried apricots, or amardine, *are used to make this dessert, but individually dried apricots can be used as well. These dried apricots vary in sweetness, so adjust the sugar to suit your taste. Cornstarch is traditionally used in many Arab recipes, but it is not actually necessary in most cases, so you may omit it here if you like.*

1 lb (500 g) dried apricots or apricot leather
4 cups (32 fl oz/1 l) water, or to cover
1 cup (8 oz/250 g) plus 2 tablespoons sugar, or to taste
2 tablespoons cornstarch (cornflour) dissolved in ¼ cup (2 fl oz/60 ml) water (optional)
1 cup (8 fl oz/250 ml) heavy (double) cream
2 teaspoons orange-flower water
2 teaspoons grated orange zest (optional)
2 tablespoons chopped toasted pistachio nuts

Place the apricots in a bowl and add the water. Let stand overnight.

The next day, transfer the apricots and their soaking water to a saucepan, adding more water if necessary to cover, and bring to a boil. Reduce the heat to medium and simmer until the apricots are very soft, about 30 minutes.

Transfer the apricots and their cooking liquid to a food processor fitted with the metal blade or to a blender and purée. Alternatively, pass the apricots through a food mill or a sieve.

Return the purée to the pan and bring to a simmer. Stir in the 1 cup (8 oz/250 g) sugar and the cornstarch mixture (if using). Simmer, stirring occasionally, until thickened, 2–3 minutes. Transfer to 6 individual serving bowls. Cover and refrigerate.

At serving time, whip the cream with the 2 tablespoons sugar (or more to taste) until soft peaks form and then beat in

Clockwise from left: Bread and Honey Pudding with Kaymak, Amardine Cream, Almond Rice Pudding

the orange-flower water until the peaks are of a medium stiffness. Fold in the orange zest (if using). Place a dollop of cream on each serving. Top with chopped pistachio nuts and serve.

SERVES 6

LEBANON

MAHALLABIA

Almond Rice Pudding

The name means "made with milk." Unlike some rice puddings prepared with cooked rice, this uses ground rice or rice flour. Some recipes add a little cornstarch as a thickening agent. This pudding can be flavored with rosewater or orange-flower water and garnished with toasted coconut, chopped pistachios or almonds, or pomegranate seeds. In Turkey, a tablespoon of ground coffee dissolved in hot water is added to the mixture.

4½ cups (36 fl oz/1.1 l) milk
1 cup (4 oz/125 g) ground blanched almonds
1 cup (8 oz/250 g) sugar
¼ teaspoon freshly grated nutmeg or ground cinnamon
¼ cup (4 oz/125 g) rice flour (see glossary)
2 tablespoons cornstarch (cornflour)
2 tablespoons orange-flower water or rosewater, or to taste
chopped almonds or pistachios (optional)
toasted coconut (optional)
pomegranate seeds (optional; see glossary)

❀ In a 2-qt (2-l) saucepan bring 4 cups (32 fl oz/1 l) of the milk to a boil. Stir in the ground almonds, sugar and nutmeg or cinnamon and remove from the heat. Steep the mixture for 30 minutes.

❀ In a bowl stir together the rice flour and cornstarch. Gradually add the remaining ½ cup (4 fl oz/125 ml) cold milk to the flour mixture, stirring until a smooth paste forms. Bring the sweetened almond milk back to a boil. Add a little of the hot almond milk to the rice flour paste, stirring constantly. Then pour all of the rice flour paste into the saucepan and cook over low heat, stirring very often, until the mixture thickens, 10–15 minutes. Do not allow the mixture to scorch and do not scrape the bottom of the pan.

❀ Stir in the flower water and cook, stirring, for 3–4 minutes longer. Remove from the heat and divide among 6–8 dessert bowls. Cover and refrigerate until cold.

❀ Serve plain or garnish with nuts, coconut or pomegranate seeds.

SERVES 6–8

MOROCCO

M'HENCHA

Coiled Pastry Filled with Almond Paste

*A traditional Moroccan almond dessert. It is shaped like a coiled snake (*m'hencha *means, literally, "the snake") and makes a dramatic presentation.*

FOR THE FILLING:

1½ cups (8 oz/250 g) blanched almonds
1 teaspoon almond extract
¼ cup (2 oz/60 g) unsalted butter, melted
¾ cup (3 oz/90 g) confectioners' (icing) sugar
3–4 tablespoons orange-flower water

Coiled Pastry filled with Almond Paste

1 egg
½ teaspoon ground cinnamon (optional)

12 *filo* sheets (see glossary)
5 tablespoons (2½ oz/75 g) unsalted butter, melted
1 egg, beaten with a little water
confectioner's (icing) sugar
1 teaspoon ground cinnamon

❀ To make the filling, in a food processor fitted with the metal blade, combine all the ingredients. Pulse well to combine. Turn out onto a work surface and knead until it holds together. Divide into 12 equal portions and form each portion into a ball. Cover and chill well.

❀ On a work surface and using the palms of your hands, roll each chilled ball into a log about ½ in (12 mm) in diameter.

❀ Preheat an oven to 350°F (180°C).

❀ Place a *filo* sheet on the work surface and brush with melted butter. Cover with a second sheet and brush with butter. Place 4 logs, end to end, along a long edge of the stack, placing them about 2 in (5 cm) from the edge. Fold the 2-in (5-cm) border over the logs and roll up tightly, tucking in the ends as you do. Repeat with the remaining 10 *filo* sheets and logs, forming 6 rolls in all.

❀ Brush a cake pan or baking sheet with melted butter. Coil one roll in the center of the pan. Continue to coil the rolls, sticking the ends of the rolls together with a little of the beaten egg, so that the rolls join to look like one long coiled snake. Brush the entire pastry with the beaten egg.

❀ Bake until crisp and pale gold, about 30 minutes. Invert onto another pan or baking sheet, return to the oven and crisp on the other side, about 10 minutes longer.

❀ Remove from the oven and invert onto a serving plate. Sprinkle liberally with the sugar. Sprinkle on the cinnamon in lines to form a pattern. Cut into wedges and serve warm or at room temperature.

SERVES 8

GREECE

KYTHONI STO FOURNOU

Baked Quinces Filled with Walnuts

In the fall and winter, quinces are a popular dessert in Greece and throughout the Balkans. Some varieties turn a delightful shade of Venetian red when cooked. If the quince you have are not the variety that turn red, or if you are not cooking them long enough for them to change color, you can cook them with pomegranate juice. If you do not have access to quince, apples can be used for this recipe.

6 large quinces
3 tablespoons butter, at room temperature
½ cup (2 oz/60 g) chopped walnuts
½ cup (4 oz/125 g) sugar
1 teaspoon ground cinnamon
¼ cup (2 fl oz/60 ml) water or pomegranate juice (see glossary)
clotted cream, *kaymak* or thickened plain yogurt for serving (see glossary)

Preheat an oven to 350°F (180°C).

Rub off the fuzz from the quinces and cut them in half lengthwise. Remove the core and seeds. Place in a buttered baking dish, hollow side up.

In a small bowl combine the butter, walnuts, sugar and cinnamon and mix well. Place a spoonful in the center of each quince half. Add the water or pomegranate juice to the pan.

Bake, basting occasionally with the dish juices, until tender, about 30 minutes. Transfer to individual dishes and serve warm or at room temperature with clotted cream, *kaymak* (cut into slices), or thickened yogurt.

SERVES 6

SYRIA

TEEKH MOURABA

Watermelon Preserves

Serve this melon conserve with chicken or roast meat.

1 lb (500 g) watermelon rind
8 cups (64 fl oz/2 l) water
1 tablespoon fresh lime juice or salt
boiling water, to cover
2 cups (1 lb/500 g) sugar
1 lemon, thinly sliced
1 cinnamon stick, about 2 in (5 cm) long

Pare the green from the watermelon rind and trim away the pink edge. Cut into 1-in (2.5-cm) cubes. In a bowl combine 4 cups (32 fl oz/1 l) of the water and the lime or salt. Add the rind and let stand overnight.

The next day, drain well and rinse with cold water. Place in a nonreactive saucepan and add boiling water to cover. Simmer for 15 minutes and then drain. In the same saucepan combine the remaining 4 cups (32 fl oz/1 l) water and the sugar and bring to a boil, stirring to dissolve the sugar. Boil for 5 minutes. Add the rind, lemon slices and cinnamon and boil rapidly over high heat until the rind is translucent, 15–20 minutes. Remove from the heat and let the rind stand in the syrup overnight.

The next day, return the rind and syrup to a boil and ladle into hot, sterilized jars. Seal according to the manufacturer's instructions. Store in a cool, dark place.

MAKES 3 PT (48 FL OZ/1.5 L)

Baked Quinces Filled with Walnuts

Left to right: Orange Brandy, Tomato Preserves, Watermelon Preserves

PROVENCE

CONFITURE DE TOMATES

Tomato Preserves

An unusual preserve that is good with cheese or spread on toast.

2½ lb (1.25 kg) ripe tomatoes, peeled and chopped
2 lb (1 kg) sugar
pinch of salt
zest of 2 lemons, cut into long, narrow strips
½ vanilla bean (optional)
¼ cup (1 oz/30 g) chopped walnuts (optional)

In a nonreactive saucepan combine the tomatoes, sugar and salt. Bring to a boil, stirring often to prevent scorching. Reduce the heat to low and simmer for about 30 minutes. Add the lemon zest and vanilla bean (if using). Continue to simmer until the mixture is very thick and the jell point is reached, 221°–224°F (105°–106°C) on a candy thermometer or until a large spoonful dropped onto a saucer chilled in the freezer sets within 2 minutes. This will take about 15–20 minutes.

If adding the nuts, stir them in at the end. Discard the vanilla bean, if used. Ladle into hot, sterilized jars and seal according to the manufacturer's instructions. Store in a cool, dark place.

MAKES ABOUT 4 PT (64 FL OZ/ 2 L)

PROVENCE

RATAFIA

Orange Brandy

Just the tonic to cure what ails you. This mixture can be prepared months ahead of time and left in a cool, dark place to be sampled on a day when a little malaise strikes.

6 oranges
2 cups (1 lb/500 g) sugar
1 teaspoon ground coriander
¼ teaspoon ground cinnamon
4 cups (32 fl oz/1 l) brandy or Cognac

Wash and dry the oranges well. Using a vegetable peeler, remove the zest (no bitter white pith), then finely chop it. Place in a large mixing bowl. Squeeze the juice from the oranges and add it to the bowl. Add the sugar, coriander, cinnamon and brandy and stir well.

Pour into a large jar or crock and cap with a tight-fitting lid. Let rest in a cool, dark place for 2 months.

Strain through a fine-mesh sieve lined with cheesecloth (muslin) and pour into a clean bottle. Close securely and store in a cool, dark place.

MAKES 4 CUPS (32 FL OZ/1 L)

GREECE

KOURAMBIEDES

Butter Cookies

Even though these rich little shortbread morsels are Christmas cookies, they are served at weddings, birthday parties, baptisms, and other celebrations because they are too good to have only once a year. They are best eaten within a day or so of baking, but they can be made a week ahead and stored in a tightly sealed tin.

1 lb (500 g) unsalted butter
2 egg yolks
3 tablespoons confectioners' (icing) sugar, plus confectioners' sugar for coating
⅛ teaspoon baking soda (sodium bicarbonate)
3 tablespoons fresh orange juice
1½ tablespoons brandy
5 cups (1½ lb/750 g) all-purpose (plain) flour
about 36 whole cloves

Preheat an oven to 350°F (180°C). Line 2 baking sheets with parchment paper.

In a heavy saucepan over low heat, melt the butter. Let it cook for a minute, then transfer it to a bowl and let cool completely. Beat the egg yolks into the cooled butter and then beat in the 3 tablespoons confectioner's sugar. In a cup dissolve the baking soda in the orange juice and brandy and add to the butter mixture. Beat well until very light in color. Gradually add the flour, beating well until a soft dough forms.

On a lightly floured surface, knead the dough until it is soft, smooth and almost silky, about 5 minutes. Roll the dough between your palms into balls 1½ in (4 cm) in diameter. You will have about 3 dozen. Place 1 clove in the center of each ball. Place the cookies, well spaced, on the prepared baking sheets. Bake until pale brown, about 20 minutes. Remove from the baking sheets to wire racks and let the cookies cool a little. They are fragile, so handle with care.

Place a little confectioners' sugar in a shallow bowl. Very gently roll each cookie in the sugar; be generous with the topping.

MAKES ABOUT 3 DOZEN

GREECE

KOPENHAYI

Almond Custard Filo Pastry

This dessert was created to honor King George I of Greece when he began his reign in 1862. He was Danish and this almond-filled filo *pastry was named for Denmark's famed Copenhagen. Some versions of this recipe have a pie crust–type bottom pastry and* filo *only on top. Some cooks grind the almonds; others separate the eggs, beat the yolks into the almond paste mixture and then beat the whites until stiff and fold them into filling.*

FOR THE SYRUP:

2 cups (1 lb/500 g) sugar
1 cup (8 fl oz/250 ml) water
2 tablespoons fresh lemon juice
1 orange zest strip, about 3 in (7.5 cm) long
1 cinnamon stick, about 2 in (5 cm) long

1 lb (500 g) almond paste (see glossary)
½ cup (4 oz/125 g) sugar
8 eggs
2 teaspoons all-purpose (plain) flour
1½ teaspoons baking powder
½ teaspoon ground cinnamon
2 tablespoons brandy (optional)
½ cup (4 oz/125 g) unsalted butter, melted and clarified or skimmed of froth (see glossary)
16 *filo* sheets (see glossary)

To make the syrup, in a heavy saucepan combine the sugar, water, lemon juice, orange zest and cinnamon stick. Bring to a boil over high heat, stirring to dissolve the sugar. Reduce the heat to low and simmer until thickened, about 15 minutes. Remove from the heat and remove and discard the orange zest and cinnamon stick. Cool the syrup completely.

Preheat an oven to 325°F (165°C).

In a bowl with an electric mixer set on medium speed, beat together almond paste and sugar. Beat in the eggs, one at a time, beating well after each addition. Add the flour, baking powder and cinnamon and continue to beat until the mixture is creamy. Beat in the brandy, if using.

Using a wide pastry brush, spread melted butter on the bottom and sides of an 11-by-16-by-2½-in (28-by-40-by-6-cm) baking pan or dish. One by one and brushing each sheet with butter, layer 8 *filo* sheets in the pan. Pour in the almond mixture to cover evenly. Top with the remaining *filo* sheets, again buttering each one. Butter the top layer generously. Using a sharp knife, score the pastry into 16–24 diamond shapes.

Bake until the top is golden, 45–50 minutes. Remove the pastry from the oven and immediately pour the cooled syrup over the hot pastry. Return to the oven for 2–3 minutes, then remove from the oven and let stand for a few hours before serving.

To serve, recut the pastry with a sharp knife.

MAKES 16–24 PIECES

GREECE

FLAOUNES KYPRIOTIKES

Minted Cheese Tart

This interesting cheese tart also appears as a dessert in Spain and as a savory tart in Cyprus (although the Cypriots sometimes add raisins and cinnamon to the mint-scented cheese). Rather than use a soft, fresh cheese like ricotta, in Cyprus they combine haloumi, mizithra *and* kasseri *cheeses (see glossary), and add a little mastic to the crust in place of the yeast.*

FOR THE PASTRY:

2 cups (10 oz/315 g) all-purpose (plain) flour
¼ cup (2 oz/60 g) lard
1 egg
1 tablespoon sugar
1 teaspoon active dry yeast dissolved in ½ cup (4 fl oz/125 ml) milk

FOR THE FILLING:

2 cups (1 lb/500 g) fresh ricotta or cream cheese
1 cup (8 oz/250 g) sugar
4 eggs
¼ cup (2 fl oz/60 ml) Pernod or anise liqueur
12 whole fresh mint leaves
pinch of ground cinnamon (optional)

To make the pastry, combine the flour, lard, egg, sugar and yeast mixture. Turn out onto a floured work surface and knead to form a smooth dough. Cover the dough with a kitchen towel or plastic wrap and let the dough rest for 20 minutes.

Alternatively, in a food processor combine the flour, sugar and lard and pulse once or twice. With the processor on, add the egg and yeast mixture. Process until combined.

On a lightly floured surface, roll out the dough into a round large enough to fit a 10-in (25-cm) tart pan with a removable

Top to bottom: Butter Cookies, Almond Custard Filo Pastry, Minted Cheese Tart

bottom. Transfer the dough round to the pan and ease it into the pan. Trim off the excess dough.

❀ Preheat an oven to 350°F (180°C).

❀ To make the filling, in a bowl with an electric mixer set on medium speed, beat together the cheese, sugar and eggs until creamy. Add the liqueur and beat well. You can chop 2 of the mint leaves and stir them in, if you like, along with the cinnamon (if using).

❀ Pour the cheese mixture into the pastry shell. Arrange the whole mint leaves on top and push them down just a bit. Bake until set at the edge but still quivery in the center, 25–30 minutes. Transfer to a wire rack to cool.

❀ Cut into wedges to serve.

SERVES 8

CATALONIA

SANGRÍA

Wine Punch

Every family has a special recipe for this Spanish wine cooler. Some add brandy or liqueur; others vary the fruit or amount of soda.

1 bottle (3 cups/24 fl oz/750 ml) dry red wine
2 tablespoons brandy or orange-flavored liqueur
2 tablespoons sugar
juice of 1 lemon
juice of 2 oranges
1 lemon, sliced paper-thin
1 orange, sliced paper-thin and slices cut into quarters
3 cups (24 fl oz/750 ml) soda water
8–10 ice cubes

In a large pitcher or bowl, combine the wine, brandy or liqueur, sugar and citrus juices. Add the sliced fruits and steep for several hours in the refrigerator.

Add the soda water and ice and serve.

SERVES 6–8

CATALONIA

PANELLETS

Sweet Potato Cookies

A traditional treat on All Saints' Day, these cookies are most often rolled in pine nuts before baking. Less often a combination of pine nuts and chopped hazelnuts (filberts) is used. They will keep in tightly covered containers at room temperature for about 1 week.

½ lb (250 g) sweet potatoes (2 small or 1 large)
3½ cups (1¼ lb/625 g) almonds, chopped
2 cups (1 lb/500 g) sugar
2 egg yolks
1 teaspoon vanilla extract (essence)
1 tablespoon grated lemon zest
½ cup (2½ oz/75 g) all-purpose (plain) flour
1 cup (5 oz/155 g) pine nuts
1 cup (5 oz/155 g) hazelnuts (filberts), chopped
2 egg whites, beaten until medium-stiff peaks form

Peel the sweet potatoes and cut into chunks. In a saucepan combine the sweet potatoes with water to cover. Bring to a boil and cook until soft, about 15 minutes. Drain well, place in a large bowl and mash. Alternatively, boil the sweet potatoes whole in their skins until soft, about 30 minutes, then peel and mash. Let cool.

Add the almonds, sugar, egg yolks, vanilla and lemon zest to the cooled sweet potatoes and mix well with a wooden spoon to form a smooth dough that looks a bit like mashed potatoes. Knead for a few minutes in the bowl, then cover with a kitchen towel and allow the dough to rest for 30 minutes.

Preheat an oven to 350°F (180°C). Oil 3 large baking sheets.

Combine the pine nuts and hazelnuts in a shallow bowl. Pinch off pieces of dough the size of a walnut and roll each piece between your palms into a ball. Flatten each ball a bit. Brush on all sides with the egg white, then roll in the nuts. Place the cookies, well spaced, on the prepared baking sheets.

Bake until golden, 15–20 minutes. Remove to wire racks to cool.

MAKES ABOUT 4 DOZEN

CATALONIA

CREMA CATALANA

Caramelized Custard

Caramelized custard such as this silky dessert is served in practically every restaurant in Barcelona. It is sometimes called crema de San José, *as it is traditionally served on St. Joseph's Day. Although the custard is usually chilled and then caramelized, the most voluptuous version I can remember was one in which the custard was still a little warm and the topping very crunchy.*

1 tablespoon cornstarch
1 cup (8 fl oz/250 ml) milk
1 cup (8 fl oz/250 ml) half-and-half or heavy (double) cream
3 lemon zest strips, each about 2 in (5 cm) long

Clockwise from top left: Caramelized Custard, Sangría, Sweet Potato Cookies

1 cinnamon stick, about 2 in (5 cm) long
5 or 6 egg yolks
½ cup (4 oz/125 g) granulated sugar
⅓ cup (2½ oz/75 g) brown or ⅓ cup (3 oz/90 g) granulated sugar

❀ In a small bowl dissolve the cornstarch in a few tablespoons of the milk. In a saucepan combine the remaining milk, the cream, lemon zest and cinnamon stick. Place over medium heat and just before it comes to a boil, turn off the heat. Cover and set aside.

❀ In a bowl with an electric mixer, beat together the egg yolks and ½ cup (4 oz/125 g) granulated sugar until pale. Remove and discard the lemon zest from the warm milk. Whisk some of the warm milk into the egg yolks, then whisk the egg yolks into the milk mixture. Add the cornstarch mixture and whisk well. Place the saucepan over low heat and simmer, stirring constantly, until the mixture thickens, about 10 minutes. Strain the mixture through a fine-mesh sieve into a pitcher. Then divide the mixture evenly among six ½-cup (4-fl oz/125-ml) custard cups or shallow earthenware ramekins designed for this dish, or one 3- to 4-cup (24–32 fl oz/750 ml–1 l) ramekin. Cover and refrigerate until cool or chilled.

❀ To caramelize the custard, preheat a broiler (griller). Sprinkle a scant 1 tablespoon brown or granulated sugar over the top of each custard or the ⅓ cup (2½ oz/75 g) over the large custard. Slip it into the broiler and broil (grill) until the sugar melts and is golden. Alternatively, light a small propane torch or heat an iron plate specially designed for caramelizing to red hot over a gas flame and place atop the custard(s) until golden.Serve immediately.

SERVES 6

SICILY

Gelato di Zabaglione

Marsala Ice Cream

What could be more Sicilian than an ice cream made with Marsala? Serve garnished with berries, if desired.

¾ cup (6 fl oz/180 ml) plus 2 tablespoons sweet Marsala
4 cups (32 fl oz/1 l) heavy (double) cream
¾ cup (6 oz/185 g) sugar
pinch of salt
8 egg yolks

❀ Pour the ¾ cup (6 fl oz/180 ml) Marsala into a saucepan and boil until reduced to ¼ cup (2 fl oz/60 ml). Remove from the heat and let cool to room temperature.

❀ In a saucepan over medium heat, combine the cream, sugar and salt. Heat until just hot, stirring to dissolve the sugar; do not boil.

❀ In a bowl lightly whisk the yolks until blended. Whisk in 1 cup (8 fl oz/250 ml) of the hot cream, then whisk the egg mixture into the hot cream in the saucepan. Cook over medium heat, stirring constantly, until the mixture thickly coats a spoon, 3–5 minutes; do not boil.

❀ Pour the cream mixture through a fine-mesh sieve into a mixing bowl. Nest the bowl in another bowl filled with ice so the mixture cools down quickly. Stir in the reduced Marsala. Cover and chill well.

❀ Stir the remaining 2 tablespoons Marsala into the chilled cream. Pour into an ice cream maker and freeze according to the manufacturer's instructions.

MAKES 1 QT (1 L)

SICILY

Gelato di Pistacchio

Pistachio Ice Cream

Sicily is known for fabulous ice cream and this is one of the island's best. Don't be disappointed if your ice cream is not the bright green color that one associates with commercial pistachio ice cream. The color is added artificially.

2½ cups (10 oz/315 g) pistachios
3½ cups (28 fl oz/875 ml) heavy (double) cream

Left to right: Coffee Ice, Apricot Ice Cream, Pistachio Ice Cream, Marsala Ice Cream

1½ cups (12 fl oz/375 ml) milk
1 cup (8 oz/250 g) sugar
7 egg yolks

❀ Preheat an oven to 350°F (180°C). Spread the nuts on a baking sheet and toast until fragrant, 6–8 minutes. Transfer to a food processor fitted with the metal blade and process to chop coarsely. Or chop by hand. Set aside.
❀ In a large saucepan combine the cream and milk and heat to boiling. Add all but ½ cup (2 oz/60 g) of the nuts and let steep for 2 hours.
❀ Line a sieve with cheesecloth (muslin) and strain the cream through it into a bowl, pressing on nuts to extract as much flavor as possible. Return the cream to the saucepan with ½ cup (4 oz/125 g) of the sugar and bring to a boil, stirring to dissolve the sugar.
❀ In a bowl whisk together the egg yolks and the remaining ½ cup (4 oz/125 g) sugar until combined. Whisk in 1 cup (8 fl oz/250 ml) of the hot cream, then whisk the egg mixture into the hot cream in the saucepan. Cook over medium heat, stirring constantly, until the mixture thickly coats a spoon, 3–5 minutes; do not boil.
❀ Pour the cream mixture through a fine-mesh sieve into a mixing bowl. Nest the bowl in another bowl filled with ice so the mixture cools down quickly. Then cover and refrigerate overnight.
❀ Pour into an ice cream maker and freeze according to the manufacturer's instructions. Fold in the reserved nuts just before the ice cream is set.

MAKES 1 QT (1 L)

SYRIA

Dondurma Mish Mish

Apricot Ice Cream

Fruit-flavored ice creams are popular in the Middle East. If sahleb *is not in your pantry, use cornstarch.*

½ lb (250 g) apricots
2 teaspoons grated orange zest (optional)
1 teaspoon *sahleb* (see glossary) or 1½ tablespoons cornstarch (cornflour)
2 cups (16 fl oz/500 ml) milk
1 cup (8 fl oz/250 ml) light (single) cream
⅔ cup (5 oz/155 g) sugar
2 teaspoons rosewater or orange-flower water

❀ Bring a saucepan three-fourths full of water to a boil. Add the apricots and blanch for about one minute. Drain and, when cool enough to handle, peel, pit and slice. Place in a food processor fitted with the metal blade or in a blender. Add the orange zest (if using) and purée until smooth.
❀ Dissolve the *sahleb* or cornstarch in a little of the milk and set aside.
❀ In a saucepan combine the remaining milk, the cream and sugar. Bring slowly to a boil over medium heat, stirring until the sugar dissolves. Add the apricot purée and *sahleb* or cornstarch mixture. Cook over low heat, stirring, until mixture thickens enough to coat the back of a spoon, about 3 minutes. Remove from the heat, stir in the flower water and beat with a spoon until thickened. Let cool.
❀ Pour into an ice cream maker and freeze according to the manufacturer's instructions.

MAKES 1 QT (1 L)

SICILY

Granita di Caffè

Coffee Ice

A granita *is a refreshing alternative to ice cream during hot weather.*

½–¾ cup (4–6 oz/125–185 g) sugar
3 cups (24 fl oz/750 ml) hot, strong brewed espresso
1½ cups (12 fl oz/375 ml) heavy (double) cream
3 tablespoons sugar
2 teaspoons ground cinnamon (optional)

❀ Stir the sugar into the hot espresso until it dissolves. Pour into a shallow metal pan. Cover and place in the freezer until ice crystals begin to form, 2–3 hours, depending upon the freezer.
❀ Break up the crystals with a fork, re-cover and freeze again. Repeat this process every 30 minutes until the mixture is slushy, 2–3 hours.
❀ Pour the cream into a bowl and beat until thick. Add the sugar and cinnamon (if using) and beat until soft peaks form. Place a dollop of cream on the bottom of each of 4–6 dessert glasses. Divide the *granita* evenly among the dishes. Top with the remaining cream. Eat at once before it melts!

SERVES 4–6

Left to right: Fig Conserve, Quince Preserves

TURKEY

AYVA REÇELI

Quince Preserves

Great spread on bread or as a cookie filling.

2 lb (1 kg) quinces
3 whole cloves (optional)
1 cinnamon stick, about 2 in (5 cm) long (optional)
4 cups (32 fl oz/1 l) water
4 cups (2 lb/1 kg) sugar
¼ cup (2 fl oz/60 ml) fresh lemon juice
¼ cup (2 fl oz/60 ml) rosewater (optional)

Peel and core the quinces, then grate them and place in a nonreactive saucepan. Tie the peel and seeds of the quince and the cloves and cinnamon stick, if using, in a piece of cheesecloth (muslin) and add to the pan. Add cold water to cover. Bring to a boil and boil until tender, about 30 minutes. Pour through a sieve, collecting the liquid in a pitcher or bowl; reserve the quinces and cloth bag. Measure the liquid and add hot water, if necessary, to measure 1¾ cups (14 fl oz/440 ml).

Pour the liquid into a saucepan, bring to a boil and boil for 2 minutes. Add the reserved quinces and cloth bag and boil, uncovered, for 5 minutes. Remove from the heat and let stand until the mixture turns pink, about 3 hours.

Bring to a boil again, add the lemon juice and cook until the jell point is reached, 221°–224°F (105°–106°C) on a candy thermometer or until a large spoonful dropped onto a saucer chilled in the freezer sets within 2 minutes. This will take 20–30 minutes.

Discard the cloth bag. Stir in the rosewater, if desired. Ladle into hot, sterilized jars and seal according to manufacturer's instructions. Store in a cool, dark place.

MAKES 4 PT (64 FL OZ/2 L)

PROVENCE

CONFITURE DE FIGUES

Fig Conserve

Great on walnut bread or any kind of toast. This is the taste of summer.

4 cups (2 lb/1 kg) sugar
2 cups (16 fl oz/500 ml) water
grated zest of 1 lemon
2½–3 lb (1.25–1.5 kg) figs, peeled, stemmed and quartered
½ vanilla bean (optional)
1 teaspoon aniseeds or fennel seeds (optional)
1 cinnamon stick, about 2 in (5 cm) long (optional)
2 whole cloves (optional)
¼ cup (2 fl oz/60 ml) fresh lemon juice

In a large nonreactive saucepan combine the sugar and water. Slowly bring to a boil, stirring until sugar is dissolved. Remove from the heat and add the lemon zest and figs. Tie the seeds, cinnamon sticks and/or cloves, if using, in a piece of cheesecloth (muslin) and add to the pan. Let stand at room temperature for a few hours or overnight.

Bring the fig mixture to a boil. Reduce the heat to medium and simmer until thickened to a jam consistency, or until a candy thermometer reads 221°–224°F (105°–106°C). Alternatively, drop a large spoonful onto a saucer chilled in the freezer; it should set with in 2 minutes. This simmering process should take about 2 hours. Add the lemon juice during the last 30 minutes of cooking.

Discard the cloth bag. Ladle into hot, sterilized jars and seal according to the manufacturer's instructions.

MAKES ABOUT 3½ PT (56 FL OZ/1.75 ML)

ALGERIA

ACIR

Citrus Drinks

Very refreshing on a hot day. The juice infusions can be made ahead of time and the chilled mineral water added when served.

FOR THE LEMON-GRAPEFRUIT DRINK *(acir el qaress):*

juice of 6 large lemons
juice of 1 grapefruit
⅔ cup (5 oz/155 g) sugar

FOR THE ORANGE-LEMON-GRAPEFRUIT DRINK *(acir tchina):*

juice of 1 orange
juice of 1 lemon
juice of 1 grapefruit
½ cup (4 oz/125 g) sugar
1 orange, peeled and thinly sliced

ice cubes
3 cups (24 fl oz/750 ml) mineral water

Select one of the drinks to make. Both the drinks are made the same way: Combine the juices and sugar in a pitcher and stir to dissolve the sugar. For the orange-lemon-grapefruit drink, add the orange slices to the juice mixture.

Fill 3 or 4 tall glasses with ice and pour one-third or one-fourth of the infusion into each glass. Top off with mineral water and serve.

EACH DRINK SERVES 3 OR 4

Citrus Drinks

S Y R I A

MA'MOUL

Stuffed Butter Cookies

These Syrian Easter cookies are easy to prepare once you master folding the dough around the filling. They can be stuffed with a date or a nut filling. Choose the filling that appeals to you. Store in an airtight tin at room temperature for up to 1 week.

FOR THE DATE FILLING:

1 lb (500 g) pitted dates, chopped
½ cup (4 fl oz/125 ml) water
grated zest of 1 orange
½ teaspoon ground cinnamon

FOR THE NUT FILLING:

2 cups (8 oz/250 g) chopped walnuts, almonds or pistachios
1 cup (8 oz/250 g) granulated sugar, or to taste
1 tablespoon rosewater
2 teaspoons ground cinnamon

1 cup (½ lb/250 g) unsalted butter, at room temperature
2 tablespoons granulated sugar
2 cups (8 oz/250 g) sifted all-purpose (plain) flour
1 tablespoon rosewater or orange-flower water
2–4 tablespoons milk or water
sifted confectioners' (icing) sugar

Choose either the date or the nut filling. To make the date filling, in a saucepan combine the dates and the water and bring to a boil. Reduce the heat to low and simmer, uncovered, stirring occasionally, until the dates form a paste, about 5 minutes. Stir in the orange zest and cinnamon. To make the nut filling, in a bowl stir together all the ingredients.

Cookie platter: (outside ring) Stuffed Butter Cookie, (inside) Almond Cookies, Mint Tea

❀ Preheat an oven to 300°F (150°C).
❀ In a bowl and using an electric mixer, beat together the butter and granulated sugar until light and fluffy. Beat in the flour and then beat in the milk and flower water. Knead in the bowl until the dough holds together and is easy to shape.
❀ Pinch off a walnut-size piece of dough. Roll it between your palms into a ball and hollow it out with your thumb. Pinch the sides up to form a pot shape. Place a spoonful of filling into the hollow, then pinch the dough closed over the filling. Press and then score the sealed edge, if desired.
❀ Place the filled balls on an ungreased baking sheet. Bake until firm and fully set, about 20 minutes; do not brown. Carefully transfer the cookies to wire racks. Sprinkle them generously with confectioners' sugar while still warm, then cool completely.

MAKES ABOUT 2½ DOZEN

ALGERIA

MAKROUD EL LOUSE

Almond Cookies

To grind nuts without making them oily or pasty, place them, in batches, in a food processor or blender with the sugar. These cookies are sweet and chewy and can be made a week ahead of time and kept in a covered container.

1¼ lb (625 g) blanched almonds, finely ground (about 3 cups)
1¼ cups (10 oz/315 g) granulated sugar
1 tablespoon grated lemon zest
2 eggs
all-purpose (plain) flour for dusting
1 cup (8 fl oz/250 ml) water
1 tablespoon orange-flower water
2 cups (8 oz/250 g) confectioners' (icing) sugar

❀ Preheat an oven to 350°F (180°C). Line 2 large baking sheets with parchment paper or leave ungreased.
❀ In a large bowl combine the almonds, 1 cup (8 oz/250 g) of the granulated sugar and the lemon zest and stir to mix. Make a well in the center and add the eggs to the well. Gradually mix the dry ingredients into the wet ingredients. Continue to mix until a smooth dough forms.
❀ Divide the dough in half. On a heavily floured surface and using floured palms, roll each half into a log about 18 in (45 cm) long and 1½ in (4 cm) in diameter. Flatten the log into an oblong about 1½ in (4 cm) thick and 2 in (5 cm) wide. Cut on the diagonal into slices 1½ in (4 cm) thick. Dust the slices with flour and place on the prepared baking sheets about 1 in (2.5 cm) apart. Bake until pale gold, about 15 minutes. Transfer to wire racks to cool.
❀ In a saucepan combine the remaining ¼ cup (2 oz/60 g) granulated sugar and the water. Bring to a boil over high heat, stirring until the sugar dissolves. Cook over high heat, uncovered, until a thin syrup forms. Pour into a shallow bowl and let cool. Stir the flower water into the cooled syrup.
❀ Spread the confectioner's sugar in a shallow pan. Dip the cooled cookies first in the syrup and then in the sugar. Set on a rack to dry.

MAKES ABOUT 6 DOZEN

MOROCCO

CHAY

Mint Tea

The drama of tea service is most important here. The tea is poured into glasses from high in the air, to aerate the tea on its way to the vessel and thereby heighten its flavor.

2 tablespoons green tea
6 tablespoons (3 oz/90 g) sugar
1 large handful stemmed fresh mint leaves
6 cups (48 fl oz/1.5 l) water, boiling
a few orange zest strips or 1 teaspoon orange-flower water (optional)

❀ Place the tea on the bottom of a teapot. Top with the sugar, then the mint leaves and finally the orange zest strips or flower water. Holding the kettle about 1 ft (30 cm) above the teapot, pour in the boiling water. Stir well and then let steep for 10–15 minutes.
❀ Pour out 1 glass of tea, then pour it back into the pot, again to aerate it. To aerate the tea further, again pour the tea into the glasses from about 1 ft (30 cm) above them. Serve hot.

SERVES 6

GLOSSARY

ALI-OLI
Sometimes written *aioli*. Spanish version of French aioli, a garlic-infused mayonnaise.

ALMOND
White oval nut used throughout the Mediterranean as both an ingredient and a garnish. Sold whole, slivered or sliced; blanched or unblanched; or even still in its beige pitted shell.

ALMOND PASTE
Made from ground blanched almonds, sugar and a little glycerine or a similar ingredient, to keep it malleable, almond paste is sweeter and coarser than its close relative marzipan. Sometimes almond extract is added to intensify its flavor. Used mainly for pastries; in Morocco used as a stuffing for fish.

AVGOLEMONO
Egg-and-lemon mixture used in Greek cooking. In its thin form, it is added to soups and stews and served spooned over stuffed grapeleaves (recipe on page 61). In its thick form, it accompanies meat-filled zucchini or other stuffed vegetables. To make a thin *avgolemono,* beat 2 or 3 whole eggs or 3 egg yolks with 4–5 tablespoons (about 2 fl oz/ 60 ml) fresh lemon juice. Gradually add 1 cup (8 fl oz/ 250 ml) stock from the dish being cooked and whisk constantly. Heat, stirring constantly, until warmed through and thickened, or stir into the soup or stew you are flavoring and stir until thoroughly combined and heated through. Alternatively, beat 3 egg whites until stiff, and then fold the yolk–lemon juice mixture into the whites before adding the stock. To make a thick sauce, melt 2 tablespoons unsalted butter in a saucepan over medium heat. Whisk in 2 tablespoons all-purpose (plain) flour until smooth and cook, stirring, a couple minutes. Gradually add 2 cups (16 fl oz/500 ml) boiling stock and continue whisking until it comes back to a boil. Reduce the heat to low. In a small bowl, beat together 3 whole eggs or egg yolks and 4–5 tablespoons (about 2 fl oz/60 ml) fresh lemon juice. Slowly add a little of the hot sauce to the egg mixture, whisking well, then stir the mixture into the pan. Whisk constantly until heated through but do not boil.

BOUQUET GARNI
A neatly tied bundle of herbs and other seasonings that is added to soups, stews and other dishes to impart flavoring, and is easily removed after cooking. The contents of a bouquet garni varies with the dish being cooked.

BRIK
Tunisian deep-fried savory pastry. Filled with cooked meat, poultry or fish and usually a whole egg.

BRIOUAT
Moroccan pastry made from *ouarka* (q. v.), which is both savory or sweet. It is either filled with meat, poultry, seafood or nuts, baked until crisp and golden and then dipped in honey.

BULGUR
Also known as burghul. Hulled wheat that has been steamed until partially cooked, then dried and ground. Sold in fine, medium and coarse grinds. Recipes usually specify which grade should be used. For example, tabbouleh requires fine bulgur. The flavor is nutty and the texture somewhat crunchy. Available in shops specializing in Middle Eastern foods and in natural-foods stores that sell whole grains in bulk.

BUTIFARRA
A white pork sausage from Catalonia spiced with cinnamon, nutmeg and cloves. Italian sweet sausage can be used as a substitute.

CACIOCAVALLO
A southern Italian cheese that originated in Campania but is now also made in Sicily. Its name means "cheese on horseback;" it comes from the fact that the cheese is dried by hanging it in pairs astride a horizontal pole, which makes it appear as if it is hung over a saddle. It also is formed into horse shapes in Palermo and Apulia. This pale yellow cow's milk cheese can be eaten fresh or aged. It is sometimes smoked as well.

CAPERS
The buds of a Mediterranean bush, prepared by pickling in brine or packing in salt. (Sometimes the leaves are pickled as well.) Harvested in early summer, the buds are cleaned and sun-dried before preserving. They take about 1 month to cure and can be stored for about 1 year. Rinse before using to remove excess brine or salt. Buy small imported capers for the finest flavor.

CHORIZO
Spanish cured pork sausage heavily flavored with paprika and garlic. Unlike Latin American versions, Spanish chorizo is mild rather than hot. It is used as an ingredient in cooking and is eaten as a cold cut.

CLARIFIED BUTTER
Unsalted butter that has been slowly melted, thereby separating the milk solids (which sink to the bottom of the pan) and water from the butter itself. The white foam is skimmed off from the top, and the golden, clear liquid is carefully poured off into another container; the milk solids on the pan bottom are then discarded. Clarified butter has a higher smoking point than regular butter and is ideal for sautéing, as the milk solids that cause the butter to burn have been eliminated. It will keep longer in the refrigerator than regular butter because the milk solids promote rancidity. *Smen* (q.v.) and *samneh* are related.

CLOTTED CREAM
A specialty of Devonshire, England, made by gently heating rich unpasteurized milk until a semisolid layer of cream forms on the top. After cooling, the thick cream is removed. It can be stored in the refrigerator for about 4 days and is similar in texture to *crème fraîche,* but not tangy or nutty in taste. Used as a topping for desserts, especially in place of the traditional Turkish *kaymak* (q.v.).

COGNAC
A fine brandy from the region of Cognac in France that is double distilled and aged in Limousin oak for at least 3 years.

COUSCOUS
Staple starch of North African cuisine, couscous is a tiny pastalike pellet made from semolina flour and salted water. It is available prepackaged in boxes labeled by grain size (moyen, or medium, is most common) and most of it is of the instant variety. Traditionally steamed in the top perforated pan of a *couscousière,* over a lower pan holding

simmering stew or water. It can also be prepared in a regular saucepan or baking dish by pouring the hot liquid over the grains, about 1½ cups (12 fl oz/375 ml) liquid to 1 cup (5 oz/155 g) couscous.

CUMIN
Tiny yellow-brown seeds with a pungent, spicy taste. Commonly available already ground, although for fullest aroma it is best to grind them just before using. They can be easily reduced to a powder in a spice mill or a blender.

CURRANTS see *Raisins, currants*

FETA
Originally a Greek cheese, feta is a soft, crumbly white cheese made from goat or sheep's milk. Feta is now made in many other countries, such as France, Israel, Bulgaria and Romania. Firmer fetas are made from cow's milk and can be used in salads or appetizers. To keep feta for a long time, be sure it remains covered with salted whey or the original brine, in a refrigerated container.

FAVA BEAN
Also known as broad bean. When very young, the whole beans, pods and all, are eaten. When mature, the fresh beans are shelled. The beans themselves have a tough skin that should be removed before cooking. Dried favas range in color from green to purplish brown; they are commonly available already peeled. A variety of small fava bean is used in Egyptian *ful mudammas* (recipe on page 214).

FILO
Also spelled phyllo; means "leaf" in Greek. Paper-thin dough sheets used in Greek, Turkish and Middle Eastern sweet and savory preparations such as baklava, *spanokopitta,* borek and so on. Can be used as a substitute for *ouarka* (q.v.) and *malsouqua,* respectively the Moroccan and Tunisian paper-thin dough used in such pastries as *b'stilla, brik* and *briouat.* Can be purchased fresh or frozen; if frozen, thaw in the refrigerator. *Filo* dries out easily, so it must be kept covered well when not using.

HALOUMI
Salty sheep's milk cheese with a stringlike consistency. Made in Cyprus, where it is flavored with mint, and in Lebanon, where black cumin is added.

HARISSA
North African hot sauce made from chili pepper and cumin. Can be purchased in tubes or jars. Tunisian *harissa* may have caraway and coriander added. To make *harissa,* combine 1½ tablespoons cayenne, ¼ cup (2 oz/60 g) ground cumin and ½ cup (4 fl oz/125 ml) olive oil in a mortar and grind with a pestle until a paste forms. Add a little salt to taste and up to 2 teaspoons ground caraway.

HAZELNUT
Also called filberts. Rich-flavored pale yellow nut covered by brown skin and a hard shell. To remove the skins, shell the nuts and then toast in a 350°F (180°C) oven for 7–10 minutes, or until the skin begins to flake, then wrap in a kitchen towel and rub vigorously while the nut is warm to remove as much of the skin as possible.

KASSERI
Hard Greek sheep's milk cheese, with a few scattered tiny holes. Popular as a table cheese, or it can be cooked in butter or olive oil and served with lemon wedges (see *saganaki* on page 48).

KAYMAK
Turkish thickened cream, also known as *eishta,* used principally for desserts. It is cooked until it is so thick that it sets up firmly enough to be rolled and sliced. To make *kaymak,* pour 2 cups (16 fl oz/500 ml) heavy (double) cream into a wide, deep saucepan and place over low heat. Bring just to a boil, then cook over low heat, stirring often, for about 1½ hours. Every now and again, lift out some of the cream with a ladle and then pour it back into the pan. The cream has thickened sufficiently when the bubbles that form are large. Pour the cream into a shallow pan, cover lightly and let stand in a warm place for 2–6 hours, then refrigerate for 6–8 hours until fully set. To unmold, run the point of a knife around the edges of the cream to loosen it and invert onto a large plate or flat baking sheet. At serving time, roll up the cream into a cylinder and slice crosswise into pieces about 1 in (2.5 cm) wide or simply cut as desired. If the cream does not set up completely, it can be scooped out with a spoon for serving. Clotted cream (q.v.) or French *crème fraîche* can be used in place of *kaymak.*

KEFALOTIRI
A common Greek grating cheese. Hard and yellow, it is made from unpasteurized sheep or goat's milk. The fresh (8 months old) cheese can be eaten as a table cheese.

KIBBEE
Arabic mixture of pounded lamb and bulgur (q.v.). Can be served raw, baked or fried (recipe on page 182).

MARSALA
Wine first made by John Woodhouse in 1773 for the English, who loved such fortified wines. Production centers in the town of Marsala and neighboring towns in western Sicily. Marsala can be sweet or dry and is about 18 percent alcohol.

MASTIC
This resin extracted from a small evergreen acacia tree has long been used as a chewing gum. It is powdered and added to sweet yeast breads, milk puddings and ice cream for flavoring. Available in shops specializing in Greek and Middle Eastern foods.

MELOKHIA
Edible green leaf of the hibiscus family, related to okra, it gives off a similar viscous and gluey liquid, but its taste is more like spinach or sorrel. Used to make a classic Egyptian soup (recipe on page 111) and can be purchased dried in stores that specialize in Middle Eastern foods.

MERGUEZ
A North African sausage, quite spicy, made with lamb or beef (recipe on page 182).

MIZITHRA
A Greek soft-curd "cottage" cheese made from the whey that remains from the making of a feta cheese (q.v.). Fresh ricotta is substituted as *mizithra* is not exported.

MORTADELLA
A popular Italian sausage. It has a distinctive pattern that is achieved by the mixing of finely ground (minced) pork with coarsely diced pork fat. The slowly cooked sausage, which usually measures 6 in (15 cm) in diameter, is a popular sandwich meat or stuffing for pasta and meat dishes.

MOZZARELLA
A rindless, white southern Italian cheese traditionally made from the milk of the water buffalo, but now commonly made from cow's milk.

OLIVES
Green and black cured olives are popular throughout the Mediterranean (recipe on page 41). There are many different varieties and ways to flavor them. Among the most common types are niçoise, small brownish black Provençal brine-cured olives packed in olive oil; Kalamata, brine-cured black Greek olives packed in vinegar; Gaeta, small salt-cured Italian black olives; and dark green cracked olives popular in Provence and Greece.

OLIVE OIL
Fundamental to the cooking of all the Mediterranean countries. Olive oil is labeled according to different grades, which are based on acidity. The best olive oils are called extra-virgin, first cold pressing. Other grades include superfine, fine, virgin and pure. Extra-virgin oils lose their bouquet when cooked; use them for cold dishes or add them at the end of cooking. Mild olive oils are suitable for sautéing.

ORANGE FLOWER WATER
A fragrant liquid distilled from orange blossoms used for flavoring syrups and pastries. Available at stores that specialize in Middle Eastern foods and in gourmet sections of fine food stores. Because of its intense flavor, add it judiciously.

OUARKA
Paper-thin leaves of semolina pastry used in Moroccan cuisine to make *b'stilla, briouat* and *brik*. Known as *malsouqua* in Tunisia. *Filo* (q.v.) or Chinese spring roll wrappers can be used as a substitute.

PANCETTA
Italian cured pig belly, the same cut used to make bacon. Most often rolled into a sausagelike shape, but sometimes available flat. Flavored with cloves and black pepper, it is cured for at least 20 days. Occasionally available smoked.

PECORINO CHEESE
One of Italy's best-known sheep's milk cheeses. It is served fresh (2 weeks old) as a slightly salty table cheese, or aged as a grating cheese. The most popular varieties are from Rome *(pecorino romano)* and Sardinia *(pecorino sardo)*.

PEPPERS
Both chili peppers and sweet peppers (capsicums) are used in Mediterranean cooking. Among the fresh chilies used is a long, dark green hot pepper that is wider at the stem end and tapers to a point, and the cayenne, a small, thin pepper that is commonly dried and ground. To roast and peel fresh peppers, place the peppers directly over a gas flame on the stove top, under a preheated broiler (griller) or atop a charcoal fire and, turning as needed, blacken evenly on all sides. Transfer to a closed paper bag and let sweat for 10–15 minutes, then peel away the blackened skin. Remove the stem, seeds and ribs and cut as directed in individual recipes.

PICADA
Unique to Catalonia, this paste or finely minced mixture of garlic, saffron, fried bread, nuts and occasionally unsweetened chocolate is used as a thickening agent and is added to soups, stews and so on, usually at the end of cooking.

PINE NUT
The long, thin nut of the stone pine tree. Used in many dishes both sweet and savory, throughout the Mediterranean. An Asian variety of pine nut is sometimes stronger in flavor and not as desirable for use in Mediterranean dishes.

PISTACHIO NUT
Native to the Middle East, the pistachio nut is enclosed in a light brown shell that is easily opened. The nut itself is covered by a brown papery skin and it has green flesh. Used in both sweet and savory dishes.

POMEGRANATE JUICE AND SEEDS
Juice and seeds of an ancient fruit of the Middle East that is a symbol of fertility and abundance. The fruits are sold in specialty markets and keep well for months in a cool, dry place if not picked too ripe. The pomegranate is enjoyed as a fruit, and the sweet-tart juice extracted from its seeds is used for syrups, sherbets and in drinks. The juice is also available in bottles in Middle East shops. The seeds also are used as a garnish for soups, puddings and so on, and can be frozen.

POMEGRANATE SYRUP
A bottled concentrate made from pomegranate juice. To dilute the syrup to make juice, add about 1½ tablespoons syrup to 1 cup (8 fl oz/250 ml) of water.

PORCINI
Large, wild mushrooms (Boletus edulus), known as *cèpes* in France and *steinpilz* in Germany, prized for their meaty texture and woodsy flavor. They have two seasons, early spring and fall. When fresh, they are commonly grilled whole or sliced and sautéed. They are also one of the best mushrooms for drying, and are widely available in this form year-round. To use dried porcini, rinse well to remove surface dirt, cover with hot water and soak for 1 hour. Strain the soaking liquid through a cheesecloth-lined sieve to remove any dirt or sediment; reserve the liquid for cooking, as it is quite tasty.

PRESERVED LEMONS
An important condiment in Moroccan cooking. To make at home, scrub 16 lemons (about 4 lb/2 kg) with a stiff-bristled brush and place in a nonreactive container. Add cold water to cover and let stand for 3 days, changing the water at least once a day. Drain the lemons, then, using a sharp knife, slice lengthwise but leave attached at the top and bottom. Push 1 tablespoon coarse salt into the center of each lemon. Then place 1 tablespoon coarse salt in the bottom of several small sterilized jars. (Small jars are best to use because the lemons do not keep long once the jars are opened.) Pack the salted lemons tightly into the jars, add fresh lemon juice to cover and tightly seal the jars. (Some cooks add boiling water in addition to the lemon juice, but plain lemon juice is best.) Store in a cool, dry place for 3–4 weeks before using. Turn the jars occasionally during this period and do not be alarmed if a white film forms on the lemons; it will wash off and will not affect the flavor. Once the jars are opened, be careful not to get any oil in them or touch the lemon you are removing with a greasy spoon, as you will spoil the remaining lemons in the jar. Refrigerate after opening. To use the lemons, rinse well under running water. Squeeze out the juice and remove the pulp; discard the juice and pulp. Cut the peel as directed in individual recipes.

PROSCIUTTO
Raw salt-cured ham that has been aged to produce moist, lightly veined, intense pink meat with an edge of fat.

PROVOLONE
Southern Italian cheese made with cow's milk. Available in a variety of shapes and sizes—round, oval, pear shaped, cylindrical. Young provolone is sweet; strong provolone has been aged for up to 1 year. Available smoked as well.

PURSLANE
Wild green with reddish stalks used as a salad ingredient for the *fattoush* (recipe on page 45) of Syria and Lebanon and in salads in Greece and other nearby countries. Discard the stalks before using the tender, fleshy leaves.

RAISINS, CURRANTS
Dried fruits used extensively in Mediterranean cooking. They can be added directly to stews if they will have time to simmer in liquids and soften. If not, plump them in hot water to cover (or wine, if specified in the recipe) for about 30 minutes, then drain. If you like, reserve the soaking liquid for adding to the dish.

RAS EL HANOUT
Commonly used in meat and game dishes, this Moroccan spice mixture translates as "top of the shop." Usually includes ginger, peppercorns, cinnamon, allspice, cloves, cardamom, black cumin, aniseed, coriander, cayenne, ginger or galingal, lavender, mace or nutmeg and turmeric, as well as such exotics as belladonna, cantharides, rosebuds and so on. Many of these exotic spices are reputed to be aphrodisiacs. Available in shops specializing in North African foods.

RICE
Rice, both short grain and long grain, is widely used in Mediterranean cooking. In Italy four different kinds of rice are grown: *ordinario,* a very short round rice used for puddings; *semifino,* a round grain of medium length used for soups and salads; *fino,* a round longer grain rice used for risotto; and *superfino,* a fat longer grain rice that is ideal for risotto. The best varieties of superfino are Arborio and Carnaroli. These are cooked uncovered and the liquids are added gradually. In Spain most of the rice is cultivated in the province of Valencia and it is a short-grain variety. It is cooked uncovered, all the liquid is added at once and the rice is usually finished off the heat. The rice is used in paella and other rice-based dishes, as well as in soups, salads and so on.

Although some short grain rice is used in the Middle East for puddings, the majority of rice is of the long-grain variety. Its grains are fluffy but firm and separate. The best and most fragrant is basmati ("queen of fragrance"), which is aged to reduce its moisture content. This thin, long rice can be found in markets that specialize in Indian and Middle Eastern foods. In the Middle East rice is usually soaked before cooking and is always cooked covered. In Syria the water is salted and brought to a boil and the drained rice is added; butter or oil is added after the rice is cooked. In Lebanon the butter or oil is added to the cooking water. In Egypt the rice is sautéed in butter or oil, and then the water and salt are added. In all cases the rice boils hard for 2 minutes, the heat is reduced to a simmer and the pan is tightly covered. The rice cooks for about 20 minutes or until small holes appear on the top. Then the heat is turned off and the rice rests for 10 minutes before serving.

RICE FLOUR
A powdery flour made from white rice used in baked goods.

RICOTTA
The name means "recooked," the cheese is made by heating the whey of another cooked cheese like mozzarella or provolone. Soft, white mildly sweet and a little grainy but creamy in texture, ricotta is used in desserts such as *cannoli* and *cassata,* and in fillings for ravioli and other filled pastas. Aged, salted ricotta is a specialty of Sicily. There are also smoked ricottas.

ROMESCO
Also spelled *romescu.* Catalan olive oil–based sauce seasoned with hot pepper, almonds, garlic and tomato. Served with shellfish, meat, grilled leeks.

ROSE WATER
Distilled from fragrant rose petals and used as a flavoring for desserts and syrups. It can be very powerful, so use with caution.

SAFFRON
Saffron, the Arab word for "yellow," is the golden yellow stamens of a purple crocus flower and the world's most high-priced spice. The use of saffron originated in Asia Minor, but most of the best saffron now comes from Spain. Do not be fooled by cheap imitations, which are often crushed marigold petals or turmeric. Available in powdered and in thread form; the latter is preferred. To use the threads, pound in a mortar and steep in warm liquid to bring out the flavor.

SAHLEB
A beige powder made from the dried tubers of a species of orchid. It has a gelatinous quality similar to cornstarch or arrowroot. In Greece and Turkey it is made into a hot drink with milk and sugar. In Lebanon and Syria it is used as the thickener for the custard base for ice cream.

SALT COD
Fresh cod that has been roughly filleted and then salted. Normally, if soaked for 24 hours in cold water to cover, salt cod is ready to use. Depending upon its origin and the length of time it has been in salt, this timing can vary from 12 to 36 hours. Check with your merchant about soaking time when buying salt cod. To soak, immerse the cod in a large bowl of cold water; refrigerate, changing the water several times over the period of soaking. It will have whitened and doubled in bulk when it is ready to be cooked.

SAUSAGE CASINGS
Can be purchased from your butcher. The casings are usually lamb intestines and come cleaned and heavily salted. Soak overnight in water to cover, then rinse thoroughly, holding them under the tap so the cold water rushes through them.

SEEDS OF PARADISE
A combination of equal parts aniseeds, fennel seeds, brown sesame seeds and black caraway seeds; used as a topping for Tunisian bread. Not to be confused with grains of paradise, a kind of peppercorn.

SEMOLINA
Also known as pasta flour. A hard-wheat flour made from durum wheat; prized for pasta-making because it produces a dough that cooks up firmly.

Nicholas DeVore 69, 96, 99; Tony Stone Worldwide/ Richard Passmore 72t, 191; Tony Stone Worldwide/Joe Cornish 98; Tony Stone Worldwide/George Grigoriou 116–17; Tony Stone Worldwide/David Hanson 151; Tony Stone Worldwide/Linny M. Cunningham 156b; Tony Stone Worldwide/Leonard Nadel 186; Tony Stone Worldwide/Sylvain Grandadam 189b, 190, 221

Harold Sund 20,120,148, 152t, 153

Westlight/Jim Zuckerman cover; Westlight/Lawrence Manning endpapers; Westlight/Jon Gardey 19; Westlight/ Craig Aurness 22, 103; Westlight/Brent Bear 224

and a diplomatic and commercial center of the ancient world by 1250 B.C.

NORTH AFRICA: This Moroccan pendant, designed to emulate a hand holding a fish, symbolizes a respect for the life-giving powers of the Mediterranean. From the earliest known civilizations, the sea has been a vital link for sustenance and commerce.

SMEN

North African herb-flavored cooked salted butter, slightly pungent in flavor. Related to *samneh,* Arabic clarified butter made from cow or sheep's milk.

SQUID

To clean a squid, pull the head and clinging innards free from the body pouch. Pull out and discard the transparent quill-like cartilage from the pouch. Squeeze out the small beak from the mouth at the base of the tentacles and, using scissors, cut away the eyes. Using your fingers, clean out

TABIL

Tunisian spice mixture of garlic, caraway, coriander, and hot pepper, in almost equal parts.

TAGINE

Name for a Moroccan terra-cotta cooking utensil and for the stew that is cooked in it.

TAHINI

Also spelled *tahina.* A thick, oily paste of ground sesame seeds used in Middle Eastern cooking in savory and sweet

INDEX